S0-CCW-474

Milton's Epics and the Book of Psalms

MILTON'S EPICS
and the Book of Psalms

MARY ANN RADZINOWICZ

Princeton University Press
Princeton, New Jersey

Published by Princeton University Press,
41 William Street,
Princeton, New Jersey 08540
In the United Kingdom:
Princeton University Press,
Guildford, Surrey

Library of Congress
Cataloging-in-Publication Data
Radzinowicz, Mary Ann.
Milton's epics and the Book of Psalms / Mary Ann Radzinowicz.
p. cm. Bibliography: p. Includes index.
ISBN 0-691-06759-7 (alk. paper)
1. Milton, John, 1608–1674. Paradise lost.
2. Milton, John, 1608–1674. Paradise regained.
3. Epic poetry, English—History and criticism.
4. Christian poetry, English—History and criticism.
5. Bible. O.T. Psalms—Criticism, interpretation, etc.
6. Bible in literature. I. Title. PR3562.R27 1989 821'.4—dc19 88-34383 CIP

This book has been composed in Linotron Bembo

Clothbound editions of Princeton University Press books
are printed on acid-free paper, and binding materials
are chosen for strength and durability. Paperbacks,
although satisfactory for personal collections,
are not usually suitable for library rebinding

Printed in the United States of America
by Princeton University Press,
Princeton, New Jersey

for

SARAH POYNTZ

CONTENTS

PREFACE

MILTON'S POETRY is a vehicle of his faith, a faith nourished by reading the inspired Hebrew poets whom he honored through Jesus' words of praise in *Paradise Regained*. The history of the intertwined growth of Milton's poetical creativity and admiration for Psalms is well known.[1] He recognized the early presence of Psalms in forming his sense of vocation by the publication of his adaptations of Psalms 114 and 146 with the explanation that they were "done by the Author at fifteen years old," and by thanking his father for urging him to study "Palæstinus . . . vates" ("Ad Patrem" 85).[2] The accomplishment of the Nativity Ode—a poem not only based on Luke's New Testament psalms but composed of numerous topoi from the Psalms set by the Book of Common Prayer to be read at Christmastime—apparently prompted Milton's decision to write a full sequence of Christian poems moving through the year's festivals and the events of the life of Christ. The Book of Psalms had already been adapted for such cyclical worship, of course, and Milton drew extensively on the Psalter for the themes and images of the group of four poems constituting his own cycle: "The Passion," "On Time," "Upon the Circumcision," and "At a Solemn Musick." Ten years after his first psalm translations, Milton turned again to the Book of Psalms and translated Psalms 80 through 88 into rhyming verse, dating them April 1648; five years later he translated Psalms 1 through 8 into a variety of metrical forms. Finally in the last of his published poems, *Paradise Regained*, Milton spoke through Jesus his lifelong conviction that "*Sion*'s songs, to all true tasts excelling," are incomparable lyric poems, "Where God is prais'd aright, and Godlike men" (*PR* 4.347–48).

In Milton's prose, too, the history of persistent interest in Psalms is equally clear. His first letter, a letter to Thomas Young that Parker dates 1627, thanks his former tutor for a "Hebrew Bible, your very welcome gift."[3] *Of Education* proposes an ideal curriculum in which "the Hebrew tongue" should be learned so "that the Scriptures may be

[1] See my *Toward* Samson Agonistes, 188–226, for that history.

[2] *CE* 1:11; *CE* 1:276. All citations from Milton's poetry are from *The Works of John Milton* [*CE*], ed. Frank Allen Patterson et al., 18 vols. (New York: Columbia University Press, 1931–40). Line references will appear in the text.

[3] For the date of the letter, see Parker, "Milton and Thomas Young, 1620–1628," *Modern Language Notes* 53 (1938): 399–407; and Parker, *Milton: A Biography*, 2:724, 734; for the text, see *YP* 1:311–12.

now read in their own originall"; Edward Phillips indicates how far Milton put that into practice by teaching his own pupils "*Hebrew, Chaldee* and *Syriac*, so far as to go through the *Pentateuch*, or the Five Books of *Moses* in *Hebrew*, to make a good entrance into the *Targum*, or *Chaldee* Paraphrase, and to understand several Chapters of *St Matthew* in the *Syriac* Testament."[4] Phillips records, too, that Milton put his students to work "writing from his own dictation, some part, from time to time, of . . . a perfect System of Divinity," a preliminary to *Christian Doctrine*. That psalm-saturated work, begun in the early 1640s, was in a fair copy by the early 1660s, and was still being added to until his death in 1674.[5] In the tractate Milton repeatedly cited 126 of the 150 psalms, relating them both individually and in thematically established groups to the principal topics of his theology. Although in my conclusion I concentrate on a handful of psalms that have some claim to be particularly Miltonic, Milton's interest in Psalms was not an affection for some dozen or so. In deriving his theology in *Christian Doctrine*, he took evidence from nearly four-fifths of the psalms.[6] Some of those not consulted for doctrinal evidence, he otherwise singled out, however; he translated three of them, for instance.

If the history of Milton's lifelong interest in Psalms is clear with respect to both his poetry and his prose, however, there exists no full description of the pervasiveness of psalms in the epics *Paradise Lost* and *Paradise Regained*, and no full critical account of the literary consequences of that saturation, although important and valuable analyses do exist of Milton's knowledge and use of some psalms or groups of psalms in some works.[7] My purpose in writing this book is simply to supply such a description and criticism. The poetical experience of the poet John Milton included early and late psalm reading and translation. His study of Psalms in Hebrew, Latin, and English enabled him to discover the principles of psalm genre and poesis. The religious experience of the religious poet included early and late psalm analysis. His study of Psalms proceeded by reconsidering their thematic interrelationships under the doctrinal topics widely used among Puritans and

[4] *YP* 2:400; Phillips in Darbishire, *The Early Lives of Milton*, 61.

[5] See Maurice Kelley, *YP* 6:15–35.

[6] Psalms 9, 11, 13, 20, 21, 43, 47, 48, 57, 65, 70, 76, 79, 83, 85, 87, 96, 98, 100, 107, 108, 114, 117, 121, 124, 128, 129, 131, 132, 134, 136, 138, 142, and 150 are not cited in *Christian Doctrine*. He translated 83, 85, and 87 among those, however.

[7] I shall acknowledge these in place, but should mention in advance one book of great value in examining the diffusion of Psalms in Milton's epics, the pioneering book by James Sims, *The Bible in Milton's Epics*, and one of great value in understanding the literary consequences of that prevalence through the constitutive genres of Psalms, the recent book by Barbara Lewalski, Paradise Lost *and the Rhetoric of Literary Forms*.

derived by him from William Ames and John Wolleb. Although Milton read all of the Bible alive to its literary and intellectual force, what is particular to his reading of Psalms is his response to their lyricism, his turning to Psalms to shadow the strong moments in his epics when characters respond to the numinous. Hence, my book is perhaps not only a study of the Psalms as sources and analogues for Milton's two major poems but also an attempt to relate to each other two remarkable poetic oeuvres—one an anonymous, powerful, ancient, worship-centered, lyric oeuvre; the other an individually determined, revolutionary, heroic oeuvre. The longer I spent with Psalms and with Milton, that is, the more independently luminous each seemed; my book is meant to give to the reader an account of the enrichment of Milton's two epics from his reading of Psalms, but I will be disappointed in it if it does not turn readers of Milton into readers of Psalms.

Since the reader will follow my argument most easily with an English text of the Book of Psalms to hand, I have taken all my citations from the King James (Authorized) Version, a 1612 edition of which he owned, and not from the Geneva Bible; although he also owned a copy of the Geneva Bible as well as Latin Junius-Tremellius, the modern reader would find the Geneva Bible hard to come by and difficult to use.[8] The edition I have used, like many but not all, italicizes words added to the Hebrew by translation; all italics in my citations of Psalms, save for those specifically noted as adding emphasis, are such italicized additions in translation. Any King James Version may be conveniently used with my book.

Finally I should explain that my book begins, in a breach of chronology, in Part One with an examination of Psalms in *Paradise Regained* and then goes on in Part Two to an examination of Psalms in *Paradise Lost*. Nothing in my argument is lost by such a breach of chronology, since I neither consider that Milton's thematic and generic interest in Psalms changed during the period of the composition of his epics nor believe that he abandoned or lost in *Paradise Regained* poetic skills or strategies he mastered in writing *Paradise Lost*, even when he turned to a new, plainer style for the brief epic. If nothing is lost by breaching chronology, I have a teacher's reason for thinking something is gained. I believe that my readers will find it helpful to their understanding to move from simple to complex, unitary to manifold, and plain to richly decorated adaptations of Psalms. While the scriptural adaptations in *Paradise Regained* are thoroughgoing and interesting in themselves, they serve the purposes of a lucid sharpness and pith, a rhetorical econ-

[8] See p. 200 below, for a discussion of Milton's Bible.

omy as though the mazy ripeness the poet found in *Paradise Lost* had been distilled for the later work. That makes *Paradise Regained* a particularly direct and useful place to begin an analysis both of Milton's interest in the Book of Psalms and what he may have learned from it that bears on his writing of epics. The very compression in Milton's brief epic, its remarkable achievement of the psalmic, provides an economical basis for understanding the more variable and complex strategies of *Paradise Lost*.

While there is doubtless a sense in which it is true to say that Milton learned biblical poesis gradually, imitating Psalms in *Paradise Lost* and then applying his techniques with greater compression and consistency to *Paradise Regained*, it is just as true to say that he learnt thoroughly in advance of either by direct study of Psalms to understand the Hebrew medium. Before either epic endeavor, he recognized it as a parallelistic medium incorporating rhetorical, poetic, and prosodic figures. What he found admirable and beautiful in that medium was thus available to him for imitation not only in the epics but also in *Samson Agonistes*. In conformity, therefore, with my plan to move from the single, simple use of biblical models for the genres and themes in *Paradise Regained* to the more complex, varied, and multiform use in *Paradise Lost*, I also describe Milton's echoes of psalm versification first in the brief epic and then in the diffuse epic, in an interchapter between Parts I and II, taking up the English imitation of the Hebrew medium. I should explain that my reason for a more compressed treatment of Milton's echoing or imitating of the Hebrew medium than of his imitating psalm themes and genres is my disinclination to insist on influences and divergences that may be conjectural. For the same reason, in the interchapter on psalm poesis I link Milton's translations of Psalms 1–8 with *Paradise Regained* and his translations of Psalms 80–88 with *Paradise Lost*, the moods and themes of the two groups suggesting the alignment, but the point being to evidence my claims for Milton's psalmic poesis by reference to his practice as a translator before finding psalmic transumptions in his English verse. I do not claim that his imitations result in a verse experienced as Hebrew by readers of Hebrew verse, only that they result in a verse experienced as psalmic by readers of English poetry, mediated in translations many of which Milton consulted in making his own translations from the Hebrew.[9] The elementary classical Hebrew, much eroded by time, that

[9] See Douglas Bush, *Variorum* 2:991–1006, for summaries of the major arguments concerning Milton's use of Hebrew originals and of metrical and other translations.

I learnt at Cambridge University from my friend Hedva Ben-Israel, now Chairman of the Faculty of History at Hebrew University in Jerusalem, puts me at a disadvantage with respect to Milton; the modesty of my claims for the Hebraicism of his imitations reflects my own limited Hebrew. Milton's willingness to translate eight psalms in a wide variety of meters without imposing a single traditional English one suggests that he thought Hebrew verse observed its own kind of ancient freedom, analogous to the freedom he saw in Greek verse. Like the verse of Pindar, that of David privileged *rhythmus* over *metrum*. The second group of psalm translations, Milton's work on Psalms 1–8 is, I think, of primary importance in his response to the Hebrew medium. But his earlier translations of Psalms 80–88 are useful in showing Milton's responses to psalm style in the verse of *Paradise Lost*.

Milton's understanding of the laws of brief epic led him to make a compressed and rigorous use of psalms in *Paradise Regained*, drawing on the Book of Psalms with respect to its literary genres, its poetical medium, and its principal themes. In imitating its poetry, he chose one principal device, biblical parallelism, in order to secure for *Paradise Regained* the beauty of biblical plain style. The Book of Psalms affords many other poetical devices and tropes, and Milton takes advantage of them in *Paradise Lost*. But Luke and the writer of Hebrews especially valued the apothegmatic conciseness so well structured by parallelism, and Milton sought for his New Testament–based brief epic the same effect. Similarly, because the New Testament adapted from the Old Testament for its own purposes of succinct persuasion the proverbial, parabolic, and historical veins represented by the wisdom song, Milton too especially drew on that literary genre for *Paradise Regained*. Finally, the writers of the New Testament quoted parts of royal or messianic psalms and took it for granted that they prefigured and proved the sonship of Jesus Christ; Hebrews in particular spelled out the typological hermeneutic applicable to psalms. On that basis Milton constructed an interpretive combat between Jesus and Satan, concerning the themes of those psalms Jesus read to discover his role.

The laws of diffuse epic, however, are otherwise. In *Paradise Lost* Milton's wishes for tonal variety and affective richness or complexity directed him to an imitation of most of the genres of psalms he found to be good models of worship. As the most comprehensive of the *genera mista*, epic builds into its structure the effects proper to drama, narrative, and lyric. Milton's Christian epic does that too; when drawing on the lyric, he takes advantage of all the resources of the full roster of lyrical genres present in psalms. Moreover, he uses them not only where their expressiveness assists the local need for foregrounding, continuity, and variety but also where their worship charges individual moments with a sense of overarching coherence. Milton finds those moments helpful in the conversion of extended narrative into a single religious act. In the sphere of ideas and themes, the laws of the brief and the diffuse epic also prompt different uses of the Book of Psalms. Intellectually the brief epic searches single-mindedly after the dramatization of correct or founding doctrine; the diffuse epic moves toward the intellectually encyclopedic, and Milton's habitual clustering of psalms into thematic groups in *Christian Doctrine* makes an important contribution to the encyclopedism of *Paradise Lost*.

To turn from the map to the history of my book, I should say that earlier and partial versions of some of the material have appeared in "*Paradise Regained* as Hermeneutic Combat," in a special issue of *University of Hartford Studies in Literature* 15/16 (1983–1984): 99–107, edited by William L. Stull, entitled *Literature and Religion: Essays on Renaissance Literature and Contemporary Criticism*; "Psalms and the Representation of Death in *Paradise Lost*," in *Milton Studies*, volume 23, edited by James D. Simmonds, published 1987 by the University of Pittsburgh Press, revised and used by permission of the publisher; and "How Milton Read the Bible: The Case of *Paradise Regained*," in *A Cambridge Companion to Milton Studies*, edited by Dennis Danielson, Cambridge University Press, forthcoming. I am grateful to the presses involved for permission to reprint material to which they hold copyright.

The inception of the book was the invitation by Scott Elledge to introduce the subject of Milton's heroic use of the Psalms at a meeting of The Milton Seminar in 1981, soon after I joined the English Department at Cornell University. The original research for the project was supported by a grant in 1982 from the John Simon Guggenheim Memorial Foundation. Part I was finished while I held a Hurst Professorship at Washington University in 1986. I finished the book during a Cornell sabbatical leave spent in Ireland in the winter and spring of 1987. I am grateful to those institutions for their encouragement and material help. Of the libraries that have facilitated my work, I owe my special thanks to the Cambridge University Library, the Folger Shakespeare Library, the Olin Library of Cornell University, and the Library of Washington University. Among those who have read parts or versions of the manuscript, I am grateful to Irene Samuel, Gerard Cox, William Stull, Achsah Guibbory, and Dennis Danielson. Ann Whitaker proofread, and Anne Krook read the whole twice and checked all the citations and references: I cannot possibly thank them enough. My dedication to Sarah Poyntz, whose love of the poetry of nature is so strong, carries the hope that where Milton and the Psalms intersect may be found enough of that poetry to make my book acceptable.

Ithaca, New York
Ballyvaughan, County Clare, Republic of Ireland

ABBREVIATIONS

CE	*The Works of John Milton*, edited by Frank Allen Patterson et al., 18 vols. (New York: Columbia University Press, 1931–40).
PL	*Paradise Lost*, in above.
PR	*Paradise Regained*, in above.
YP	*Complete Prose Works of John Milton*, edited by Don M. Wolfe et al., 8 vols. (New Haven, Conn.: Yale University Press, 1953–82).

Milton's Epics and the Book of Psalms

INTRODUCTION

How Milton Read the Book of Psalms: His Formal, Stylistic, and Thematic Analysis

MILTON READ the Book of Psalms as the record of a journey through life traversing all the tempers, moods, passions, and uneven reactions that mark the psalmist's search for an adequate faith. Such a mode of reading was common to Englishmen in his day, guided by the Geneva Bible's representation of Psalms as a course of life by which "at length [to] atteine to [an] incorruptible crowne of glorie."[1] Since the journey is not a consistent progress toward enlightenment, individual psalms register backsliding, fear, self-deception, even inadequacy of response no less truly than nobility of spirit. Milton did not congratulate the psalmist or censure him for this or that response.[2] Rather, the generation of each psalm from an occasion in the life of its speaker gave him examples of the impassioned voices in which human beings record significant moments in their life's journey. He thought its whole course showed the power of experience to ripen the human soul.

Milton read Psalms, however, not simply as an anthology of moral, intellectual, and psychological episodes in the journey. He also read it as encompassing a variety of genres, each marked by a distinctive decorum, rhetorical structure, and poetical figures. While many English psalm paraphrasts grouped some psalms by mood or theme, Milton showed awareness of a fuller range of psalm kinds.[3] He did not distribute psalms among various psalmists and attributed none to any poet other than David. When he translated Psalms 80 through 88, for example, he ignored the superscriptions to Asaph and to Heman the Ezrahite.[4] He particularly noticed, however, the variety of distinctive

[1] *The Geneva Bible: A facsimile of the 1560 edition*, 235.

[2] Neither did he correct Job's friends for their smugness when he wrote in *Of True Religion, Heresy, Schism and Toleration*, "God will assuredly pardon . . . the friends of *Job*, good and pious men, though much mistaken." *YP* 8:424.

[3] See Lewalski, *Protestant Poetics and the Seventeenth-Century Religious Lyric*, 39–53.

[4] Milton was not unaware of differing or uncertain authorship, but he made nothing of it. Thus, in *The Tenure of Kings and Magistrates*, he calls David "likeliest to bee Author

speaking parts that David plays in Scripture—musician, believer, prophet, teacher, witness, and penitent among them. By distinguishing in David that range of feelings and intentions, Milton registered the genres or formal kinds in the Book of Psalms.[5] Hence he was able to write into *Paradise Lost* a range of lyrics based on a variety of psalm genres. He imitated hymns, laments, wisdom songs, thanksgivings, blessings, and prophecies, each genre by convention having an appropriate form and structure, a distinctive decorum and rhetoric, an individual voice and stance. Milton's recognition of psalm kinds put at his disposal a variety of religious lyrics to be incorporated into the epic, brief or diffuse, to function there in much the same way that individual genres in the religious anthology of the personal and national journey in the Book of Psalms contribute variety and emotional strength to the comprehensive spiritual achievement that the book as a whole traces. He read it as a book unified by its paideutic journey; he stressed the aptness of single psalms for special occasions in the religious life of each believer;[6] he responded to the patterns of genres that move across the Psalter, interrelating individual songs.

A consequence of interweaving diverse psalm genres in both *Paradise Regained* and *Paradise Lost* is what we may call multivocality, and that multivocality plays an important role in the architecture of each epic. Each is received by the reader not just as one speaker's continuous delivery of a transcendent mimesis drawn either from Luke or from Genesis and its aftermath, but also as a blending of many voices, rhetorically as well as psychologically and intellectually distinctive. Thus each epic reveals both a powerful, unifying, personal impulse urging Milton to express in poetry a lyrical act of worship and an equally powerful, comprehensive, impersonal impulse urging him to express in poetry a fullness of knowledge. Milton nowhere claimed to have seen in the

---

of the *Psalm* 94," although Psalm 94 is not one of the seventy-three naming him in its heading. *YP* 3:211.

[5] In *An Apology against a Pamphlet*, the phrase "*David* . . . wiser than [his] teachers," *YP* 1:923, implies wisdom song; in *Animadversions*, "holy *David*," *YP* 1:665, implies hymn; in *A Defence of the People of England*, "king David, repenting in bitter grief," *YP* 4:361, implies lament; in *A Second Defence*, "that passage . . . from David the prophet," *YP* 4:651, the prophetic psalm; in *Eikonoklastes*, "*David* . . . suffering without just cause, learnt that meekness and that wisdom by adversity," *YP* 3:571, lament converted to thanksgiving; in *Christian Doctrine*, "the prophet David," "disclosing God's law and teaching [in] an upright way of life," "This divine . . . man," and "Of particular repentance we have examples in David," *YP* 6:367, 469, indicate prophetic psalm, wisdom song, hymn, and lament.

[6] "And so have wee our several Psalmes for severall occasions. . . ." *Animadversions*, *YP* 1:686.

unified diversity of the Book of Psalms a comprehensive formal pattern for epic; other books of the Bible performed that function for him, when he looked to scriptural authority to strengthen classical models for epic—Genesis for *Paradise Lost*, Job for *Paradise Regained*. Rather his attentiveness to the psalms taught him something not learnt elsewhere about the generation of a long heroic poem out of the impassioned speech of brief poems. The distinctive psalmic genres act as choral voices creating multivocality for the epic, as arcs uniting the work while spacing the process of change and variety within it. To some of the genres or kinds, Milton adds his own voice. He too laments, warns, hymns, expostulates, and teaches upon occasions anticipated by the groups of psalms, in decorum anticipated by their intentions. But he is not limited to them, nor obliged to give his own voice to all. When, for example, in *Paradise Lost*, the proems draw on prophetic psalms or the angelic songs imitate hymns, Milton capably unites his voice to that of bard or angel. To some of Adam's laments he adds his personal voice, while from others he withholds it to encourage our ironic awareness of original, ordinary self-pity. As the Book of Psalms in Milton's reading is more than the sum of its lyrical parts in representing a journey of wisdom learned through suffering, so the multivocality of *Paradise Lost* draws all speakers and the audience as well into *paideia*. Similarly, in the briefer narrated dialogues of *Paradise Regained*, Milton constructs from psalms the two angelic hymns and the laments of Mary and of the disciples, now more rarely but pointedly merging his voice with those of his speakers. His epics are not univocal but multivocal; the vatic voice is not composed of short self-reflexive songs but takes its color from alterations in mood and occasion; the unity of the heroic intellectual enterprise not only controls, but is qualified by, a diversity of lyric energies.

Milton's recognition of psalm genres coexisted with his reading of the unity of the Book of Psalms as an encyclopedic representation of the heroic idea that human suffering is purposive and educative. The limitations of lyric from Milton's point of view drove him to write the heroic poem; the lyrical effects of intensity and unity checked for him the potential endlessness of epic. The heroic poem confronts for a whole society those threats to high achievement posed by its own experience of chaos. The narrative of that confrontation glorifies the active virtues its society must attain as alone sufficient to perfect its culture. The epic poet undertakes to narrate the deeds of heroic figures best suited to exemplify the actual or potential achievements of his civilization in that confrontation. His own responses—lyrical, reflexive, or didactic—are part of the story; he encompasses in his own person a quest for the heroic mode. But the virtues that preserve a state and make it happy are as many as are the dangers that threaten it; the poet seeking to render them in epic faces a centrifugal energy in the conception of his poem that puts him to the choice between what Milton called a "diffuse" and a "brief" model. No matter how well-made either model might be, a proliferation of journeys or tests, of achievements or educative failures, endangers the coherence of his epic, as the unity of *The Faerie Queene*, for example, may be threatened by the multiplicity of virtues Spenser represented as generative of the achievement of English Renaissance civilization. It is then that an equivalent lyric impulse—to interject one's own passion to control chaos in one's own voice in lyric compression—acts to check epic endlessness. Psalm reading was of enormous value to Milton in showing him models both of intense lyricism and of comprehensive heroism, just as it was of value in showing him models of generic multivocality and of an intellectually unified journey toward abstract comprehensive knowledge.

Milton, then, practiced a threefold reading of psalms. He made a thematic analysis of the whole Book of Psalms as figuring both a personal and public religious journey, both of the individual believer and of the Hebrew people. He made a generic analysis of the individual kinds to be found in the Book of Psalms, and he made a further stylistic or figural analysis of its tropes and prosody. He read the psalms as inspired truth, as individual instances of psalmic genres, and as compositions in a scriptural poetic medium. Only reading in the first or thematic way did Milton read Scripture differently from any other literary text. The third kind of analysis of Scripture, the stylistic, he actually blended with techniques grounded in his education in classical literature and in classical and Renaissance rhetoric.

Milton acknowledged in *The Reason of Church Government* that classical poetry as well as Scripture contained precedents for both high and serious lyric and far-ranging and profound epic. No one doubts that he interwove classical and scriptural models in *Paradise Regained* and *Paradise Lost*,[7] although some, mistakenly, argue that the classical is present as a rejected or discountenanced model rather than an inspiration. Milton did not reject what he certainly revalued. In the interweaving of sacred and secular precedents, he upheld the historical and

[7] For the classical models for "Lycidas," see Hunt, Lycidas *and the Italian Critics*; for the scriptural models, Wittreich, *Visionary Poetics*, chap. 2. For the classical models for *Paradise Regained*, see Low, "Milton, *Paradise Regained*, and Georgic"; for the scriptural see Lewalski, *Milton's Brief Epic*, chap. 2. For the classical models for *Paradise Lost*, see Webber, *Milton and His Epic Tradition*, chap. 1; for the scriptural, *Milton and the Art of Sacred Song*, ed. Patrick and Sundell, pt. 1.

aesthetic priority of biblical over classical model, working within a humanistic educational tradition that constructed a harmony from both. Just as Milton read psalms as falling into formal kinds that had classical analogues as well as biblical precedents and imitated both in his epics, so too he identified psalm figures and described them in classical terminology before imitating them stylistically.

For *Paradise Lost* and *Paradise Regained* Milton viewed Scripture as a work of authoritative truth and poetical beauty, from which later poetical beauties derive or toward which they should aspire. He used Scripture as a metonymy for God's creativity, just as he said Nature was; together they were books "wherein to read his wondrous Works." He too, like Jesus in *Paradise Regained*, held Hebrew poetry a model for verbal excellence in times to come:

> *Sion*'s songs, to all true tasts excelling,
> Where God is prais'd aright, and Godlike men,
> The Holiest of Holies, and his Saints;
> Such are from God inspir'd.
> (4.347–50)

While the psalms take priority over secular texts by virtue of their inspired truth, they enjoy historical priority as well:

> our Psalms with artful terms
> inscrib'd,
> Our Hebrew Songs and Harps in *Babylon*,
> That pleas'd so well our Victors ear, declare
> That rather *Greece* from us these Arts deriv'd.
> (4.335–38)

In *Paradise Regained* Jesus rejects Satan's claim that since "[t]he *Gentiles* also . . . write, and teach / To admiration, led by Natures light," imitation of them can produce "the secret power / Of harmony" (4.227–28, 254–55); he maintains that the Hebrews write better than the Gentiles, are divinely inspired, and taught the Greeks their art.

Milton nowhere doubts the possibility of concurrence between "divine and humane things" in poetry. In *Of Education* the "morall works of *Plato*, *Xenophon*, *Cicero*, *Plutarch*, *Laertius*, and those *Locrian* remnants" are to be "reduc't in their nightward studies . . . under the determinat sentence of *David*, or *Salomon*, or the Evangels and *Apostolic* scriptures."[8] In *The Reason of Church Government* Milton finds both pa-

[8] *YP* 2:396–97. In "Of . . . Tragedy," Milton adds, "The Apostle *Paul* himself thought it not unworthy to insert a verse of *Euripides* into the Text of Holy Scripture." *CE* 1:331.

gan and biblical tragedy "doctrinal and exemplary to a Nation" and "the magnifick Odes and Hymns [of] *Pindarus* and *Callimachus*" generically similar to "those frequent songs [in scripture which] not in their divine argument alone, *but in the very critical art of composition* may be easily made appear over all the kinds of Lyrick poesy, to be incomparable."[9] Similar collocations of the classics and Scripture appear in the stylistic annotations in marginalia in Milton's library, suggesting that Hebrew and Greek poetry were introduced to him as objects of comparison at Saint Paul's School through a critical method derived from Greek and Italian Renaissance rhetoricians.[10] Thematic or linguistic parallels between classical and biblical passages are carefully noted. A note to Pindar *Olympia* II, antistrophe 4, for example, reads:

> "The songs of love burn bright." See Eustathius on *Iliad V*, discussing the flame that appeared above the head and shield of Diomedes, where by fire he understands a light. On the other hand in Luke 22.56 light is used for fire.[11]

Brief stylistic annotations to his reading abound. Marginalia in Milton's copy of Sir John Harington's 1591 translation of *Orlando Furioso*, for example, enumerate more than 130 similes, sentences, proverbs, oracles, descriptions, imprecations, periphrases, epitaphs, dissimulations, and homilies.[12] From his school days on, then, Milton was accustomed to read Hebrew, modern, and classical poetry by the same critical methods.[13]

[9] *YP* 1:815–16, emphasis added. The passage is discussed in Hunt, Lycidas *and the Italian Critics*, 54–55.

[10] Clark, in *Milton at Saint Paul's School*, 185–86 and 198–208, describes that training. In a Latin letter to Alexander Gill, Milton explains his inspiration to adapt Psalm 114 "to the rules of Greek Heroic song" as "since I left your school . . . the first and only piece which I have composed in Greek" (*YP* 1:321–22). To recast in Greek a work by "the truly divine poet" suggests both Milton's comfortableness in each tradition and his future recasting of Hebrew psalms in English. See Boswell, "Library, Milton's," *A Milton Encyclopedia*, 5:23–25, for an account of Milton's postuniversity book buying.

[11] *CE* 18:281. Similarly, a note to *Pythian* III, strophe 3 notes: "Incantations were famous remedies among the ancients, now disused among the Christians" (*CE* 18:292); to Euripides *Ion* 65: "See Grotius in [his work] on the truth of the Christian Religion (on the subject of virgin births)" (*CE* 18:318).

[12] *CE* 18:330–36.

[13] Milton not only read and marginally annotated Ariosto as a school boy, he returned to him when making notes in his Commonplace Book; Parker suggests the later reading may have been in preparation for his Italian journey (*Milton: A Biography*, 2.804). The practice of subjecting biblical poetry to rhetorical analysis was not unique to Milton or to the Renaissance. Augustine in *De Doctrina Christiana*, book four, Cassiodorus in *De institutibus divinarum litterarum* and the commentary on Psalms, and Bede in *De schematis*

Milton's stylistic analysis of the psalms, natural and habitual to him, resulted in an imitation in *Paradise Regained* and *Paradise Lost* that goes far beyond the simple echoing of phrases or ideas. Verbal echoes can be heard, of course, both to the King James Version and the Coverdale translation in the Book of Common Prayer. But Milton sought to grasp the genius of Hebrew poetry by means of classical rhetorical tools and thought he found within its characteristic parallelism the well-known tropes and schemes that delighted him in classical art. He imitated Psalms not only by alluding to or echoing the metaphors and music of Hebrew poetry but by reconstituting and adapting Hebrew poetry to blank verse. His stylistic analysis saw in the psalms the truest poetry, a storehouse of "artful terms," a model for "harmony . . . and various-measur'd verse," a unified medium from which acts of worship might find appropriate models (*PR* 4.335, 255–56).

The distinction between Milton's generic and stylistic analysis is somewhat artificial. For Milton "decorum" is the "grand master peece to observe" in the arts of imitation;[14] the identification of a psalmic kind carries with it the notion of figures suitable to the genre and speaker. Nonetheless, a difference of strategy in the imitation of the Psalms appears in the two epics, bearing on the distinction. *Paradise Lost* draws particularly on generic analysis, *Paradise Regained* on stylistic. In *Paradise Lost* Milton uses the Hebrew poetical medium in its distinctive genres, each dominated by a decorum recognizing as suitable certain characteristic schemes and tropes. Milton's imitation of the decorum of psalm kinds in *Paradise Lost* within, for example, angelic hymns or the laments of men or fallen angels is more striking than an imitation of Hebrew poetry as a pervasive medium. The contrary is true of *Paradise Regained*, where, for example, the Son is characterized in opposition to Satan by their contrastive interpretations of psalm themes, but each reflects the Hebraic medium itself rather than the diversity of its psalmic kinds. The plain style of the entire brief epic owes a good deal to Milton's sense of psalmic poesis. *Paradise Lost* imitates an Old Testament action within which actions of the New Testament are predicted; it adapts psalm kinds drawn from the recognized occasions in the community's religious life to analogous occasions in the plot of the epic. The Old Testament worshiper is always alert to the connection between a psalm and its occasion. *Paradise Regained* imitates a New Testament action and adapts in particular those psalms referred

---

et tropis sacrae liber identified scriptural figures by classical names, a procedure continued in such Reformation handbooks as Melanchthon's *Institutiones Rhetoricae*.

[14] *Of Education*, *YP* 2:405. See Sanchez, "Persona and Decorum in Milton's Prose," 6–10.

to in the New Testament. The New Testament treats those psalms with a relative disregard for their psychological and historical contexts to emphasize genre-neutral typological and prophetic elements in them. Of course generic analysis is not absent from *Paradise Regained.* The differences in the Son's voice and demeanor when he is alone in thought and when he confronts Satan point toward private lament and thanksgiving as sources for the former and hymn, blessing, and wisdom song as sources for the latter. Equally, *Paradise Lost* reflects a concern with the psalmic medium itself. Nevertheless, *Paradise Lost* is sensitive to the genres of psalms throughout the Old Testament collection, whereas *Paradise Regained* reflects a typological reading of the New Testament.

With respect to the thematic mode of analysis, in *Christian Doctrine* and in *Paradise Lost* Milton claimed for Psalms the authority of a sacred text requiring a serious literal reading; he treated psalms as doctrine-bearing and appropriate subjects for human reason. In *Christian Doctrine*, Milton winnowed them for their constitutive truths and therefore grouped them into clusters by themes. One brief example may illustrate the way he combined thematic and generic analysis. In Book II, chapter 10, "Of the Second Kind of Virtues Connected with a Man's Duties towards Himself," Milton treated "those [virtues] which are exhibited in our repulsion or endurance of evils."[15] He specified two: "fortitude and patience." He cited eight psalms—Psalms 3, 8, 23, 37, 46, 56, 112, and 118—in proof of the value of fortitude. Of those eight, Psalm 3 is a lament from which renewed trust arises; Psalm 8 is a hymn glorifying God as creator; Psalm 23 is a messianic psalm; Psalm 37 is a wisdom song composed of proverbs; Psalm 46 is a hymn testifying to God's strength; Psalm 56 is a lament turning toward thanksgiving at its close; Psalm 112 is a hymn on the blessedness of the fear of God; Psalm 118 is a liturgy of thanksgiving. In bringing together proof texts from those psalms, Milton disregarded their formal diversity to group them by an idea in some of their verses. The verses he treated as definitive rational statements; the psalms he considered a thematic group.

[15] *YP* 6:738. In translating *Christian Doctrine*, Carey translated all proof texts literally, including those from the Book of Psalms, rather than using the King James (Authorized) Version for them. He noted, "the Authorized Version . . . frequently differs from anything Milton's Latin proof text can be taken to mean." He added, "At the time of writing the *Christian Doctrine* Milton availed himself of the Junius-Tremellius Latin Bible. But, his mind well stored in addition with the Hebrew and Greek texts, and his energies concentrated on the pursuit of an argument, he frequently altered the Latin to suit his immediate purpose" (translator's preface, xiv). Psalms cited from *Christian Doctrine* follow Carey. Elsewhere all quotations from psalms are taken from the King James (Authorized) Version.

When Milton then took up the theme of fortitude in *Paradise Lost*, he echoed psalms in the thematic cluster within an imitation of the appropriate psalm genre.

The value of fortitude, for example, is the subject of Adam's last words in *Paradise Lost*, making a hymn that may illustrate how Milton amalgamated formal and thematic readings of psalms in the epic. Adam said to Michael:

> Henceforth I learne, that to obey is best,
> And love with fear the onely God, to walk
> As in his presence, ever to observe
> His providence, and on him sole depend,
> Mercifull over all his works, with good
> Still overcoming evil, and by small
> Accomplishing great things, by things deemd weak
> Subverting worldly strong, and worldly wise
> By simply meek; that suffering for Truths sake
> Is fortitude to highest victorie,
> And to the faithful Death the Gate of Life;
> Taught this by his example whom I now
> Acknowledge my Redeemer ever blest.
> (12.561–73)

Here Adam composes a psalm according to the decorum of the hymn, whose substance owes more to the thematic group Milton brought together in *Christian Doctrine* than to materials present in such formal hymns as Psalms 8, 19, 29, 33, 103, or 104. Adam echoes Psalm 56.12,[16] "In God have I put my trust; I will not be afraid what man can do unto me," together with Psalm 23.4, "though I walk through the valley of the shadow of death, I will fear no evil," and Psalm 18.32, "*It is* God that girdeth me with strength, and maketh my way perfect." Milton cited many psalms repeatedly in *Christian Doctrine* in single verses to prove this or that truth, thus forming psalm clusters by themes. In *Paradise Lost*, Milton rhetorically and structurally adapts a genre, the hymn, from the Book of Psalms both to direct the reader's response and to imitate the speaker's feelings; he fills that lyric form with thematic echoes from relevant intellectually derived psalm clusters.[17]

[16] Milton numbered the verses of psalms in the *Christian Doctrine* from the Septuagint, not the King James Version; John Carey retained that numbering in the translation. When quoted from Milton's prose, psalm verse citations will bear the numbering of the Septuagint. When I quote from the King James Version, I use its verse numbers. *YP* 6:738.

[17] To see both the generic and thematic usefulness of psalms to *Paradise Lost* is to notice

Few passages in *Paradise Lost* reveal only one way of studying Scripture. From his thematic analysis, Milton imported a good deal of characteristic psalm thought into the epic. On such subjects as the creation and human history, the nature and attributes of God, the qualities of fallen and unfallen angels, sin, work, penitence, and death, he had collected proof texts in *Christian Doctrine* yielding clusters of concepts that played a role in generating and buttressing his thought. When affective moments and acts such as lament, blessing and cursing, prayer, praise, or teaching were to be rendered, the poet's formal analysis led him to other groupings of psalms. His responsiveness to the schemes and tropes of the Hebrew poetry of the psalms prompted a biblicism in his style. In Adam's closing hymn, for example, Milton composed with an ear for psalm parallelism:

> Mercifull over all his works, with good
> Still overcoming evil, and by small
> Accomplishing great things, by things deemd weak
> Subverting worldly strong, and worldly wise
> By simply meek.
> (12.565–69)

Echoing Psalm 145.9, "The Lord *is* good to all: and his tender mercies *are* over all his works," Milton produces a parallelism by isocolon (good overcoming evil: small accomplishing great), ellipsis and antimetabole (things weak subverting strong: [subverting] worldly wise by [things] meek), common devices in the psalms. In Psalm 145 itself, verse 18 illustrates antimetabole with ellipsis: "The Lord *is* nigh unto all them that call upon him, to all that call upon him in truth [the Lord is nigh]."[18]

---

a greater permeation of the text than has heretofore been recognized. In *The Bible in Milton's Epics*, Sims gathers evidence primarily from verbal echoes. His treatment of Psalm 2 in *Paradise Lost* is instructive. Psalm 2 is cited thirteen times in *Christian Doctrine*, nine times citing verse 7: "I will declare the decree: the Lord hath said unto me, Thou *art* my Son; this day have I begotten thee." Sims discovers eleven echoes to Psalm 2 in *Paradise Lost*, none to verse 7, and five to verse 4, "He that sitteth in the heavens shall laugh: the Lord shall have them in derision." Sims's catalogue correctly calls our attention to strict verbal echoes. But Psalm 2 is a royal proclamatory psalm; its rhetorical structure and decorum are imitated across the band of angelic and human hymns in the epic, whenever kingship or vicegerency is praised. The thematic value Milton assigned to verse 7, moreover, is reflected in the dialogue in heaven in Book III and the debate between Lucifer and Abdiel in Book V.

[18] Isocolon is the use of phrases of equal length and corresponding structure. Ellipsis is the omission of a word or phrase to be understood. Antimetabole or chiasmus is an inversion of the order of repeated words.

Milton's interpretive mode in reading Scripture combines the literal with the typological.[19] He explained it in *Christian Doctrine* 1.30: "Holy Scriptures were not written merely for particular occasions. . . . They were written for the use of the church throughout all succeeding ages, not only under the law but also under the gospel." The Old and New Testaments are consistent with each other: "Almost everything in the New Testament is proved by reference to the Old." Both are intended to teach and "if studied carefully . . . are an ideal instrument for educating even unlearned readers in those matters which have most to do with salvation." For that reason, "each passage of scripture has only a single sense, though in the Old Testament this sense is often a combination of the historical and the typological." To reach that single sense, Milton devised a "right method" for literal reading: "The requisites are linguistic ability, knowledge of the original sources, consideration of the overall intent, distinction between literal and figurative language, examination of the causes and circumstances, and of what comes before and after the passage in question, and comparison of one text with another." He enforced a distinction between literal and figurative language in order to inhibit allegorical interpretation and warned against "beliefs . . . deduced from scripture by a process of human reasoning which does not carry any conviction with it."[20] His own "comparison of one text with another" produced the thematic clusters which he deployed in *Paradise Lost*. The clusters are chosen more critically than comprehensively.

Extrinsic evidence for Milton's practice of generic analysis is more scattered than the evidence for his thematic or literal hermeneutic, but it nonetheless exists. Conceiving of Scripture as meant "for the use of the church throughout all succeeding ages," Milton saw in it patterns or models for subsequent acts of worship. In *Christian Doctrine* 2.4–6, discussing "external [Worship] . . . usually called RELIGION," he registered his awareness of the distinct genres of psalms by considering the kinds of speech acts involved in worship. He divided worship into invocation and sanctification, invocation dealing with the things a faithful worshiper might say and sanctification those a zealous worshiper might both say and do. He subdivided invocation into petition and thanksgiving on the one hand and oath taking and lot casting on the other. Under petition, he specified the lament and the blessing or curse. He identified the hymn both with petition and thanksgiving:

[19] See Conklin, *Biblical Criticism and Heresy in Milton*; MacCallum, "Milton and the Figurative Interpretation of the Bible"; Sims, "Bible, Milton and the," *A Milton Encyclopedia*; and Knott, *The Sword of the Spirit: Puritan Responses to the Bible*.

[20] YP 6:575, 576, 578–79, 581, 582, and 590.

"Invocation, and particularly thanksgiving, is sometimes accompanied by singing, and by hymns in honor of the divine name." Discussing petition, he characterized lament as "uttered in whispers or even in groans" and defined its ideal rhetoric: "[t]autological repetitiveness and empty verbiage are to be avoided. . . . But that repetitiveness which results from vehement disturbance of the mind is not to be counted vain." Under petition he noted that "we are even commanded to curse . . . the enemies of God and the church, fellow-Christians who have proved false, and anyone who commits major sins against God or even against ourselves," citing "the example of some of the holiest men . . . in many . . . Psalms." He warned against "rash curses," adding that "[t]he godly themselves sometimes fall in this way." Though the partial genres of beatitude and imprecation rarely fill an entire psalm or stand alone, they are thus defined as intrinsic but abusable forms of expressive worship.[21]

In all three of the chapters considering worship, Milton justified his analysis of worship by proof texts from Psalms—twenty-two in chapter 4, ten in chapter 5 (augmented by eight references to David's speeches in 1 Samuel), three in chapter 6 (plus one further reference to David's practice). What they proved was the existence of modes of worship used by the Jews that might be recommended to the church in his own day; Milton proposed biblical models as formal examples. He noted, "Even the Lord's Prayer is a pattern or model, rather than a formula to be repeated verbatim either by the apostles or by the churches today."[22] In the course of proving the indifference of time, place and physical posture in worship, he spoke in passing so as to distinguish petition—thus far consisting of lament and of blessing and cursing—from prophecy; and he defined prophecy so as to identify it with the wisdom song. What he wrote of prophecy in considering invocation did not point, that is, to what a modern reader would recognize as prophetic or oracular psalms, but to didactic or wisdom songs.[23] He explained:

> Paul says, on this subject, . . . *any man praying or prophesying with his head covered brings shame upon his head: but any woman who does*

[21] *YP* 6:683, 671–72, 675, 677.

[22] *YP* 6:670. Since Luke (11.2) had written, "When ye pray, say, Our Father . . ." but Matthew (6.9), "After this manner therefore pray ye: Our Father. . . ." Milton thought it necessary to specify.

[23] Milton regularly used the word prophesy to mean to teach and not only to deliver apocalyptic truth under divine inspiration. In *Christian Doctrine*, he wrote, "under the gospel the simple gift of teaching, especially of public teaching, is called *prophecy*." *YP* 6:572.

> *not keep her head covered when she prays or prophesies brings shame upon her head. . . .* Why was this? Because at that time it was a sign of subjection for either a man or a woman to have the head covered. As a result men prayed and prophesied with their heads uncovered. But nowadays it is a sign of subjection for a man to be bare-headed, and a sign of authority for him to have his head covered. The result is that in most churches, particularly those of Europe, it is the custom to praise God bare-headed in order to show reverence, since that is the way we show it in everyday life, but to prophesy with the head covered, as a sign of authority. It is also customary to listen to prophecy with the head covered, as befitting mature and free-born sons. Thus the spirit, not the letter of the law is observed, which is as it should always be.[24]

He distinguished prayer (reverent, obedient petition) from prophecy (free, reflective teaching) within a historical gloss that makes the point that, while customs and usages change, the impulses of worship are constant. The prophet-teacher addresses himself to "mature and free-born sons" in wisdom songs.

In chapter 5, "Of Oath-taking and the Casting of Lots," Milton continued his discussion of invocation, having identified lament, thanksgiving, hymn, benediction, curse, and wisdom song as modes of invocation. Before considering Milton's views on oath taking and lot casting, it may be helpful here to say something about the general Ramist structure of *Christian Doctrine.* Ramist logic is an essentially spatial logic that mnemonically arranges information by a repeated binary division of knowledge into opposing axioms, arranged from the most general to the most specific.[25] As a Ramist scholarly work on the intellectual discipline of Christian dogmatics, *Christian Doctrine* first divides its subject into two exhaustively general branches—faith or the knowledge of God, and love or the worship of God. Milton's systematic headings were not original with him but came from such standard Reformation doctrinal handbooks as those of Ames and Wolleb. Milton could, however, give them brief or extended treatment. Those propositions of particular interest to him he developed fully; those of least interest he repeated from his sources or handled sketchily. Having exhausted all the topics involving faith, the first branch of the disci-

[24] *YP* 6:673.

[25] As Milton explained, "I do not teach anything new in this work. I aim only to assist the reader's memory by collecting together, as it were, into a single book texts which are scattered here and there throughout the Bible, and by systematizing them under definite headings, in order to make reference easy." *YP* 6:127.

pline, Milton turned to worship and quickly took the usual methodical steps dividing the causes of worship into either God or the virtues, dividing virtues into general and special, dividing special into duties toward God and toward man, dividing duties toward God into internal and external, before at length taking up the external duties toward God or worship, dichotomized into its parts and its circumstances. As we have seen, the fearful symmetry of the method produced two parts, invocation and sanctification; invocation demanded two double members: petition and thanksgiving, oaths and the casting of lots; sanctification fell into two single topics: zeal and the profession of faith.

Ramist spatial logic is an awkward form in which to arrange any kind of historical analysis, although it is adequate for synchronic empiricism. In oath taking and lot casting, however, Milton saw a change from Hebrew religious practices generated by particular historical situations into Christian adaptations of them under altered conditions. Although he took up both in *Christian Doctrine* because Ramist method in Ames and Wolleb demanded the discussion, he briefly treated them as possible liturgical models undergoing historical change. In *Christian Doctrine*, that is, Milton accepted the concept of the evolution of psalm genres in changed cultural circumstances.

Oath taking and lot casting are interrelated forms of petition that seek to use God's own words to speak to him. Endorsing the taking of oaths, Milton quoted two psalms. From those models he drew in *Paradise Lost* scenes of the Father's decrees.[26] His principal proof text came from Psalm 95, in which God reminds his people of an earlier vow:

> Harden not your heart, as in the provocation, *and* as *in* the day of temptation in the wilderness:
>
> When your fathers tempted me, proved me, and saw my work.
>
> Forty years long was I grieved with *this* generation, and said, It *is* a people that do err in their heart, and they have not known my ways:
>
> Unto whom I sware in my wrath that they should not enter into my rest.

Oath taking is a ceremony present frequently in Psalms. By and large Milton contented himself with adapting the mode in *Paradise Lost* to plot and character; in *Christian Doctrine* he recommended it as a mode of pious self-commitment.

[26] Kelley notes oaths of God in *Paradise Lost* at 2.352; 5.607, 811; and 12.346–47 (*YP* 6:684). Similar decrees or promises can be found in such places as *PL* 4.427; 5.814; 8.333; and 11.83.

Similarly, the casting of lots is an ancient technique by which the Jews sought God's answer to specific problems. Lots, usually pieces of wood marked to identify the persons or options to be chosen among, were placed in a special receptacle and shaken by someone in authority—a temple prophet, seer or leader—until one fell into his lap deciding the issue. The practice was not confined to Israel, but it can be found in a number of places in Scripture, many noticed by Milton, to which might be added 1 Samuel 14.42: "And Saul said, Cast *lots* between me and Jonathan my son. And Jonathan was taken." Milton defined it as "in effect an APPEAL TO THE DIVINE POWER FOR EXPLANATION . . . IN UNCERTAIN OR CONTROVERSIAL MATTERS" and tried to dissociate it from "superstitious purposes or in gaming or in trickery."[27] Satan in *Paradise Regained*, nevertheless, is ironic at the expense of "the Oracle / *Urim* and *Thummim*, those oraculous gems" (3.13–14). In its own historical period, the practice was closely related to the consultation of tribal prophets, whose inspired delivery of God's will produced the prophetic psalms.[28]

Milton examined texts of a historical period which generated both prophetic psalms and lot casting. In the tractate, he linked lot casting to oath taking and adapted them uneasily to his own time, relating the worshiper in both actions to the prophet as seer. Prophecy reveals the true nature of the God of Israel; the prophetic psalmist is the spokesman of God to the people. In the epic poems, where the prophetic psalmist becomes the narrative poet, Milton only ironizes lot casting and restricts oath taking to God.

In next treating "Sanctification," Milton distinguished between the hallowing of God's name in every circumstance of human life and the open profession of true religion, describing each so as to point to one genre of psalm, the wisdom song. When he contrasted a holy sanctification of God's name with blasphemy, for example, he noted: "Those who, in all sincerity, and with no desire to stir up controversy, teach or discuss some doctrine concerning the deity which they have quite apparently, as they see it, learned from the Holy Scriptures, are

[27] *YP* 6:690.

[28] Mowinckel explains the practice: "[t]he ancient Israelite did not feel that there was any contrast between the unconstrained oracle and utterance of a spontaneous inspiration and the oracle that had been won by technical means; for it required a supra-normal equipment . . . to be able to handle the casting of lots in such a way that the right oracle would appear. Even at the time of Jesus, Judaism ascribed to the high priest an official prophetic inspiration: he was able to prophesy because of his 'being the high priest that year' (John 11.51). Even the technical oracle of the priest, found for instance by the casting of lots, would often have to be given the proper form and style . . . ; this was also an outcome of 'wisdom' and inspiration." *The Psalms in Israel's Worship*, 2:57.

in no sense guilty of the sin of blasphemy." And when he offered proof texts for "open profession of the true religion," he quoted Psalm 119.46: "*I shall speak of your testimonies before kings, and shall not be ashamed.*" He set forth, that is, the two principal functions of wisdom literature—teaching and testifying (or, in the technical term of Reformation theology, "witnessing"); he cited the most prominent of the wisdom psalms.[29]

This extrinsic evidence of Milton's generic analysis of Psalms confirms the evidence of his variously naming the psalmist musician or singer, man of piety, prophet, penitent teacher, and the like. Milton's awareness of the structures of various kinds of psalms gave him lyric models for songs in both epics: the hymn became the model for a broad spectrum of songs of praise, most but not all spoken or sung by angels in *Paradise Lost*, and for the two angelic hymns framing the central action of *Paradise Regained*. The biblical lament patterned a range of laments in *Paradise Lost*, most but not all uttered by the human pair, and the expressions of anxiety by Mary and the disciples in *Paradise Regained*. The wisdom song shaped diverse didactic odes, especially those delivered by and to Abdiel in *Paradise Lost* and the summary stages of the Son's self-analysis in *Paradise Regained*. Similarly, the thanksgiving served as model for a group of brief expressions of gratitude, particularly following moments of penitence; the blessing served as model for expressions of benediction, not free-standing but contained in hymn and wisdom song; finally, the prophetic psalm served as model for the proems. Moreover the admixture of genres in some psalms, especially change-of-mood psalms, inspired generic variety in Milton's adaptations: the proems, for example, open like hymns, develop through lament and didactic comment, turn to thanksgiving, and end in prophecy. Both the Book of Psalms and *Paradise Lost* propose a full paideutic journey for the believer through a moral, political, and social landscape, colored by moods found in the situations of various personalities. Both dramatize and represent diverse voices to display the analogy between the poet's, the actors', and the audience's experience of moral growth and augmented insight. The multivocality of both Psalms and *Paradise Lost* produces the rich texture of epic affect. Not the mixed-mode psalms but two groups of psalms similarly influence and enable the brief epic—the wisdom song contributes to its didacticism and witness; the New Testament psalms of Luke contribute to its messianic prophecy.

While Milton's formal analysis of Psalms led him to recreate and

[29] *YP* 6:700, 701.

bind together many genres across the texture of *Paradise Lost*, those genres acting as poetical ribs and particularly influencing the emotional reading of the epic as a powerfully varied poem, and to echo wisdom songs and Lukean psalms in his plainstyle brief epic, his concurrent thematic analysis led to intellectual strengthening of each poem. Milton considered that he made his poetry out of ideas as much as words and disliked the "toylsom vanity" of aiming at "verbal curiosities."[30] The truth of his poetry was as vitally grounded in the Book of Psalms as its style and formal multiplicity. From *Christian Doctrine* one may discover the meaning Milton gave to a multitude of verses of psalms, so that a curious reader may relate psalms to Milton's Christology, psalms to Milton's eschatology, and so forth. Perfect retrieval of scriptural truth was his aim. He wrote at length on issues alive to him, more briefly when the subject seemed to him tolerably well-examined elsewhere, or self-evident. The subjects of work and death were of special interest to him; because he thought he understood them better than most thinkers, he gave extended treatment to mortalism and works of faith, gathering multiple psalm citations in those areas. They resonate in both his epic poems. Wherever Milton took up a theme of great personal significance to him in the theological handbook, a dense and complex analytical handling of psalm texts followed, the result of a systematic winnowing of psalms into substantive clusters. The themes of Jesus' sonship and human witness were themes of profoundest concern to Milton; to his psalm clusters in those areas and their presence in the brief epic, I now turn.

[30] *YP* 1:811.

PART I

Paradise Regained

ONE

"Where God is prais'd aright"

Psalm Themes

WHEN MILTON began to write *Paradise Regained* on the model of Job, he brought to the new poem hermeneutic habits made precise and boldly imaginative by having written both *Christian Doctrine* and *Paradise Lost.* The new theme came to him inspired and authorized by the Book of Psalms, "Where God is prais'd aright, and Godlike men" (4.348). *Paradise Regained* quickly exposes the inadequacy of the term *literal* to describe Milton's thematic analysis of psalms and directs the modern reader to reinstate the distinction English Reformed exegetes sought to make in using the terms *carnal* and *spiritual* for biblical interpretation. Psalms are "strew'd" throughout Milton's New Testament sources for *Paradise Regained,* the most important being Luke, Matthew, John, Revelation, and the Epistle to the Hebrews, Luke providing plot and structure for *Paradise Regained* in addition to ideas. Those are also the New Testament books, together with the Acts of the Apostles and the Epistle to the Romans, densest in psalm allusions. When psalms were transferred from their Old Testament context to the New Testament, they were of course subjected to new readings by the early Christian redactors,[1] who used a messianic interpretation certainly not literal to Hebrew midrash.[2] Milton thought, "Each passage of scripture has only a single sense, though in the Old Testament this sense is often a combination of the historical and the typological."

[1] When Milton uses psalms as proof texts in *Christian Doctrine,* and those proof texts are likewise quoted in New Testament contexts, Milton regularly cites the New Testament context as well, associating a New Testament typological hermeneutic with the thematic cluster.

[2] Midrash is the rabbinical exegesis of Old Testament writings. Governed by the theological assumption of what Hartman and Budick call "divine unicity and the inviolability of the sacred text" (*Midrash and Literature,* xi), midrash is committed to interpret scripture so as to make a claim for its truth; it does so by asserting that its exegesis adds nothing not already present in or literal to the text. At the same time, midrash makes a constantly altering sense of Scripture in its revisions and explications. Commentary freshens the text, keeps it alive and open, but claims to protect the text and retain its simplicity.

When he set forth the correct way of interpreting scripture in *Christian Doctrine* to reach that single sense, he adduced psalm texts to instance doctrines found in the Old Testament, to show how the early Christian hermeneutic developed Old Testament materials, and finally to argue his own independent readings. In correlating the Old Testament with the New as proved by the Old, he took both to be intended "for the use of the church throughout all succeeding ages."[3]

Milton argued that the historically prior text, the Old Testament, is authoritative because it is divinely inspired and was also "handed down . . . in an uncorrupted state"; the later New Testament text, although much more difficult to establish, since it was "entrusted throughout the ages . . . to a variety of hands, some more corrupt than others" and since "[w]e possess no autograph copy: no exemplar which we can rely on as more trustworthy than the others," is authoritative because it was inspired to be "*useful for teaching*" and proves its doctrine by reference to the Old Testament.[4] Then turning to the New Testament interpretation of the Old Testament Scripture, Milton cited a number of psalms in sequence with Luke and Acts, both establishing that the Old Testament contains saving truth and showing its congruence with the New.[5] Finally, still interweaving New Testament examples with the Old, Milton established areas of "indifference" in Scripture and proved the "liberty of prophesying" or the right and duty of each

[3] *YP* 6:581, 575.

[4] *YP* 6:588, 589, 577. See also *YP* 6:576–77: "Almost everything in the New Testament is proved by reference to the Old. The function of the . . . New Testament is made clear in . . . II Tim. iii.15–17: *that you have known the Holy Scriptures from childhood, and they are able to make you wise and lead you to salvation through the faith which is in Christ Jesus. All scripture is divinely inspired, and useful for teaching, for reproof, for correction, for discipline in right living, so that the man of God may be fully prepared and equipped for every good work.* It is true that the scriptures which Timothy is said to have *known from childhood* . . . seem to have been only the books of the Old Testament. It is not apparent that any book of the New Testament had been written when Timothy was a child. However, in the next verse the same claim is made for the whole divinely inspired scripture. This claim is that it is *useful for teaching.*"

[5] "Thus the scriptures are, both in themselves and through God's illumination absolutely clear. If studied carefully and regularly, they are an ideal instrument for educating . . . in those matters which have most to do with salvation. Psal. xix.8: *the doctrine of Jehovah is perfect, restoring the soul; the testimony of Jehovah is true, making the unlearned wise* . . . , and cxix.105: *your word is a lamp to my feet and a light to my path,* cxix.130: *the entrance of your words gives light, it gives the simple prudence*—another proof that the scriptures ought to be read by everyone; cxix.18: *open my eyes, that I may see marvels out of your law* . . . ; Luke xxiv.45: *he opened their minds, so that they should understand the scriptures;* Acts xviii.28: *in public he convinced the Jews more and more, showing . . . that Jesus was the Christ.*" *YP* 6:578–79.

reader to interpret for himself.[6] Milton concluded with the concept of the "double scripture," privileging "the internal scripture of the Holy Spirit" to the "external scripture of the written word."[7]

Milton endorsed a personal insight derived from the spirit within man, when that faculty undertook a sustained comparative analysis of Scripture, technically known as "the analogy of faith." He qualified any meaning he might derive from a single text by reference to the progressive understanding he had of the whole. Thus spiritual inner light in Milton is not a beam shining now on this, now on that notion but a sustained self-correcting reason, continuously cross-questioning parts of the text against the whole or retrospectively considering moments of insight against a total understanding progressively achieved. He called this manner of breaking out of the hermeneutic circle manly freedom; he thought the alternative of submitting interpretation to an established church to be childish and monkish.

This line of argument may seem the familiar polemic by which Milton used Scripture to argue divorce by consent or the presbyterian way of organizing the church. In *Paradise Regained*, however, Milton became a poetic witness who suspended biblical polemic to offer a testimony of faith; his biblical hermeneutic now upheld a new imaginative strategy. The thematic use of psalms in *Paradise Regained* involves a particularly interesting dramatic deployment of the concept of "double scripture." The poet, dividing literal into spiritual and carnal, split interpretation (the spirit) from text (the letter) and maneuvered them into dialogic confrontation. In *Paradise Regained* Satan quotes Scripture in his own cause, and the Son generates interpretations that wrest Scripture back from him again. Milton constructed a dramatic conflict

[6] "The rule and canon of faith, therefore, is scripture alone: Psal. xix.10: *the judgments of Jehovah are truth itself.* . . . Apparently not all the instructions which the apostles gave the churches were written down, or if they were written down they have not survived. . . . We should conclude that these instructions, though useful, were not necessary for salvation. They ought, then, to be supplied either from other passages of scripture or, if it is doubtful whether this is possible . . . from that same Spirit operating in us through faith and charity. . . . So when the Corinthians asked Paul about certain matters on which scripture had not laid down anything definite, he answered them in accordance with the spirit of Christianity, and by means of that spiritual anointing which he had received: I Cor. vii.12: *I say this, not the Lord,* 25,26: *I have no command from the Lord about virgins, but I give my own opinion, as one to whom the Lord through his mercy has granted faith.* . . . Thus he reminds them that they are able to supply answers for themselves in questions of this kind." *YP* 6:585–87.

[7] "Nowadays the external authority for our faith, . . . the scriptures, is of very considerable importance and, generally speaking, it is the authority of which we first have experience. The pre-eminent and supreme authority, however, is the authority of the Spirit, which is internal, and the individual possession of each man." *YP* 6:587.

by opposing to Satan's literal but "carnal" reading of psalms an evolving higher reading of them by the Son. Satan tries by an adversarial, worldly, or ironic use of psalms to trap the Son into betraying their spiritual values to achieve earthly or "carnal" messiahship; contrariwise, the Son uses a clairvoyant reading through an inspired hermeneutic to defeat Satan's strategy, eluding entrapment and achieving true messiahship by his higher reasoning.

The contest between them concludes in the epic as it concluded in Luke 4.10–13 with Satan's abused interpretation of Psalm 91.11–12: "For he shall give his angels charge over thee, to keep thee in all thy ways. They shall bear thee up in *their* hands, lest thou dash thy foot against a stone." Satan pretends that the psalm advises "master reality through your power over servant angels," as though reality were established by kicking a stone or resorting to angel-propelled levitation to avoid it. Christ's reply opposes a spiritual or prophetically literal reading of the psalm. Not only the climax of the poem depends on freeing a psalm from abuse, however: the whole dialogue between Satan and the Son contests the meaning of messianic clues found in psalms. Satan tries to play on the Son's sense of his vocation, "born to promote all truth, / All righteous things" (*PR* 1.205–6), by treating psalm verses as though their referents were always worldly leadership; the Son offers him an inward sense of psalm meaning.

The principal psalms at issue in this hermeneutic contest are those regularly taken by Christians to prophesy the Son. The New Testament model for the Son's self-interpretation by way of messianic psalms is the Epistle to the Hebrews. The long debate between the Son and Satan focuses on Psalms 2, 8, 10, 78, 91, and 110, interpreted in Hebrews and thence in *Paradise Regained* to identify the Son's triple function as prophet, king, and high priest but carnally read by Satan simply as royal psalms attesting to paternal inheritance. A brief preliminary example of one conflict between Satan and the Son concerning glory may usefully illustrate Milton's method.

At the beginning of the third book of *Paradise Regained*, Milton exhibits tireless Satan in renewed attack, urging the Son to misinterpret his kingly function and to intervene in the politics of his day. He reads fame and glory as heroic impulses towards empire. The Son coolly dismisses fame, defines true glory as achieved "when God / . . . with approbation marks / The just man, and divulges him through Heaven" (3.60–62), and stipulates its proper means "By deeds of peace, by wisdom eminent, / By patience, temperance" (3.91–92). He concludes by repudiating human vainglory for godly witness: "I seek not mine, but his / Who sent me, and thereby witness whence I am" (3.106–7).

At this juncture, the "Tempter murmuring" places before the Son a group of thematically related creation and royal psalms,[8] giving them an ironic "carnal" gloss:

> Think not so slight of glory; therein least
> Resembling thy great Father: he seeks glory,
> And for his glory all things made, all things
> Orders and governs, nor content in Heaven
> By all his Angels glorifi'd, requires
> Glory from men, from all men good or bad,
> Wise or unwise, no difference, no exemption;
> Above all Sacrifice, or hallow'd gift
> Glory he requires, and glory he receives
> Promiscuous from all Nations, Jew, or Greek,
> Or Barbarous, nor exception hath declar'd;
> From us his foes pronounc't glory he exacts.
> (3.109–20)

Satan weaves together Psalms 19.1, "The heavens declare the glory of God"; 33.6, 8, "By the word of the Lord were the heavens made," "let all the inhabitants of the world stand in awe of him"; 8.1, "O Lord our Lord, how excellent *is* thy name in all the earth! who hast set thy glory above the heavens"; 90.16, "Let thy work appear unto thy servants, and thy glory unto their children"; 115.3, "But our God *is* in the heavens: he hath done whatsoever he hath pleased"; 86.9, "All nations whom thou hast made shall come and worship before thee, O Lord; and shall glorify thy name"; and 104.1, 31, "thou art clothed with honour and majesty," "The glory of the Lord shall endure for ever: the Lord shall rejoice in his works." From those verses, Satan reads God as an emperor who created the universe to exercise his limitless power and who exacts glory as a tribute from men.

From the same psalm cluster, the Son constructs a "spiritual" reading, interpreting creation as God's generosity and glory as human thanksgiving:

> To whom our Saviour fervently reply'd.
> And reason; since his word all things produc'd,
> Though chiefly not for glory as prime end,
> But to shew forth his goodness, and impart
> His good communicable to every soul
> Freely; of whom what could he less expect

[8] The psalms are those Milton grouped in *Christian Doctrine* when he discussed God's nature and attributes. *YP* 6:130–52.

> Then glory and benediction, that is thanks,
> . . . .
> But why should man seek glory? who of his own
> Hath nothing, and to whom nothing belongs
> But condemnation, ignominy, and shame?
> (3.121–36)

The Son here revisits each psalm Satan has used; to Satan's Psalm 33.6, 8 he adds 33.4–5, "all his works *are done* in truth," "the earth is full of the goodness of the Lord"; to Satan's 8.1 he adds 8.4–5, "What is man, that thou art mindful of him? and the son of man, that thou visitest him? For thou hast made him a little lower than the angels, and hast crowned him with glory and honour"; to 90.16 he adds 90.17, "And let the beauty of the Lord our God be upon us: and establish thou the work of our hands upon us; yea, the work of our hands establish thou it"; to 19.1 he adds 19.13–14, "Keep back thy servant also from presumptuous *sins* . . . O Lord, my strength, and my redeemer"; to 115.3 he adds 115.1, "Not unto us, O Lord, not unto us, but unto thy name give glory, for thy mercy, *and* for thy truth's sake"; and finally to 104.1 he adds 104.34, "My meditation of him shall be sweet: I will be glad in the Lord."

To answer Satan's carnal literalism by the Son's spiritual literalism that insists on regard for context, Milton adapted a dialogue between Jesus and the Pharisees found in John 8.12–50. That dialogue ends, "And I seek not mine own glory," the saying that opens the Son's rebuke of Satan; it begins, "I am one that bear witness of myself, and the Father that sent me beareth witness of me," the saying that closes his rebuke: "I seek not mine, but his / Who sent me, and thereby witness whence I am" (*PR* 3.106–7). In John 8.12–50, Jesus confronts the chief priests, scribes and Pharisees in a sequence of interpretive challenges. He tells them, "Ye judge after the flesh," adding "Why do ye not understand my speech? *even* because ye cannot hear my word. Ye are of *your* father the devil." The disputation between the Son and Satan over the true meaning of glory puts psalms in a dialogic confrontation modeled on John. Where the priests' spokesmen for the Law insisted on their literal "single sense" of the Old Testament, the Son answered them with a spiritual reading of how the gospel fulfilled the law. John 8.50, "And I seek not mine own glory," is itself a Christian midrash of Psalm 115.1, "not unto us, but unto thy name give glory." This intricately simple instance may introduce Milton's full-scale practice of dialogically placed psalm interpretations in *Paradise Regained*, where messianic psalms interpreted in Hebrews are gathered within the plot structure of Luke to shape the confrontation of Satan and the Son.

Messianic psalms—in particular Psalms 2, 8, 10, 22, 78, 82, 91, and 110—are used by Satan across the poem to question the meaning of Jesus' sonship. He defines sonship either so broadly as to include even himself or so narrowly as to exclude "the perfect man." The Son's increasing self-knowledge counters with the same group of Psalms given a New Testament gloss. Essentially, Satan and the Son contest the potentially conflicting implications of Psalm 2.7, "the Lord hath said unto me, Thou *art* my Son; this day have I begotten thee," and 82.6, "I have said, Ye *are* gods; and all of you *are* children of the most High." Their contest spans all four books of *Paradise Regained.* Satan concerns himself with those two texts sometimes plainly, sometimes indirectly; they are never far from his words. His apparently sincere and his ironic interpretations, reasonably and strategically offered, are "carnal." The Son gives the same group of psalms a "spiritual" reading, his study and progressively intuitive self-knowledge leading him toward the New Testament positions found in Milton's biblical sources. Hebrews, containing the greatest number of psalm allusions in any of Milton's sources other than Revelation, expounds that interpretation of the Messiah that the Son in *Paradise Regained* comes to understand, teach, and finally manifest. Hebrews addresses a community of Jewish Christians whose conversion has lost impetus and for whom the Law under which it was first nurtured may be reasserting itself. Hence its writer reinterpreted traditional Jewish religious events and customs to confirm the new Christian faith, drawing on well-known psalms from the Jewish liturgy. Milton commented on the special aptness of Hebrews to scriptural teaching in *Christian Doctrine,*[9] particularly its exposition of Sonship.[10]

Milton located the central argument of Hebrews in verses 5.8–9: "Though he were a Son, yet learned he obedience by the things which he suffered; And being made perfect, he became the author of eternal salvation unto all them that obey him." They gloss the plot he took from Luke 4.1–13, and they are "proved"—that is, evidenced—by numerous psalms. To the psalms already quoted in Hebrews, Milton added cognate verses in *Christian Doctrine*, not only acknowledging the

[9] "The apostle says to Timothy, II Tim. i.13: . . . 'Hold fast the pattern,' which the author of the epistle to the Hebrews seems to have been determined to do, so as to teach the main points of Christian doctrine methodically." *YP* 6:128.

[10] "The generation of the divine nature is by no one more sublimely or more fully explained than by the apostle to the Hebrews." *YP* 6:211.

epistle's own richness in psalm reading but reinforcing it.[11] He associated the augmented psalm clusters with the three principal themes of Hebrews: that Jesus is the true Messiah, prophet, and king (chaps. 1–3), the new high priest (chaps. 4–9), and an example of perfect obedient faith (chaps. 10–13). Thus a first group of related citations of psalms and Hebrews appears in *Christian Doctrine* when Milton takes up God's nature and decrees, predestination, the Son, creation, and providence (Book I, chaps. 2–8); a second group, when he discusses Christ the redeemer, his mediatorial office, redemption, repentance, and saving faith (Book I, chaps. 14–15); and a final scattered group appears when Milton considers the behavior of the faithful in Book II. Since he thought the writer of the epistle had used a method like his own in collating spiritual texts "so as to teach the main points of Christian doctrine" (*YP* 6:128), Milton augmented Hebrews and followed it faithfully.

Milton used Hebrews and its proof texts from the psalms synchronically and abstractly in *Christian Doctrine*. In *Paradise Regained* he isolated the temptation in the wilderness from Luke as the heroic act by which the Son "[founds] A fairer Paradise" (4.613). He withdrew the temptation from its place in an accomplished life manifesting the spiritual meanings of psalms and dramatized it as an eluded entrapment. He limited each actor to such knowledge as he could naturally possess at the commencement of the temptation or gain during it. Both Satan and Jesus begin with a quantum of Old Testament learning, including Job's sufferings and the contents of the Book of Psalms. The course of the poem produces self-knowledge in Jesus and an understanding of his role equivalent to that of the writer of Hebrews; it produces in Satan a horrifying recognition of the Son and of his own fate. Both Satan's assault and the Son's obedience turn on contrastive psalm readings; Hebrews, augmented with other psalms not cited in Hebrews, supplies the ideas, readings, and often words, contested in the struggle between Satan and the Son. Although Satan continually questions the nature of the Son's kingship, while the Son takes up both the prophetic

[11] Cross-referencing Psalms and Hebrews, Milton reinforced Hebrews's citations with supplementary psalms. Hebrews 1 quotes Psalms 2, 45, 102, 104, and 110; Milton added 16, 33, 34, 90, 91, 95, and 148. Hebrews 2 quotes 8 and 22; Milton added 72 and 110. Hebrews 3 quotes 95; Milton added 141. Hebrews 4 quotes 95; Milton added 33, 137, 139, 147. Hebrews 5 quotes 2, 110; Milton added 90. Hebrews 6 quotes 110; Milton added 94. Hebrews 7, 8, and 9 quote no psalms, but Milton linked them respectively with 51 and 58, 90 and again 90. Hebrews 10 quotes 40; Milton added 2, 90, and 119. Hebrews 11 and 12 cite no psalms; Milton quoted them respectively with 15, 16, 17, 19, 49, 37, 78 and 15, 24, 26, 90, 94, 103, 116, 119. Hebrews 13 cites 118; Milton added 26, 119.

and kingly functions of his mediation as well, the crucial contest in *Paradise Regained* as in Hebrews is over priesthood.

The brief proem to *Paradise Regained* sets the large theme—

> Recover'd Paradise to all mankind,
> By one mans firm obedience fully tri'd
> Through all temptation
> (1.3–5)

—with the very emphasis of Hebrews 2.18: "For in that he himself hath suffered being tempted, he is able to succour them that are tempted." Action begins with Satan "Nigh Thunder-struck" by the sound of the Father's proclamation of the Son at his baptism still in his ears. The proclamation[12]—"This is my Son belov'd, in him am pleas'd" (1.85)—joining Psalm 2.7, "Thou *art* my Son; this day have I begotten thee," to Isaiah 42.1, "Behold my servant, whom I uphold; mine elect, *in whom* my soul delighteth," unites the two concepts of Messiah and servant explained in Hebrews. Satan, doubtful of its significance but alert to its threat, summons his peers in a midair consistory and warns:

> Who this is we must learn, for man he seems
> In all his lineaments, though in his face
> The glimpses of his Fathers glory shine.
> (1.91–93)

A parallel scene represents God in conversation with Gabriel and concludes a brief angelic hymn. God must leave the poem when the heroic test of the "perfect Man" commences, so that the test will show that the Son's worthiness arises from his humanity; Milton highlights in God's declaration the significance of psalms in Hebrews to the ensuing test. The proclamation opens and closes with an exaltation of the Son before all the angels, as "This perfect Man, by merit call'd my Son, / To earn Salvation for the Sons of men" (1.166–67). The superiority of the Son to every created being is taught by Hebrews 1–3. God, Milton's ideal exegete since typology is literal intention to him,[13] offers a perfect interpretation in advance of the action to Satan's con-

[12] Matthew 3.17: "And lo a voice from heaven, saying, This is my beloved Son, in whom I am well pleased." Mark 1.11: "And there came a voice from heaven, *saying*, Thou art my beloved Son, in whom I am well pleased." Luke 3.22: "And the Holy Ghost descended in a bodily shape like a dove upon him, and a voice came from heaven, which said, Thou art my beloved Son; in thee I am well pleased." And Hebrews 1.5: "For unto which of the angels said he at any time, Thou art my Son, this day have I begotten thee?"

[13] See Lewalski, *Milton's Brief Epic*, 164–82.

tinuous question of what it means that the man Jesus is called the "son of God": Jesus earned the title and is called the Son "by merit."

Like the author of Hebrews, Luke, too, quotes psalms selectively, controlling his allusions not only by a messianic vision so similar to Hebrews as to have suggested his authorship of the epistle to some, but also by a strong sense of literary form. His gospel is organized into five well-defined parts, like acts in a play: Jesus' early years (1.5 to 1.80), his preparation for his ministry (3.1 to 4.13), his actual ministry in Galilee (4.14 to 9.50), his journey to Jerusalem (9.51 to 19.46), and his crucifixion and resurrection (19.47 to 24.53). The gospel focuses its longest attention upon the episodes of Jesus' journey toward Jerusalem, previewed in Luke 9.51: "he stedfastly set his face to go to Jerusalem."[14] In Luke, the temptation in the wilderness is the final preparation for that journey. Milton endows it with the centrality in Jesus' life suggested by Luke's treatment of it as the symbolic event that initiates the ministry.[15] He confirms in Luke's exposition the thematic emphasis of Hebrews.[16] God tells Gabriel that the temptation in the wilderness is a decisive preliminary exercise:

> There he shall first lay down the rudiments
> Of his great warfare, e're I send him forth
> To conquer Sin and Death the two grand foes,
> By Humiliation and strong Sufferance:
> His weakness shall o'recome Satanic strength
> And all the world, and mass of sinful flesh.
> (1.157–62)

The symbolic value of the temptation to Luke, the author of Hebrews, and Milton lies in Jesus' confirmed obedience tested by suffering.

[14] See Kermode, *The Genesis of Secrecy*, 69, on the nativity stories in Luke.

[15] In Luke the temptation is framed symmetrically to create that sense of symbolic force. It opens, "And Jesus being full of the Holy Ghost returned from Jordan [his baptism], and was led by the Spirit into the wilderness, Being forty days tempted of the devil" (4.1–2). It closes, "And when the devil had ended all the temptation, he departed from him for a season. And Jesus returned in the power of the Spirit into Galilee: and there went out a fame of him through all the region round about" (4.13–14).

[16] Hebrews 2.9–10, 16–18: "But we see Jesus, who was made a little lower than the angels for the suffering of death, crowned with glory and honour; that he by the grace of God should taste death for every man. For it became him, for whom *are* all things, and by whom *are* all things, in bringing many sons unto glory, to make the captain of their salvation perfect through sufferings. . . . For verily he took not on *him the nature of* angels; but he took on *him* the seed of Abraham. Wherefore in all things it behoved him to be made like unto *his* brethren, that he might be a merciful and faithful high priest in things *pertaining* to God, to make reconciliation for the sins of the people. For in that he himself hath suffered being tempted, he is able to succour them that are tempted."

From the obedience comes not only his moral value as an example to mankind, but his priestly value as one who both makes sacrifice and is the sacrifice for mankind, that priesthood being the core theme of Hebrews (2.14–18).[17] In Luke, the temptation in the wilderness ended with the misconstrued Psalm 91.11–12, "For he shall give his angels charge over thee, to keep thee in all thy ways. They shall bear thee up in *their* hands, lest thou dash thy foot against a stone," provoking from the Son the absolute authority of Deuteronomy 6.16, "Ye shall not tempt the Lord your God." On those suggestions, Milton arranges debate between the Son and Satan on the messianic psalms quoted in Hebrews and in Luke, together with cognate psalms.

As God is the best of all Milton's scriptural exegetes, Satan naturally is the worst. In his opening speech he exposes both a carnal hermeneutic and a sophisticated skepticism in applying it to the problem of Jesus. When Satan recounts the baptism of the Son, his gloss unmistakably defines a call to kingship. John the Baptist

> *Pretends to wash off* sin, and fit them so
> Purified to receive him pure, or *rather*
> *To do him honour as their King.*
> (1.73–75; my emphasis)

Satan's irony gives edge to his confidence that he can see through the appearances of pious ritual to their functionality. Nonetheless, as he continues, his questions cloaked in suavity reveal an uncertainty grounding Milton's drama:

> [I saw] on his head
> A perfect Dove descend, what e're it meant,
> And out of Heav'n the Sov'raign voice I heard,
> This is my Son belov'd, in him am pleas'd.
> His Mother then is mortal, but his Sire,
> He who obtains the Monarchy of Heav'n,
> And what will he not do to advance his Son?
> His first-begot we know, and sore have felt,
> When his fierce thunder drove us to the deep;
> Who this is we must learn.
> (1.82–91)

[17] "Seeing then that we have a great high priest, that is passed into the heavens, Jesus the Son of God, let us hold fast *our* profession." "Forasmuch then as the children are partakers of flesh and blood, he also himself likewise took part of the same; that through death he might destroy him that had the power of death, that is, the devil" (Hebrews 4.14 and 2.14).

Satan links the Father's exaltation of the Son "to whom shall bow / All knees" (5.608–9) in *Paradise Lost* to his proclamation of this Son, glossing the psalm formula "this is my son" as the announcement of a rival heir to usurp his own worldly leadership "Supream on Earth." He resolves "to subvert whom he suspected rais'd / To end his Raign on Earth so long enjoy'd" (1.124–25). One prong of his subversive attack is to strike a treaty with the claimant Son; all knees may bow to him, if he will bow to Satan. Another prong is to alienate Father from Son, by making this son unworthy of his inheritance. Satan sees a way to attack the moral worth of Jesus, through a carnal reading of Psalm 2.6–7: "Yet have I set my king upon my holy hill of Zion. I will declare the decree: the Lord hath said unto me, Thou *art* my Son; this day have I begotten thee."

The first day's action is delayed one last time, however, by a representation of the Son in soliloquy, he too thinking of psalm interpretation. The angelic hymn hinted at scriptural right reading in predicting the Son's victory "not of arms, / But to vanquish by wisdom hellish wiles" (1.174–75). Milton draws on the account of Christ's childhood and youth, given only in Luke, to show Jesus recalling the self-knowledge that took him to the Temple to teach and prophesy:[18]

> [T]herefore above my years,
> The Law of God I read, and found it sweet,
> Made it my whole delight.
> (1.206–8)

He had proposed to himself "victorious deeds . . . heroic acts" but "held it more humane, more heavenly" to "teach the erring Soul." When his mother told him of the annunciation, an event again recorded only in Luke, she encouraged his heroic aspirations. To learn what "matchless Deeds" might "express [his] matchless Sire," he read Scripture, "searching what was writ / Concerning the Messiah," and discovered from Psalm 22 that his "way must lie / Through many a hard assay even to the death" (1.263–64). He then went to John the Baptist, the promise of whose birth, too, is exclusive to Luke, and heard himself proclaimed in "the sum of all, my Father's voice" (1.283). At that point in his musings, Jesus offers his reading of Psalm 2.7 against Satan's. The Father's voice prophesied no coronation; it signaled divine authority to begin a life of public witness,

[18] Sims, *The Bible in Milton's Epics*, 274, notes an echo of Psalm 119.103, "How sweet are thy words unto my taste!" Psalm 119, a wisdom psalm extolling the Law, contains many hints for the soliloquy, for example 119.34–35: "Give me understanding, and I shall keep thy law; . . . . Make me to go in the path of thy commandments; for therein do I delight."

> by which I knew the time
> Now full, that I no more should live obscure,
> But openly begin, as best becomes
> The Authority which I deriv'd from Heaven.
> (1.286–89)

As the Son trustfully enters the wilderness, "For what concerns my knowledge God reveals" (1.293), he enacts Psalm 16.11, "Thou wilt shew me the path of life."

The action of Book I, the temptation to turn stones into bread, commences when Satan in disguise suggests that the Son relieve their hunger. A dry and curt Jesus, very like the Lukean Jesus answering lawyers and Sadducees, declines:

> Think'st thou such force in Bread? is it not written
> (For I discern thee other then thou seem'st)
> Man lives not by Bread only, but each Word
> Proceeding from the mouth of God.
> (1.347–50)

Here what is written in Luke 4.4, "And Jesus answered him, saying, It is written, That man shall not live by bread alone, but by every word of God," is based on Deuteronomy 8.3 and Jeremiah 31.33 as glossed in Hebrews 6.5 and 8.10, "[The enlightened] have tasted the good word of God" and "I will put my laws into their mind, and write them in their hearts: and I will be to them a God, and they shall be to me a people."[19] Satan, rebuffed, poses as God's loyal opposition and man's friend, offering "advice by presages and signs, / And answers, oracles, portents and dreams" (1.394–95). At once the Son knows that he alone is now to speak God's word; as the writer of Hebrews 1.1–2 put it, "God, who . . . spake in time past unto the fathers by the prophets, Hath in these last days spoken unto us by *his* Son." The scene ends with the Son assuming his prophetic role:

> No more shalt thou by oracling abuse
> The Gentiles; henceforth Oracles are ceast,
> . . . .
> God hath now sent his living Oracle
> Into the World, to teach his final will,
> And sends his Spirit of Truth henceforth to dwell
> In pious Hearts, an inward Oracle

[19] Deuteronomy 8.3 reads, in part, "man doth not live by bread only, but by every *word* that proceedeth out of the mouth of the Lord doth man live." Jeremiah 31.33 reads, in part, "After those days, saith the Lord, I will put my law in their inward parts, and write it in their hearts; and will be their God, and they shall be my people."

> To all truth requisite for men to know.
> (1.455–56, 460–64)

He combines, that is, the prayer of Psalm 43.3, "O send out thy light and thy truth: let them lead me," and its answering benediction in Psalm 72.18, "Blessed *be* the Lord God, the God of Israel, who only doeth wondrous things."

While Satan holds firm to a blanket definition of the Son as royal heir, each temptation allows Jesus to see in his sonship its constitutive prophetic, kingly, and priestly spiritual functions; at each stage he argues from the group of thematically linked psalms Milton brought together in *Christian Doctrine*. The close of the first temptation, the temptation to banquet as Satan's guest, introduces the kingly function of sonship by contesting the meaning of Psalm 95.8–9, "Harden not your heart, as in the provocation, *and* as *in* the day of temptation in the wilderness: When your fathers tempted me, proved me, and saw my work." Hebrews 3.7–12 glosses the "provocation" in the psalm as "an evil heart of unbelief." When Satan returns to the task of subverting the Son, he flourishes the banquet table as a kingly tribute from Nature to its creator's heir. The Son rejects the banquet at first simply as though recalling Psalm 141.4, "[W]ith men that work iniquity . . . let me not eat of their dainties." But ultimately he addresses the Satanic "provocation":

> Why shouldst thou then obtrude this diligence,
> In vain, where no acceptance it can find,
> And with my hunger what has thou to do?
> Thy Pompous Delicacies I contemn,
> And count thy specious gifts no gifts but guiles.
> (2.387–91)

The obtrusion of guileful "diligence" is the "provocation in the wilderness" of Psalm 95.7, narrated in Psalm 78.17–19: "And they sinned yet more against him by provoking the most High in the wilderness. And they tempted God in their heart by asking meat for their lust. Yea, they spake against God; they said, Can God furnish a table in the wilderness?" Satan's taunt, "What *doubt'st thou Son of God*? sit down and eat," and Jesus' reply, "I can at will, *doubt not*, as soon as thou, / Command a Table in this Wilderness" (emphasis added), reveals that the struggle is won by the Son's faith, not mere temperance or prudence (2.377, 383–84).

The trial of kingship in Satan's offer of alliance with Parthia or Rome similarly opposes a carnally read Psalm 22.28, "For the kingdom *is* the Lord's: and he *is* the governor among the nations," to the

Son's spiritual reading of Psalm 33.16, "There is no king saved by the multitude of an host: a mighty man is not delivered by much strength," reinforced by Psalm 103.19, "The Lord hath prepared his throne in the heavens; and his kingdom ruleth over all," in a scenario using the implied dialogue of 145.11, 13: "They shall speak of the glory of thy kingdom, and talk of thy power; . . . . Thy kingdom *is* an everlasting kingdom, and thy dominion *endureth* throughout all generations." So Satan first recommends Parthia as a politic ally, since "prediction still / In all things, and all men, supposes means" (3.354–55) and then Rome. The Son is not less shrewd. The Parthian alliance, for all its "ostentation vain of fleshly arm, / And fragile arms," cannot save nations too morally corrupt to save themselves; the Roman alliance assures only earthly kingdom:

> Know therefore when my season comes to sit
> On *David*'s Throne, it shall be like a tree
> Spreading and over-shadowing all the Earth,
> Or as a stone that shall to pieces dash
> All Monarchies besides throughout the world,
> And of my Kingdom there shall be no end.
> (4.146–51)

While his rejection fulfills Daniel's prophecy, it also draws together Psalm 2.9, "thou shalt dash them in pieces like a potter's vessel," and Psalm 145.13, "Thy kingdom *is* an everlasting kingdom," with possibly a hint of Psalm 1.3, "And he shall be like a tree planted by the rivers of water."

Finally, the storm tower sequence likewise deploys contrasting psalm readings. Satan's consistent preoccupation with worldly kingship culminates in crude ironies. He summarizes the Son's moral and intellectual triumphs so that his rejection of "offer'd aid, / Which would have set thee in short time with ease / On *David's* Throne; or Throne of all the world" (4.377–79) appears a provincial shrinking from the "mighty work" of "Saviour to Mankind." Satan then threatens the Son with astrology, finding in "what the Stars . . . give me to spell" a malevolent taunt that predicts the passion:

> Sorrows, and labours, opposition, hate,
> Attends thee, scorns, reproaches, injuries,
> Violence and stripes, and lastly cruel death.
> (4.386–88)

While Satan continues to manipulate carnal readings of the messianic psalm group Milton brought together in *Christian Doctrine* 1.2–5, in this prefiguration of the passion, Milton moves forward to consider the block of interrelated psalms and Hebrews texts he brought together in *Christian Doctrine* 1.14–15, discussing Christ as redeemer, his mediatorial office, and redemption. To Psalms 2 and 22 are added Psalms 37, 40, and 94. Satan promises "opposition and hate" from Psalm 2.2: "The kings of the earth set themselves, and the rulers take counsel together, against the Lord, and against his anointed," passing over the psalm's foretelling of their failure, "He that sitteth in the heavens shall laugh: the Lord shall have them in derision" (v. 4). He predicts "scorns, reproaches, injuries . . . and lastly cruel death" from Psalm 22.6, 15, "[I am] a reproach of men, and despised of the people" and "thou hast brought me into the dust of death," choosing not to notice its promise, "he hath not despised nor abhorred the affliction of the afflicted; neither hath he hid his face from him; but when he cried unto him, he heard" (v. 24). Satan derives "violence and stripes" from Psalm 37.14, "The wicked have drawn out the sword, and have bent their bow . . . to slay such as be of upright conversation," ignoring its reassurance that "evildoers . . . shall soon be cut down like the grass, and wither as the green herb. Trust in the Lord, and do good" (vv. 1–3). Similarly Satan hints at Psalm 40.12, "innumerable evils have compassed me about," without its hope that though "I *am* poor and needy; *yet* the Lord thinketh upon me" (v. 17) and Psalm 94.5, "They break in pieces thy people, O Lord, and afflict thine heritage," without its reassurance, "For the Lord will not cast off his people, neither will he forsake his inheritance" (v. 14).

When these abusive taunts and the ensuing storm equally fail to terrify the Son, Satan threatens him by the misprision of Psalm 91 from Luke 4.9–13: "And he brought him to Jerusalem, and set him on a pinnacle of the temple, and said unto him, If thou be the Son of God, cast thyself down from hence: For it is written, He shall give his angels charge over thee, to keep thee: And in *their* hands they shall bear thee up, lest at any time thou dash thy foot against a stone. And Jesus answering said unto him, It is said, Thou shalt not tempt the Lord thy God." Satan used the storm as a "sure fore-going sign" (4.483) of the "dangers, and adversities and pains" (4.479) which he predicts for the Son; Milton uses it symbolically to recall the darkening of the sun at the crucifixion. But the assault on Christ's political kingship, always Satan's thrust, does not rely only on fear to produce submission; it relies on pride as well. Satan considers that the Son's desire to attract national support for his kingship will tempt him to perform a miracle, stage-managed so that the Father will be alienated. Either terror or pride may be the lever by which finally and brutally to subvert the prophesied reign. Hence, though after the storm Satan comes "with no new device . . . [but] resolv'd / Desperate of better course, to vent his rage," and though he apparently concedes victory, "Thou shalt be what thou art ordain'd, no doubt; / For Angels have proclaim'd it" (4.443–45, 473–74), the Son recognizes Satan's maneuver to manipulate him:

> Who knowing I shall raign past thy preventing,
> Obtrud'st thy offer'd aid, that I accepting
> At least might seem to hold all power of thee,
> Ambitious spirit, and wouldst be thought my God,
> And storm'st refus'd, thinking to terrifie
> Mee to thy will.
> (4.492–97)

Satan's storm tower final temptation—full of pique, rage, and violence—is not bankrupt in its resort to naked force, however. His conceded impotence on an earlier occasion cloaked a considered attack, and so it does now.

Milton's musical and figural accompaniment for the confrontation between carnal and spiritual understanding throughout the poem is the contrast between noise and silence, passion and calm, and perverted nature and innocent. At nightfall wild beasts become mild in the presence of the Son, "nor sleeping him nor waking harm'd" (1.311), reflecting the promise of Psalm 8.7–8: "[Thou hast put under his feet] All sheep and oxen, yea, and the beasts of the field; The fowl of the air, and the fish of the sea, *and whatsoever* passeth through the paths of the seas." The morning greets him with the "chaunt of tuneful Birds," for whom too God provides, as in Psalm 104.12, "the fowls of the heaven have their habitation, *which* sing among the branches." In contrast, Satan's banquet table is withdrawn violently "[w]ith sound of Harpies wings, and Talons heard" (2.403); his "vain importunity" is likened to a "swarm of flies in vintage time" that "[b]eat off, returns as oft with humming sound" (4.17); he bears the Son furiously off to the pinnacle "without wing / Of *Hippogrif*." The tumultuous storm is so noisily and unnaturally produced by Satan, hidden but "feigning to disappear," that when he ends it, even he seems "glad . . . Of this fair change" (4.441–42).

The storm heralding the last temptation does not appear in Milton's source in Luke, but its interpolation is not only based on Job but inspired by Psalms, as Barbara Lewalski has already suggested. She notes that Psalm 91, the authority for God's angels bearing the Son up lest he dash his foot against a stone, contains in an earlier verse the suggestion of intimidation by night—"Thou shalt not be afraid for the terror by night."[20] Satan's inspiration also derives from a misappropriation of Psalm 90.5–7: "Thou carriest [the children of men] away as with a flood; they are *as* a sleep. . . . For we are consumed by thine anger, and by thy wrath are we troubled." Satan reads the night flood, the sleeping man, the threat of destruction, and the flash of God's anger as pyrotechnical hints and omits the confession of trust in the psalm's closing prayer. The Son, incapable of a merely carnal psalm reading, can "contemn" the bullying storm as "false portents, not sent from God, but thee." Psalm 110.3, the psalm quoted in Hebrews as establishing his priesthood, gives the Son's morning mood—"in the beauties of holiness from the womb of the morning: thou hast the dew of thy youth"; the epiphanic hymn of Psalm 148.8 conveys his true knowledge of how God manifests himself in Nature—"[Praise the Lord] Fire, and hail; snow, and vapours; stormy wind fulfilling his word."

In the temptation of the tower, at length, occurs the well-remarked carnal abuse of Psalm 91, when the devil scornfully suggests that Jesus call upon angels to keep his foot from being dashed against a stone. The Son opposes to it the words Luke ascribes to him: "it is also written, Tempt not the Lord thy God." The scene is a midrash of Psalm 94.18: "When I said, My foot slippeth; thy mercy, O Lord, held me up"; it illustrates the Son's obedience in contrast to the Jews' disobedience "*in* the day of temptation in the wilderness" (Ps. 95.8). It fulfills Psalm 8.6, "thou hast put all *things* under his feet." *Paradise Regained* immediately ends with an angelic hymn to Christ's priesthood that concludes:

> Hail Son of the most High, heir of both worlds,
> Queller of Satan, on thy glorious work
> Now enter, and begin to save mankind.
> (4.633–35)

Standing on the pinnacle of the temple as man's representative and example before God, angels and the devil, the Son reveals his mediatorial function. The best accounts we have of *Paradise Regained* suggest that the Son defeats Satan three times and the last time leaves him thunderstruck. True as that is, the final scene also completes an overarching dramatic confrontation between Satan and the Son, interpreting Luke through Hebrews. Satan's persistent probing at the literal meaning of royal heredity takes no account of what Milton and Reformation dogmatics distinguished as the "triple function of the mediatorial office,

[20] See Lewalski, *Milton's Brief Epic*, 305–6.

PROPHETIC, PRIESTLY and KINGLY."[21] Satan asks only whether the phrase "son of God" applies so specifically to Jesus as to end forthwith his own reign on earth, but Milton wrote into each temptation, not only the last, a privileging of priesthood over the other functions derived from Hebrews and consonant with his own lifelong detestation of prelacy. Not only does each part of the Son's testing involve carnal versus spiritual readings of psalms, each contains a scene not properly accounted for without consulting the epistle and the psalms it quotes, together with those psalms Milton added as reinforcement. The scenes taken together consider hereditary priesthood; there are four of them, one in each book; together they give dramatic coherence to the theme uppermost in the poem, the question of Christ's priesthood.

In Book I, during the temptation to turn stones to bread, Satan curtly asks permission to visit the Son, just as an atheist priest is permitted to stand at the altar. In Book II, before the temptation of the banquet, he debunks the authority of hereditary office. In Book III, before the temptation of kingdom, power and glory, he asks the Son to mediate between him and the Father. In Book IV, between the storm and tower episodes, he summarizes the Son's exemplary manhood. The four scenes involve New Testament readings of psalms to test the connection between exemplary and vicarious action. In each the Son both teaches and manifests the redemptive faith expounded in Hebrews. Milton must control the interpretation of his readers so that heroic self-sacrifice may be manifested without contamination from superstition or prelatical traditions, the Son's singularity not preserved at the expense of his moral exemplification, the poet's compassion not swallowed up in his didacticism. The writer of Hebrews perhaps faced a similar problem with respect to his audience. Certainly he and Milton adopted similar solutions—a density of psalm allusion directed to show how the Son as priest not only offers but is both gift and sacrifice. In the scenes to which I now turn, while Satan continues to offer expedient readings of inheritance, the Son does not halt at the assertion that his kingdom is of the spirit and not of the world but adds that his triumph consists in humiliation and suffering. He uses the humiliation to teach self-sacrifice as heroic self-fulfillment; Milton represents the pity and awe in it to move his readers to faith.

In the first brief glance at priesthood, Satan makes an ironical request out of his chilly knowledge of clergy:

> Thy Father, who is holy, wise and pure,
> Suffers the Hypocrite or Atheous Priest

[21] *YP* 6:432.

> To tread his Sacred Courts, and minister
> . . . .
> . . . disdain not such access to me.
> (1.486–88, 492)

Patronizing professional ministers, Satan mocks Psalm 15.1–2: "Lord, who shall abide in thy tabernacle? . . . He that . . . speaketh the truth in his heart," and its fellow Psalm 24.3–4: "who shall stand in his holy place? [He who hath not] sworn deceitfully." The Son's reply, "I bid not or forbid" (1. 495), elicits from Satan a mock clerical obeisance: "Satan bowing low / His gray dissimulation, disappear'd" (1. 497–98). But Milton plucked the Son's answer from Hebrews 5.5, which cites Psalm 2.7: "So also Christ glorified not himself to be made an high priest; but he that said unto him, Thou art my Son, to-day have I begotten thee." A man-made priesthood open to Satan's scorn gives way to the Son's true priesthood. Hebrews concedes the imperfection in the best professional priests: "For the law maketh men high priests which have infirmity," but claims for the Son (9.24), "Christ is not entered into the holy places made with hands, *which are* the figures of the true; but into heaven itself, now to appear in the presence of God for us." The scene creates a space between Satan's challenge that priests are self-perpetuating tithesmen and the Son's acquiescence in the self-sacrifice appointed for him.

In the next of the four scenes of priesthood, Jesus, aware of hunger for the first time, wholly ignores it. As he walks in the wilderness, he not only thinks like psalm texts—Psalm 34.10, "The young lions do lack, and suffer hunger: but they that seek the Lord shall not want any good *thing*," or Psalm 107.9, "[He] filleth the hungry soul with goodness"—but manifests them, thereby witnessing to the Father, part of his "end of being on Earth." Meanwhile Satan asks advice from the other fallen angels a second time, now linking the new man genealogically to the old Adam but distinguishing them intellectually and morally. The whole thrust of the scene concerns hereditary power and inherited office. The previous temptation was introduced by Satan's attempt to relate and distinguish the firstborn Son from the man by merit called the Son. Now about to test the relationship of birth to calling, Satan reports in consistory:

> Far other labour to be undergon
> Then when I dealt with *Adam* first of Men,
> Though *Adam* by his Wives allurement fell,
> However to this Man inferior far,
> If he be Man by Mothers side at least,

> With more then humane gifts from Heaven adorn'd,
> Perfections absolute, Graces divine,
> And amplitude of mind to greatest Deeds.
> (2.132–39)

While Satan interrogates the Son's humanity on his mother's side, he represses a question about his father's side; whether or not the Son *inherited* humanity, he was surely *given* divine gifts. Satan's smile at Adam's succumbing to the allure of his wife does not inhibit Belial from suggesting the "ennervement" of the Son by women. Satan listens to Belial with his thoughts still on the absurd possibility that he is dealing with the kind of hero from classical fiction, half god, half man. When he rejects Belial's suggestion, he repudiates both the idea of cross-mating between gods and human beings and the recommendation of sensuality, a too easily resisted bait:

> Before the Flood thou [Belial] with thy lusty Crew,
> False titl'd Sons of God, roaming the Earth
> Cast wanton eyes on the daughters of men,
> And coupl'd with them, and begot a race.
> Have we not seen, or by relation heard,
> In Courts and Regal Chambers how thou lurk'st,
> In Wood or Grove by mossie Fountain side,
> In Valley or Green Meadow to way-lay
> Some beauty rare, *Calisto*, *Clymene*,
> *Daphne*, or *Semele*, *Antiopa*,
> Or *Amymone*, *Syrinx*, many more
> Too long, then lay'st thy scapes on names ador'd,
> *Apollo*, *Neptune*, *Jupiter*, or *Pan*,
> Satyr, or Fawn, or Silvan? But these haunts
> Delight not all.
> (2.178–92)

Satan's skepticism about godly-mortal miscegenation comes from his knowledge that ancient poets were cheated by Belial into recording a divine interest in mortal women which was no more than a cover story put about by "the dissolutest spirit that fell" (2.150). But when he calls Belial and his "lusty Crew" "false titl'd Sons of God," the possibility is left open of a true entitlement. Pagan writers inflated their heroes in supposing them demigods by blood; Jesus rejected those poets' "personating / Thir Gods ridiculous" (4.342–43). Aware of the fictitiousness of epic genealogies, Satan interprets fatherhood in a kind of strict constructionism; he limits it to literal procreation and denies divine fatherhood to the Son just as he denies the procreation by pagan gods of heroic demigods. He cannot credit another kind of fatherhood any more than he can conceive that the "greatest things" the Son will accomplish could be the "Humiliation . . . Sufferance . . . [and] weakness" (1.160–61).

Satan's strict constructionism is opposed by Hebrews. Just as a physical connection was necessary to prove election in the Old Testament and genealogies were abundantly detailed to demonstrate it, so a hereditary vocation was necessary to priesthood. It is by way of introducing a new kind of priesthood that Milton has Satan consider godly paternity. The new priesthood is one not passed on through tribe and training, where the authority of descent endorses a continuity over generations, but rather a supratribal priesthood, strong enough to break lineal authority forever by the substitution of a single eternal priest. The Son is the only priest necessary to men, his actions perfect and his priesthood complete. Hebrews interprets Psalm 110.1, 4, "The Lord said unto my Lord, Sit thou at my right hand" and "The Lord hath sworn, and will not repent, Thou *art* a priest for ever after the order of Melchizedek," as a "disannulling of the commandment going before" that priesthood derive from "the loins of [a] father" (Heb. 7.18, 10). As a strict constructionist in paternity cases who moreover knows in kingship as well as in priesthood the Hebrew laws of inheritance,[22] Satan thinks that the Son inherits the throne of David and the kingship of the world not by his father's but his mother's line; his "Father known" is a "Carpenter" transmitting only "low . . . birth." Jesus is "ordain'd / To sit upon [his] Father *David's* Throne" because David is "By Mother's side thy Father."

The third priestly scene finds Satan reminding the Son in Book III of the zeal and duty he must show in good season if his kingdom is to be secure. His carnal construction of Psalm 69.9, "the zeal of thine house hath eaten me up," and of 119.139, "My zeal hath consumed me," converts those verses into goads toward power:

> If Kingdom move thee not, let move thee Zeal,
> And Duty; Zeal and Duty are not slow;

[22] The law making priesthood heritable is found in Deuteronomy 18.5, "For the Lord thy God hath chosen him out of all thy tribes, to stand to minister in the name of the Lord, him and his sons for ever." Heritability of kingship, the king nominating one of his sons to succeed him, is found in 1 Kings 1.30 and 2 Chron. 21.3. Satan's assertion that Jesus inherited kingship through Mary rests on a traditional interpretation of Isaiah 11.1; "And there shall come forth a rod out of the stem of Jesse, and a Branch shall grow out of his roots," read so that the rod symbolizes Mary and the branch, Jesus. Satan ignores the genealogy in Matthew 1.1–16 that derives Jesus' royal descent from Adam and Seth through Shem and Boaz, Jesse and David, down to Joseph.

. . . .
Zeal of thy Fathers house, Duty to free
Thy Country from her Heathen servitude;
So shalt thou best fullfil, best verifie
The Prophets old, who sung thy endless raign.
(3.171–72, 175–78)

The Son knows the implications of his messianic priesthood, however, and replies to Satan in terms of self-sacrifice:

What if [God] hath decreed that I shall first
Be try'd in humble state, and things adverse,
By tribulations, injuries, insults,
Contempts, and scorns, and snares, and violence,
Suffering, abstaining, quietly expecting
Without distrust or doubt, that he may know
What I can suffer, how obey? who best
Can suffer, best can do; best reign, who first
Well hath obey'd; just tryal e're I merit
My exaltation without change or end.
(3.188–97)

The thematically related psalms which furnish the material of the Son's reply are Psalm 25, the psalm of the suffering servant of the Lord, which ends "Let integrity and uprightness preserve me; for I wait on thee," Psalm 118.18, "The Lord hath chastened me sore: but he hath not given me over unto death," Psalm 26.6, "I will wash mine hands in innocency: so will I compass thine altar, O Lord," and Psalm 94.12, "Blessed *is* the man whom thou chastenest, O Lord." As the Son infers his passion from these psalms, he fulfills the priestly role defined in Hebrews 5.8, "Though he were a Son, yet learned he obedience by the things which he suffered," where Hebrews also cites Psalm 22. Satan's recognition of the priestly implications in the Son's words draws from him a dramatic and reckless confession of a wish that the Son interpose between him and his "Fathers ire" "a kind of shading cool / Interposition" (3.221–22). Satan acknowledges momentarily the Son's right to be intercessor.

The final priestly scene is the divided scene in Book IV that reverts to testing the psalmic phrase "sons of God." As Satan saw, fallen angels have no particular entitlement to apply the phrase to themselves. But what of a general entitlement of all beings to be called "Sons of God" on the basis of Psalm 82.6? Satan's initial strict construction of the verse, "I have said, Ye *are* gods; and all of you *are* children of the most High," read it as skeptically as he read the ancient poets. The angels were "false titl'd" if they relied on that authority, for the psalm only claims that God, the creator of all beings, is the maker of all kings or magistrates. Divine fatherhood in that sense Satan reads merely as a metaphor for the transfer of power. Yet when circumstances suggest it, Satan also gives Psalm 82 a broad construction. Satan would disinherit the Son by distributing sonship too widely, just as willingly as he would disinherit him by restricting paternity narrowly. In the first part of the divided scene, Satan reacts to the Son's rejection of all the kingdoms of the world and their power and glory as his conditional gifts, a rejection Milton gave nearly word for word from his source in Luke 4.8: "Get thee behind me, Satan: for it is written, Thou shalt worship the Lord thy God, and him only shalt thou serve." Jesus in Luke paraphrases Deuteronomy 11.13, "I command you this day, to love the Lord your God, and to serve him with all your heart and with all your soul," recasting Psalm 81.9, "neither shalt thou worship any strange god" and Psalm 72.11, "Yea, all kings shall fall down before him: all nations shall serve him." The Son's indignation was fully aroused by Satan's audacity to offer to him that which was already and always his own, "[to] offer them to me the Son of God, / To me my own, on such abhorred pact" (4.190–91). In response to that indignant self-identification, Satan broadly construes Psalm 82, claiming his own sonship and godhood:

> Be not so sore offended, Son of God;
> Though Sons of God both Angels are and Men,
> If I to try whether in higher sort
> Then these thou bear'st that title, have propos'd
> What both from Men and Angels I receive,
> . . . .
> God of this world invok't and world beneath.
> (4.196–200, 203)

Up to a point Satan reads the psalm just as Milton read it in *Christian Doctrine*: the verse "I say, you are Gods, and all of you sons of the Most High" is "God's own words when he was addressing kings and magnates." But Milton explains, "We should notice . . . that the name 'God' is, *by the will and permission of God the Father*, not infrequently bestowed even upon angels and men (*how much more, then, upon the only begotten Son, the image of the Father*!)"[23] To Satan, "sons of God" is God's formula for the delegation of power, analogous to the titles bestowed on Satan himself by men, "God of this world invok't and world

[23] *YP* 6:213, and 6:233, my emphasis.

beneath." Hence when the Son withstands the terror of the storm, Satan recurs to the verse to test a final broad reading:

> [I] Heard thee pronounc'd the Son of God belov'd.
> Thenceforth I thought thee worth my nearer view
> And narrower Scrutiny, that I might learn
> In what degree or meaning thou art call'd
> The Son of God, which bears no *single sence*;
> The Son of God I also am, or was,
> And if I was, I am; relation stands;
> All men are Sons of God; yet thee I thought
> In some respect far higher so declar'd.
> (4.513–21, my emphasis)

But the psalm in the Hebrews interpretation does bear a single sense. And unwittingly Satan's summary of the results of their contest makes apparent to every reader that one sense:

> [I] have found thee
> Proof against all temptation as a rock
> Of Adamant, and as a Center, firm
> To the utmost of meer man both wise and good,
> Not more.
> (4.532–36)

To be "the utmost of meer man both wise and good" stands in the carnal hermeneutic of Satan as insufficient evidence that Jesus is "more . . . then man, / Worth naming Son of God" (4.538–39). It was all the evidence Hebrews required to identify the redeemer: "For we have not an high priest which cannot be touched with the feeling of our infirmities; but was in all points tempted like as *we are, yet* without sin" (Heb. 4.15). When the "utmost of meer man" does not act at all while placed upon the pinnacle of the tabernacle, he answers the prayer of Psalm 19.13: "Keep back thy servant also from presumptuous *sins*; let them not have dominion over me: then shall I be upright, and I shall be innocent from the great transgression." Luke glosses Psalm 40.6–8, "Sacrifice and offering thou didst not desire; mine ears hast thou opened: burnt offering and sin offering hast thou not required. Then said I, Lo, I come: in the volume of the book *it is* written of me, I delight to do thy will, O my God: yea, thy law *is* within my heart" so as to proclaim the one unique priest, the perfect man who "learned . . . obedience by the things which he suffered; And being made perfect, he became the author of eternal salvation" (Heb. 5.8–9). The uniqueness of the Son's priesthood is the sufficiency of his obedience to a life involving the most extreme humiliation and suffering. Milton understood the single sense of that heroic self-sacrifice as removing the need for other priesthood or mediation forever, "if Christians would but know thir own dignitie, thir libertie, thir adoption, and let it not be wonderd if I say, thir spiritual priesthood, whereby they have all equally access to any ministerial function whenever calld by thir own abilities and the church."[24]

In the end, Milton's thematic consideration of Psalms under the influence of Hebrews supplied him not only with the language and interpretation for the Son and Satan in their debate over sonship, but with an interpretation of sonship that emphasized priesthood over kingship, freeing Christians of his own day from the pretensions of prelates. To follow the trail of his thinking through his psalmic sources is to arrive at an understanding of the exemplary and vicarious standing of the Son which makes that action a once and for all sufficient atonement and example for all men.[25] If, then, it be asked whether Milton read and valued the Book of Psalms more particularly or differently than any other book of the Bible, here is the answer: the Psalter is the book of both the Old and New Testaments. Other Old Testament books enter the New Testament where it treats the decisive doctrines and events of the Christian faith, but no other Old Testament book is more pervasive in the New nor more decisively reinterpreted and reread in the very New Testament texts serving as Milton's authority. In that conjuncture, Psalms give him authority for his understanding of the meaning of the Son's life, the quality of the Son's thought, and the nature of the Son's heroism.

[24] *YP* 7:320.

[25] But see Hill, *Milton and the English Revolution*, 302, 413–16, for the argument that Milton took no particular interest in the vicarious sacrifice of Jesus Christ.

TWO

"With Hymns, our Psalms . . . our Hebrew Songs and Harps"

Psalm Genres

MILTON'S IMITATIONS of psalm genres in *Paradise Regained* reflect New Testament psalms, either those written in adaptation of Old Testament models or those psalms from the Old Testament quoted in the New Testament.[1] Just as the wisdom song has fullest representation in the New Testament, so Milton makes greatest use of that genre. He inscribes its preoccupations and themes in the very plot of the poem. Just as his text of authority, Luke's gospel, imitates hymns, so Milton frames the Son's heroic witness within two angelic songs of praise. Since that gospel shows reason for tragic lament but converts lamentation to trust and thanksgiving, Milton too deploys lament as induction to the central books of temptation, foregrounding the Son's victory against his mother's and the apostles' anxiety, sorrow, and fear. The moral thrust of New Testament Epistles is toward patience in the face of sorrow; the psalm genres they quote give priority to wisdom song, hymn, and lament. Milton's analysis of psalm genres and the decorum of his imitations of those forms in *Paradise Regained* are vital to the learned artistry of its plain style.

When Milton read Psalms, attending to the form, structure, function, rhetorical pattern and style of each genre, he read each kind asking what its traits were and how it might inspire modern worship or verse. He was unique neither in seeking a biblical poetics nor in paying particular attention to psalms. Most religious poets of his day were skilled in distinguishing lament, thanksgiving, blessing, wisdom song, and hymn, or in separating poetry from law, story, or proph-

[1] Postcanonical Hebrew psalms take the form both of poems spoken by individual New Testament characters and as free unattached poetry. The former have affinities with such poems in canonical authors outside Psalms as Hannah's hymn of thanksgiving, Jonah's prayer, or Hezekiah's thanksgiving. The latter can be found in Sirach and the so-called Psalms of Solomon, and the Qumran Manuscripts. The early Christian community both made new psalms on old models and adapted free-standing psalms. See Mowinckel, *The Psalms in Israel's Worship*, 2:114–25; and von Rad, *Wisdom in Israel*.

ecy.[2] What Milton uniquely did among the century's great religious poets, however, in becoming as far as possible a new psalmist himself, was to write biblical lyric into Bible-based narrative. What he uniquely did in *Paradise Regained* was to mine the wisdom psalm for its distinctive concern with witness and ripe time and to place wisdom song, so often imitated in gospel, within a narrative based upon gospel.

First Milton framed the central action of *Paradise Regained* within a conflation of Old Testament psalmic lament and hymn with Lukean psalms. Luke made Mary's *Magnificat*, Zacharias's *Benedictus*, the angels' *Gloria*, and Simeon's *Nunc dimittis* by imitating Old Testament songs. Milton framed and situated his brief epic within two angelic hymns; he combined the *Benedictus* and the *Gloria* with diverse hymn topoi. He wrote two laments, to preface the central action and to intensify its emotional power—laments by Mary and then by the disciples, those closest to Jesus but left behind while he sojourned in the wilderness. For Mary's interior monologue, he placed the joy of the *Magnificat* in the past and added Old Testament lament formulas of loss; for the disciples', he used Simeon's *Nunc dimittis* in a similar way. At the center of the poem he took the theme of witness in wisdom psalms to color Jesus' self-representation and the theme of ripe time in wisdom psalms to shape the ethics of heroic patience.

Witness in Wisdom Psalms and Paradise Regained

The theme of witness from wisdom psalms shapes Jesus' account of his inference of messiahship. He witnesses to his vocation in the autobiographical soliloquy placed between the angels' introductory hymn and the laments of the disciples and Mary. Wisdom psalms characteristically treat the question of the ripeness of time, and their treatments guided Milton to handle the contest between Satan and Jesus over temporal and eternal vocation across the rest of the poem between the psalmic laments and the concluding angelic hymn.

In *Christian Doctrine* Milton denied any wish to establish a modern liturgy on the prescriptive basis of Hebrew liturgy and found neither the Psalter nor the New Testament to require set forms for worship.[3] He thought set forms superstitious. Wisdom psalms are essentially nonliturgical and didactic or homiletic. They suggest a community not of worshipers ritually observing fixed holy days but of scholars listening to a teacher range between meditation and prayer on questions of faith. Although a student of comparative religion might surmise be-

[2] See Lewalski, *Protestant Poetics*, chap. 2; Martz, *The Paradise Within*, 183–94; and Patterson, "*Paradise Regained*: A Last Chance at True Romance," 187–208.

[3] *YP* 6:666, 668, 670.

hind wisdom songs a learned school with scribal leadership, perhaps on the lines of a bardic academy, Milton was entirely silent on that sort of consideration. Interested only in how such songs might be adapted to acts of faith for his own day, his analysis was thematic and formal.

Milton analyzed wisdom songs (my term, not his) when he defined "THE SANCTIFICATION OF THE DIVINE NAME IN EVERY CIRCUMSTANCE OF OUR LIFE" or "ZEAL" and "an open profession of the true faith whenever necessary."[4] He called "zealous" "[t]hose who, in all sincerity, and with no desire to stir up controversy, teach or discuss some doctrine concerning the deity which they have quite apparently, as they see it, learned from the Holy Scriptures"; to recommend such open profession he cited Psalm 119.46, "*I shall speak of your testimonies before kings, and shall not be ashamed.*"[5] "Profession" is the technical Puritan concept of "witness," the act in which the inner testimony of the conscience is seconded by outward testifying. It includes a desire to influence others in God's name and involves admonition. Describing it, Milton chose a wisdom psalm, marked by the genre's typical signs of exhortatory religious and moral instruction, linked to the stylized autobiography of the teacher. The psalm Milton cited to recommend "witness," Psalm 119, is the longest pure wisdom psalm in the Book of Psalms. Wisdom strategies can be found frequently in psalms of other genres, even in psalms clearly meant for temple worship. Their presence reflects the editorial work of generations of scribes in forming the canon of the Psalter, glossing it with moral formulas. But the genre is represented more purely in a group of psalms that Milton cited together throughout the discussion of true religion in *Christian Doctrine*, Psalms 1, 14, 19, 37, 49, 78, 112, 119, 127, and 133.[6]

Wisdom songs treat the revelation of God's will as the source of all knowledge and a guide to life. The wise man's search for knowledge is grounded in an assurance that no reality exists not controlled by God. Since God is not only the giver of wisdom but also the creator of all reality, the enlightened are not stirred to dramatize doubt or disbelief as intellectually powerful options to faith. Wisdom songs instead tend to derive a practical morality for daily life from the experience of God's behavior. Rooting the motive for morality in the fear of God, they blend wise saws with personal religious awareness, their moral wisdom typically couched in linked proverbs or wise sayings coupled

[4] *YP* 6:697, 698.

[5] *YP* 6:700, 701.

[6] To these wisdom psalms one might add four more psalms of mixed genre that Milton tended to quote with them: the related problem poems (similar to Psalm 37) Psalms 73 and 139, and the fuller historical legend poems (similar to Psalm 78) Psalms 94 and 105.

with exhortations and offered in the guise of personal experience. The psalmist introduces himself as scribe; he refers to his own words as a private meditation, confesses that he speaks from his own insight, and asks God's approval of his thoughts and words, turning his proverbial didacticism toward prayer. Although he considers himself a man of prayer, he often contrasts his former foolishness with his present understanding by way of the formula "then I understood." Although speaking personally the meditations of his own heart, he emphasizes God's law or word: the revelation of God's law began his enlightenment. A personality may only rarely be discerned behind the stylized autobiography; usually the speaker briefly mentions his age and general situation. The principal themes he considers are the contrast between the two "ways" or "paths" of life—worldly, foolish, and barrenly prosperous versus pious, honest, and ultimately favored by God; the doctrine of the ripe or proper time or season for human acts and of man's responsibility to find it; the testimony of creation and human history to God's just governance and concern with man's moral life; and, very often, proofs of God's management of retributive justice. The stylistic signature of the wisdom psalm is mnemonic enumeration of proverbs or sententiae, concise, pointed, and gnomically suggestive.

Wisdom songs are not exclusive to Psalms but are found in Proverbs, Ecclesiastes, and Job, as well as in the prophets. Milton's adaptations are contained within narrative, present in soliloquy or dialogue, and echo wisdom literature outside the Psalter as well as in it. Most notably, wisdom devices and themes are prominent in those New Testament books from which Milton took the very action, characterization of the hero, and hermeneutic strategy for *Paradise Regained.* The poem engages with the Son at that moment when, by his reading of Scripture, he understands his special role. A model for the new Christian understanding is the reinterpretation of Psalms quoted in the New Testament. Through his new psalm hermeneutic Jesus withstands Satan's temptations to misread his role and enters upon his heroic task. Milton's authorities for the action and characterization are New Testament texts themselves rich in psalms. The wisdom psalm is particularly prominent among the psalmic genres transferred to the Gospels and Epistles, claimed in their new setting to be evidential of the Son's fulfillment of Old Testament hope, and declared now to be fully understandable in their new context. Since Luke is the greatest New Testament psalmist, the richest gospel source of parable and proverb, and the fullest authority on Jesus' childhood and early manhood, Milton's preference for his account of the temptations carries with it Luke's strong tincture of personal profession and self-revelation, moral combativeness, and didactic toughness.

Proverb and parable are the Son's chosen homiletic instruments. In Luke 4.18–19, for example, after triumphing over Satan in the wilderness and defining his vocation by quoting Isaiah, "to preach the gospel to the poor . . . to preach deliverance to the captives. . . . To preach the acceptable year of the Lord," Jesus speaks in the synagogue. Skeptical Jews reject him as teacher, "Is not this Joseph's son?" He replies, "Ye will surely say unto me this proverb, Physician, heal thyself: whatsoever we have heard done in Capernaum, do also here in thy country. . . . Verily I say unto you, No prophet is accepted in his own country" (Luke 4.22–24). Proverbial wisdom is first quoted by Jesus and then rebutted from a contradictory proverb to hint at a transformed sense of role: the Son will preach to the Gentiles, rejected by his own people, and carry his truth to all nations.

Again in Luke, after choosing the twelve disciples, Jesus delivers a sermon on the plain (6.17–49). As in the Sermon on the Mount reported by Matthew,[7] so in the sermon on the plain, Jesus teaches by means of wisdom literature. He contrasts two groups of human beings, the blessed and the prosperous. He opens with a group of beatitudes that set the blessed poor, hungry, weeping, and persecuted over against the rich, full, laughing, and greatly praised; he concludes each with an antithetical warning. The contrastive form itself draws on Psalm 1. The first of Jesus' beatitudes, "Blessed *be ye* poor: for yours is the kingdom of God," echoes Psalm 10.14, "The poor committeth himself unto thee; thou art the helper of the fatherless," while the contrary, "But woe unto you that are rich! for ye have received your consolation," echoes Psalm 14.6, "Ye have shamed the counsel of the poor, because the Lord *is* his refuge," and Psalm 37.16, "A little that a righteous man hath *is* better than the riches of many wicked." The second, "Blessed *are ye* that hunger now; for ye shall be filled," echoes Psalm 146.7, "[The Lord] giveth food to the hungry," simply reversed in "Woe unto you that are full! for ye shall hunger." The third beatitude,

[7] In the Sermon on the Mount, the first beatitude, "Blessed *are* the poor in spirit: for theirs is the kingdom of heaven," reflects Psalm 1.1, 3, "Blessed *is* the man that . . . sitteth [not] in the seat of the scornful . . . whatsoever he doeth shall prosper." The third, "Blessed *are* the meek: for they shall inherit the earth," reflects Psalm 37.11, "But the meek shall inherit the earth." The fourth, "Blessed *are* they which do hunger and thirst after righteousness: for they shall be filled," reflects a wisdom section of Psalm 24.4–5: "He that hath clean hands, and a pure heart; who hath not lifted up his soul unto vanity, nor sworn deceitfully. He shall receive the blessing from the Lord, and righteousness from the God of his salvation."

"Blessed *are ye* that weep now: for ye shall laugh," and its contrary, "Woe unto you that laugh now! for ye shall mourn and weep," look back to Ecclesiastes 3.4, "A time to weep, and a time to laugh; a time to mourn, and a time to dance." The last beatitude and its contrary proposition are particularly expressive of Luke's concern for the oppressed, and both originate in wisdom song. The affirmative "Blessed are ye, when men shall hate you, and when they shall separate you *from their company*, and shall reproach *you*, and cast out your name as evil, for the Son of man's sake. . . . for in the like manner did their fathers unto the prophets" and the negative "Woe unto you, when all men shall speak well of you! for so did their fathers to the false prophets," both echo Psalm 37.7, "fret not thyself because of him who prospereth in his way, because of the man who bringeth wicked devices to pass" and Psalm 49.12, "Nevertheless man *being* in honor abideth not: he is like the beasts *that* perish," repeated at verse 20. No literary influence is more pervasive in gospel accounts of the Son's ministry than wisdom literature. In both the New Testament and *Paradise Regained*, Jesus characteristically uses Old Testament Psalms to prove New Testament doctrine, claiming to fulfill Scripture by expounding it correctly; the means he chooses both in the New Testament and *Paradise Regained* are proverb and parable, the strategies of wisdom literature.

Jesus is represented in the New Testament and *Paradise Regained* not simply as the teacher of a new form of wisdom but as the wisdom of God itself. He is both the upright man of God-fearing morality and the exemplar of the wisdom of God, who, while teaching wisdom, reveals what he declares. In the New Testament he adopts the speech of the revealer. That speech pattern contained within stylized autobiography is a regular feature of some wisdom songs. In Job 32, for example, Elihu claims the role of revealer in a typical wisdom song:

> I *am* young, and ye *are* very old; wherefore I was afraid, and durst not shew you mine opinion.
>
> I said, Days should speak, and multitude of years should teach wisdom.
>
> But *there is* a spirit in man: and the inspiration of the Almighty giveth them understanding.
>
> Great men are not *always* wise: neither do the aged understand judgment.
>
> . . . .
>
> *I said*, I will answer also my part, I also will shew mine opinion.
>
> For I am full of matter, the spirit within me constraineth me.

> Behold, my belly *is* as wine *which* hath no vent; it is ready to burst like new bottles.
> (6–9, 17–19)

Jesus transforms the revealer formula into an absolute claim in Luke 10.22: "All things are delivered to me of my Father: and no man knoweth who the Son is, but the Father; and who the Father is but the Son, and *he* to whom the Son will reveal *him*."[8] Milton characterizes Jesus as showing both the moral and metaphysical kinds of wisdom. As the first sort of sage, Jesus teaches a truer morality, making use of wisdom song formulas, concepts and strategies. Milton has him take on that role very early, when he decides "By winning words to conquer willing hearts" (1.222). As the second sort, Jesus manifests wisdom itself and does not simply speak it. The angels praise him for this vocation "to vanquish by wisdom hellish wiles" (1.175).

The wisdom genre is important to *Paradise Regained*, then, because it is important to the New Testament Gospels, especially Luke, both in sketching the character of the Son and showing how and what he teaches. The strong commitment of intellect to religion at the basis of the wisdom song has itself a double nature. On the one hand, enlightened men make practical application of an evaluative ethic. Wisdom in this sense is synonymous with reason, discipline, and prudence; it is what can be taught to others memorably and incorporated in their value systems. On the other hand, theological speculation ensues from the very concern to see meaning in daily life. Wisdom in this sense is not a gift of God on the same footing as his gifts of children, good repute, a productive life—or, as Macbeth would have it, "That which should accompany old age, / As honour, love, obedience, troops of friends"—it is an illumination. Not a system to be taught, such wisdom enters the mind as an awareness arising within quiet obedience, as though it came from outside the seer. The intense monotheism of the Jews—their demythologizing of nature, their trust in the rationality of its order because of its creator's qualities—can be expressed by both senses of wisdom. If in the Gospels the Son's teaching sometimes seems unwise, or can even be named folly, that higher teaching belongs to the tradition. The writers of the Epistles, too, quote wisdom psalms in new contexts, and by stylized autobiography lay claim to illumination and call their wisdom folly.

In *Paradise Regained*, when the Son makes a claim different from the

[8] As the case of Elihu in Job illustrates, the revealer formula is manifested whether the words of the revealer may be inspired or mistaken, confirmed or rebuked by God from the whirlwind.

ordinary sage, his claim is to wisdom authority. Satan asserts a magical power to guide men in oracles, for example; Jesus rebukes him wisely and as wisdom: he is God's "living Oracle" sent into the world to teach; he proclaims an "inward Oracle / To all truth requisite for men to know" (1.460, 463–64). That inward oracle, the revelation written on men's hearts, is the law referred to in Psalm 37.31: "The law of his God *is* in his heart; none of his steps shall slide." Holding that everything in the New Testament is proved from the Old, Milton significantly links wisdom psalms to the New Testament characterization of the Son as wisdom itself.[9]

In the brief epic, Milton intends to foster true religion by narrating the test and approval of the zeal of the hero, engaged in a sanctification of the name of the Lord at a critical juncture. While Jesus witnesses to the Father who sent him, Milton zealously sanctifies God's name. Writing psalms for his redeemer, he becomes a wisdom psalmist in his own day to his own people. Jesus divulges his vocation in "holy Meditations" before the temptations commence (1.196–293). The meditations show his prior inference of messiahship. They take the form of the didactic prayer and meditation of wisdom song, using its convention of stylized autobiography. They move twice through the two phases of wisdom witness, moral and metaphysical. Jesus then approves his zeal by deferring an ultimate witness until time be ripe. In dialogue across the last two books of the poem, Satan urges the seizing of opportunity, and the Son resists him with proverbs containing the concept of time's fullness. Jesus' answers riddle out the wisdom psalm's proverbial preoccupation with ripe time.[10]

I begin with the Son's autobiographical soliloquy and the introspective prayers of wisdom literature.[11] Alone, Jesus thinks through chron-

[9] In *Christian Doctrine* Milton elucidates the point, "fear of the Lord is called *wisdom*," by citing Psalm 25.14, "*the secret of Jehovah is with those who reverence him*," and Psalm 111.10, "*the chief point of knowledge is fear of Jehovah*," and then proving "Christ is also called *wisdom*," by citing "*he is made wisdom for us*" (1 Cor. 1.30) and "*in which are all the treasures of wisdom*" (Col. 2.3). *YP* 6:648.

[10] Tayler has suggested the "need to extricate the poem from its scriptural sources," *Milton's Poetry: Its Development in Time*, 150. LeComte endorses a suggestion of Frank Kermode that Milton identifies himself with both the Son and Cromwell, *Milton's Unchanging Mind*, 47–48; Kerrigan uses the insights of psychoanalysis on Milton and his created character, "The Riddle of *Paradise Regained*," 64–80. All find in Milton's memory of his own childhood and early tastes on the one hand and his anxieties about slow development on the other, nonscriptural sources of interest in the soliloquy.

[11] See Stein, *Heroic Knowledge*, 36–46; Elliott, "Milton's Biblical Style in *Paradise Regained*," 227–33; Fisher, "Why Is *Paradise Regained* So Cold?," 195–217; Anderson, "Is

ologically the course of his personal development, beginning and ending with confessions of his present state of mind. He confesses first to mental perturbation, figured as a "swarm" or "multitude of thoughts" (1.196–97). He concludes calmly, acquiescent to formless intuition, figured as "some strong motion" toward a goal he does not yet know (1.290–93). To read his descriptions of his mental state simply as the conscious confessions of a character possessing unquestioned interiority is to neglect in them the interrelated themes so common in wisdom literature: "Where is wisdom to be found?" and "Trust in the Lord." Jesus considers the contrast between his intuitions and the proclamations of his role on the one hand and his actual position in the world on the other. His opening image of "swarm" suggesting bees has been taken to express anxiety, its final absence to show anxiety overcome. But anxiety is uncommon to wisdom psalmists, for whom the knowledge of wisdom is as sweet as "honey" from the swarm (Prov. 24.13–14). The implications of the repeatedly invoked wisdom formula "The fear of the Lord is the beginning of wisdom" are antisuperstitious. They mean that for enlightened human beings, awe leads to an alert scrutiny of creation for signs of the order given it by God. Jesus' swarm of thoughts are like those in Psalm 49.3, "The meditation of my heart *shall be* of understanding"; his resolution is like that in Psalm 37.5, "Commit thy way unto the Lord; trust also in him; and he shall bring *it* to pass."

When Jesus then begins to remember the stages by which he has come to the wilderness, he speaks like a wisdom psalmist. He meditates on the rationality of the faithful life of obedient action. In that meditation are what Arnold Stein has seen as two stages of insight common to Milton and Jesus, followed by anticipations of two further stages unique to the Son. Not only are the stages intrinsic to wisdom literature, autobiography itself is a wisdom mode. The first of the stages concerns childhood vocation. Jesus muses:

> When I was yet a child, no childish play
> To me was pleasing, all my mind was set
> Serious to learn and know, and thence to do
> What might be publick good; my self I thought
> Born to that end, born to promote all truth,
> All righteous things: therefore above my years,

Paradise Regained Really Cold?," 15–23; Fowler, "*Paradise Regained*: Some Problems of Style," 181–89; and North, "Language and the Struggle of Identity in *Paradise Regained*," 273–83.

> The Law of God I read, and found it sweet,
> Made it my whole delight.
> (1.201–8)

The second strophe of Psalm 119 represents a youth much like Jesus' and Milton's:[12]

> Wherewithal shall a young man cleanse his way? by taking heed *thereto* according to thy word.
> With my whole heart have I sought thee: O let me not wander from thy commandments.
> Thy word have I hid in mine heart, that I might not sin against thee.
> (9–11)

A similar sense of dedication is elaborated in the more personally literal confession of Jesus Sirach in the apocryphal Ecclesiasticus: "While I was still young, before I went on my travels, I sought wisdom openly in my prayer"; "I was the last on watch; I was like one who gleans after the grape-gatherers. . . . Consider that I have not labored for myself alone, but for all who seek instruction" (Ecclus. 51.13, 33.16–17).[13]

Jesus' decision to "do / What might be publick good" (1.203–4) opens what is usually understood to mark the second stage in his conception of his role and to resemble Milton's recollection of his own development, from a will to "heroic acts," "Till truth were freed, and equity restor'd," to the decision to try "By winning words to conquer willing hearts" (1.216, 220, 222). Since wisdom psalms also combine private vocation with public, Jesus's decision has the motives of Psalm 12.5, "For the oppression of the poor, for the sighing of the needy, now will I arise, saith the Lord," and of Psalm 78.72, "So he fed them according to the integrity of his heart; and guided them by the skilfulness of his hands."

The significance of impersonal autobiography in wisdom songs is not so much its impersonality as what one might call its suprapersonality. The claim is made that the speaker is a witness to God, a witness whose testimony does not belong to him as a person but to his God, through whose prompting he turns his testimony from forensic evidence toward proclamation and teaching. As Paul Ricoeur describes

[12] Sims, *The Bible in Milton's Epics*, 274, notes that line 206 echoes Psalm 119.30 and line 207 echoes Psalm 1.2. Since Milton imitates an entire genre, the passage echoes many psalms of that genre.

[13] The stylized autobiography is analyzed in von Rad, *Wisdom in Israel*, 37–38. Quotations from Ecclesiasticus follow the Revised Standard Version.

the hermeneutics of testimony, one person witnessing for all persons attests to his vocation, not simply as someone who stepped forward but as someone sent.[14] Isaiah 43.8–10 provides the context in which Jesus' witness and vocation can be understood:

> Bring forth the blind people that have eyes, and the deaf that have ears. Let all the nations be gathered together, and let the people be assembled: who among them can declare this, and shew us former things? let them bring forth their witnesses, that they may be justified: or let them hear, and say, *It is* the truth. Ye *are* my witnesses, saith the Lord, and my servant whom I have chosen, that ye may know and believe me, and understand that I *am* he: before me there was no God formed, neither shall there be after me.

The witness is a prophet in the sense of a teacher of the truth, but more than that he is a servant; the ultimate witness is the suffering servant. Hence the chosen one acknowledges in the very impersonality of his autobiography that what matters is not that he is a particular human being (he might be either blind or deaf), but that he is a witness (yet would he have eyes and ears). The implications in the role of witness or *martus* are "Humiliation and strong Sufferance," as in Psalm 44.22: "Yea, for thy sake are we killed all the day long; we are counted as sheep for the slaughter." His authority derives from the God to whom he testifies, an exchange rendered in Psalm 50.15: "I will deliver thee, and thou shalt glorify me." Hence Milton shows Jesus turning from his resolve to teach, after he reads Scripture at Mary's prompting, to express a witnessing "Through many a hard assay even to the death" (1.264). Wisdom psalmody having gone that far in presenting the suprapersonality of the witness's autobiography, gospel determines the rest of the Son's representation of wisdom in self-portrait.[15]

The change is initiated by Jesus' recollection of what Mary taught

[14] See Ricoeur, "The Hermeneutics of Testimony," in *Essays on Biblical Interpretation*, 119–54.

[15] Jesus resolves to teach all but one sort unpersuadable by his witness, "the stubborn only to subdue." Nothing is more common to wisdom psalms than the distinction between the two ways or paths of life, unless it is the distinction between the two sort of men who choose them. In Psalm 1 the wicked are especially condemned as scorners; in Psalm 26.4 as "vain persons . . . dissemblers"; in Psalm 50.16–17, God forbids them to teach because they hate truth: "What hast thou to do to declare my statutes, or *that* thou shouldest take my covenant in thy mouth? Seeing thou hatest instruction, and casteth my words behind thee." Psalms 14 and 53 describe how willful disbelief is followed by corrupt and abominable works. The class is composed of men who have deliberately closed their minds to God and instruction. In segregating the erring from the obdurate, Jesus is a faithful wisdom teacher.

him of the annunciation and what he then read in Scripture. Her teaching, too, is significantly attributable to the wisdom tradition as embodied in Luke 1.32–33: "He shall be great, and shall be called the Son of the Highest: and the Lord God shall give unto him the throne of his father David: And he shall reign over the house of Jacob for ever; and of his kingdom there shall be no end." Mary's words in *Paradise Regained*, "By matchless Deeds express thy matchless Sire" (1.233) and "Thou shouldst be great and sit on *David's* Throne / And of thy Kingdom there should be no end" (1.240–41), recall those verses from Luke. Like Luke, they echo Daniel 2.20–23, where Daniel too sings a wisdom song.[16] In the two further parts of his soliloquy the Son first remembers his renewed systematic study of the Old Testament and discovery of the "hard assay" of his future, and he then describes his baptism and reacts to it. In the first section, the Son discovers that he is the telos of Christian typology:[17]

> I again revolv'd
> The Law and Prophets, searching what was writ
> Concerning the Messiah, to our Scribes
> Known partly, and soon found of whom they spake
> *I am*.
> (1.259–63; my emphasis)

The Son, seeing that all the patterns of God's providence are revealed in the Old Testament, can find his own life prefigured there, and so claim the deific "I am." To be read prefiguratively are the lament psalms of the unjustly accused man (principally Psalms 7, 17, 26, 35, and 69), the processional psalms of the royal Messiah (Psalms 2, 18, 45, 61, 72, 89, 110, and 118), the grieving psalms of the suffering Messiah (Psalms 22, 35, 41, 55, 69, and 109), and the prophetic psalms of

[16] Blessed be the name of God for ever and ever: for wisdom and might are his:

And he changeth the times and the seasons: he removeth kings, and setteth up kings: he giveth wisdom unto the wise, and knowledge to them that know understanding:

He revealeth the deep and secret things: he knoweth what *is* in the darkness, and the light dwelleth with him.

I thank thee, and praise thee, O thou God of my fathers, who hast given me wisdom and might, and hast made known unto me now what we desired of thee: for thou hast *now* made known unto us the king's matter.

[17] "Each passage of scripture has only a single sense, though in the Old Testament this sense is often a combination of the historical and the typological, take Hosea xi.1, for example, compared with Matt. ii.15: *I have called my son out of Egypt*. This can be read correctly in two senses, as a reference both to the people of Israel and to Christ in his infancy" (*YP* 6:581).

the second Adam, the fulfiller of human destiny (Psalms 8, 16, and 40), as well as some psalms describing God as king and creator that the Gospels will transfer to Jesus (Psalms 68, 97, and 102). To have access to typology is not to reject the ancient traditions of wisdom song, but to strengthen them by claiming them for progressive revelation.

The soliloquy closes with the Son's reflections on his baptism. Milton marks a transition between Jesus' assent to the role of suffering servant and his meditations on the Father's proclamation of his sonship by stressing his composure, "Yet neither thus disheartn'd or dismay'd, / The time prefixt I waited" (1.268–69). From the proclamation the Son concludes "the time / Now full" in which to begin his open ministry (1.286–87). Both his speeches refer to the ripeness of time—"the time prefixt," "the time now full." The Son's cognizance of ripe time is the second adaptation of wisdom psalms in *Paradise Regained*, one of the most important themes in wisdom psalms. To summarize, as a wise person Jesus drew conclusions about himself and his role by meditating on the world that God created, the historical moment in which he was born, and the revelation of God in Scripture. He inferred his messiahship and read in it his role both as wise teacher and as heroic martyr; he witnessed God in those inferences and proposed for himself a period of wisdom teaching followed by a perfect obedience in suffering. His inference does not foreclose further development or revelation; already he anticipates that what he begins as teaching must end in suffering. Wisdom literature contrives its witness by the representation of stylized autobiography. The pre-texts for *Paradise Regained* manifest both a generally applicable group of inferences about how men should live and a particular, holy sense of who the Messiah is. Milton wrote Jesus' opening soliloquy to resolve two questions, how man is to live and who the Messiah is. Readings of the character of Jesus that understand him to know in advance of all trial the essential form of his mission and at the same time take him to be capable of intellectual development and degrees of progressive understanding are better readings of Milton's biblicism than those that shape Jesus' life according to either incompatible alternative, the search for identity or the exemplification of moral choice.[18]

[18] Stein, *Heroic Knowledge*, and Teskey, "Balanced in Time: *Paradise Regained* and the Centre of the Miltonic Vision," propose the combined characterization. For the moral school see Samuel, "The Regaining of Paradise," 111–34; Patterson, "*Paradise Regained*: A Last Chance at True Romance," 187–208; and Tayler, *Milton's Poetry: Its Development in Time*. For the identity school see Nohrnberg, "*Paradise Regained* by One Greater Man: Milton's Wisdom Epic as a 'Fable of Identity,' " 83–114; Kerrigan, "The Riddle of *Par-*

Ripe Time in Wisdom Psalms and Paradise Regained

With respect to time, Jesus has one grasp of the meaning of history and Satan another.[19] The validity of each is disputed in the last two books of *Paradise Regained.* At issue between them is the role of volition and the nature of human freedom within the providential determination of the cosmos by God. The New Testament version of history, as that was interpreted by Reformation commentary, is decisively espoused by the Son in the poem. That version—arguing against a repetitive, cyclical, deterministic unrolling of time in which some heroes may fatalistically rebel or opportunistically succeed—teaches that history is accomplished or perfected in the fullness of time.[20] It orients the Old Testament christologically and is the subject of chapter 14 of *Christian Doctrine,* Book I, "OF MAN'S RESTORATION AND OF CHRIST THE REDEEMER." There Milton argues that salvation, the business of history, commenced in the Old Testament covenant and is fulfilled in Christ. Three Pauline texts are keys to that historiography. The first, Galatians 4.4, "But when the fulness of time was come, God sent forth his Son," is the text to which Jesus alludes in closing his meditation, "I knew the time / Now full" (1.286–87) and to which Satan in his final heavily ironic summary alludes before placing the Son on the pinnacle, "Now at full age, fulness of time, thy season, / When Prophesies of thee are best fullfill'd" (4.380–81). In *Christian Doctrine,* the text proved that God's promise of salvation was made to all mankind and its fulfillment expected from the moment of the fall; Milton added that the promise could also be read in the wisdom song in Job, "*I know that my redeemer lives,*" and he concluded, "The point is made even more clearly throughout the Psalms and the prophetic books."[21] The second Pauline

---

adise Regained," and North, "Language and the Struggle of Identity in *Paradise Regained,*" 273–83.

[19] On the concept of time in *Paradise Regained,* see Stein, *Heroic Knowledge,* 3–134; Chambers, "The Double Time Scheme in *Paradise Regained,*" 189–205; Zwicky, "Kairos in *Paradise Regained*: The Divine Plan," 271–77; Lewalski, "Time and History in *Paradise Regained,*" 49–81; Grant, "Time and Temptation in *Paradise Regained,*" 129–53; Samuel, "The Regaining of Paradise," 111–34; Guibbory, *The Map of Time: Seventeenth-Century English Literature and Ideas of Pattern in History,* 188–89, 204–5; Miner, "Milton and the Histories," 196, 198, 200; and Teskey, "Balanced in Time: *Paradise Regained* and the Centre of the Miltonic Vision," 269–83.

[20] See Patrides, *The Phoenix and the Ladder, The Grand Design of God,* and " 'Something like Prophetick Strain': Apocalyptic Configurations in Milton," in *The Apocalypse in English Renaissance Thought and Literature,* 207–37; Colie, "Time and Eternity: Paradox and Structure in *Paradise Lost,*" 127–38; and Stapleton, "Milton's Conception of Time in *The Christian Doctrine,*" 9–21.

[21] *YP* 6:418.

text is Ephesians 1.10: "That in the dispensation of the fulness of times he might gather together in one all things in Christ. . . ." In *Paradise Regained*, the decisive moment in history is reached when Jesus, the "glorious Eremite," was led "Into the Desert, his Victorious Field" and brought "thence / By proof the undoubted Son of God" (1.8–11). Milton's mimesis is of the events of that decisive moment, which nonetheless is a deferral of the fulness of time. The third Pauline text, Ephesians 4.13, acknowledges that history occurs in the space of the deferral of time's fulness, "[t]ill we all come in the unity of the faith, and of the knowledge of the Son of God, unto a perfect man, unto the measure of the stature of the fulness of Christ." In literary genre definition, deferral is the mode of romance;[22] for Milton, however, it is the mode of ethical historiography. The Son's deferral of his reign without end, a deferral that renders moral the space of time in which all human beings dwell, is a deferral that creates the freedom or historical indeterminacy in which human choices have ethical value and political consequences.

Paradise Regained, the quintessential New Testament poem, reads its historiography in all the New Testament literary kinds: gospel narrative, the history of events after the birth of Jesus, apocalypse as the symbolic representation of the end of time, and epistle. Gospel places the life of Jesus in a history of God's dealings with man, focusing on distinctive moments as though they were turning points between past and future. It marks the past and future by way of epiphanic events.[23] Jesus' baptism is the first such moment taken to be epiphanic in all the four Gospels; the four inform multiple references in *Paradise Regained*.[24] All imply that in the ripe time the past and future meet. Milton adapts the gospel strategy of recounting symbolic moments that change the course of history and uses it within the plot of temptation in the wilderness. Such moments reflect not only Christian historiography but also the concern of wisdom literature with ripe time. New Testament historiography in Acts interweaves past events and evidence from the psalms that what is singular and decisive in each stage of the fulfillment of history was promised earlier. A good deal of that evidence comes from wisdom psalms. The Book of Revelation symbolizes the end of time by interpreting psalms as eschatological, however little or much a Jewish reader would have found eschatology in the

[22] See Parker, *Inescapable Romance*, 10.

[23] See Frye, *The Great Code*, 129–35. See also Beardslee, *Literary Criticism of the New Testament*, 14–63.

[24] Matthew 3.13–17, Mark 1.9–11, Luke 3.21–23, and John 1.15–18; *Paradise Regained* 1.35–37, 1.67, 1.77, 1.286, 2.51, 2.83–84.

psalms John uses, a good number of them wisdom psalms. Finally, epistles commonly adopt the wisdom stance or quote wisdom psalms. Inevitably, the density of wisdom material is high in *Paradise Regained*, where ripe time is at issue.

Satan considers that while history repeats itself in cycles experienced as if time were long, it is fatally predetermined. Freedom, angelic or human, is illusory, for not only are the cycles of time rigged to move so predictably that what is to come can be magically discovered, they are also foredoomed to end. In order to defeat time or conquer doom, while the hours circle as though they were seats on a merry-go-round, an angel or a human being must jump onto an opportune moment, take the occasion randomly presented, and force it to his purpose. He may not determine but must grasp the occasion. It is possible to jump on too late, to miss one's opportunity by tardiness. Yet the moving belt has been fixed to run a preconceived course and in the end for all created beings to stop. Hence Satan alerts his peers to the arrival of a dreaded time, "And now too soon for us the circling hours / This dreaded time have compast" (1.57–58). His dread is so severe that Satan at one point seemingly wills time to race to its end, "worst is my Port, / My harbour and my ultimate repose, / The end I would attain, my final good" (3.209–11). He uses his own recklessness to goad Jesus to act too soon and in the wrong cause: "If I then to the worst that can be hast, / Why move thy feet so slow to what is best . . . ?" (3.223–24). The very fatalism of his cyclical view can at another point yield a superstitious reassurance: what has been given no date may never occur. So he reassures himself and seeks to daunt Jesus with the very determinism of history:

> but what Kingdom,
> Real or Allegoric I discern not,
> Nor when, eternal sure, as without end,
> Without beginning; for no date prefixt
> Directs me in the Starry Rubric set.
> (4.389–93)

Opposed to Satan's combined fatalism and opportunism is the Son's understanding of time as composed of epiphanic, not opportune, moments, moments that ask created beings to recognize seasonableness not made by but for them. The acknowledged and free assent to ripe time gives actions their ethical value. Wisdom literature is authority for that concept, its very aim the recognition of the right time, place, and scope of human activity in God's cosmos.

Jesus' disputation with Satan opposing ripe time to opportune moment commences in the third book of *Paradise Regained*; the first two books treated the forty days as a continuous present "with such thoughts / Accompanied of things past and to come" (1.299–300). The debate commences with Satan's advice to act at once or lose the chance. With the taunt, "Thy years are ripe, and over-ripe," he reads ancient history as the saga of opportunistic heroes—Alexander, Scipio Africanus, Pompey, Julius Caesar (3.31–42). When Jesus, instead of answering the suggestion that if time ripen it may overripen, addresses the definition of true fame or glory, Satan recurs to the matter of wasted time with the provocative question, "think'st thou to regain / Thy right by sitting still or thus retiring?" (3.163–64) He prompts the Son with zeal and duty as occasion-making, quoting scriptural history to the same point earlier supported from Greek and Roman (3.174–80). Within a group of references to the period of Maccabean wars, during the "Heathen servitude" to Antiochus when the temple was profaned, Satan alludes to Psalm 69.9, "For the zeal of thine house hath eaten me up," referring to the psalmist's commitment to restore the temple. He implies that scriptural history too advances by the self-careless urgency of heroic holy men. John quotes the psalm in his gospel when Christ drives the money-changers from the temple: "And his disciples remembered that it was written, The zeal of thine house hath eaten me up" (2.17). Apart from Psalm 22, Psalm 69 is the psalm most often quoted in the New Testament, where it is taken to prophesy the derision, abuse, and suffering the Messiah incurred by his zealous witness. Satan suppresses from his allusion what is not to his purpose, a prayer with a different notion of time, "But as for me, my prayer *is* unto thee, O Lord, *in* an acceptable time" (Ps. 69.13). An acceptable time is not a shrewdly chosen occasion; it is ripe time, the time noted in Psalm 32.6: "For this shall every one that is godly pray unto thee in a time when thou mayest be found."

Jesus' reply distinguishes occasion from ripe time in a midrash of wisdom literature like that found in John 2.4, when Jesus is quoted as saying "mine hour is not yet come." He tells Satan:

> All things are best fullfil'd in their due time,
> And time there is for all things, Truth hath said:
> If of my raign Prophetic Writ hath told,
> That it shall never end, so when begin
> The Father in his purpose hath decreed,
> He in whose hand all times and seasons roul.
> (3.182–87)

He first quotes Ecclesiastes 3.1, but he ends with that part of Psalm 69 Satan silently omitted. The Father purposes salvation; the time of its beginning is a time acceptable to him. While Satan abused Scripture to defend opportunism, Jesus interprets it to recommend patience.

Moreover, Jesus qualitatively changes Ecclesiastes when he quotes it. As it stands, the wisdom of Ecclesiastes seems as applicable to Satan's position as to the Son's. The proposition "To everything there is a season" is illustrated by the antithetical choices any moment permits: plant or uproot, kill or heal, break down or build, weep or laugh, mourn or dance, speak or be silent, love or hate, make war or peace. The passage ends with a baffled faith, "I have seen the travail, which God hath given to the sons of men to be exercised in it. He hath made every *thing* beautiful in his time: also he hath set the world in their heart, so that no man can find out the work that God maketh from the beginning to the end" (Eccl. 3.10–11). In context, the dependence of action on a right time supports a dim view of human life but a pious view of God's omniscience; a man can neither understand nor change the predetermined pattern, he can but learn to adjust his behavior to the conditions he meets. The Son makes a qualitatively different point when he uses the wisdom phrase to honor God's governance of all time and history, "He in whose hand all times and seasons roul."[25]

If *Ecclesiastes* seems to show only how human beings must dance to time's tune, psalmic wisdom teachers turn the idea of divine determinism firmly in a theological direction. Thus Psalm 139.16, "Thine eyes did see my substance, yet being unperfect; and in thy book all *my members* were written, *which* in continuance were fashioned, when *as yet there was* none of them," confirms Jesus' conviction that his career was foretold in "Prophetic Writ" and recalls Psalm 56.8, "Thou tellest my wanderings: put thou my tears into thy bottle: *are they* not in thy book?" Providence is trustworthy and prompts patience like that attributed to Jesus in Acts 1.7, "And he said unto them, It is not for you

[25] See von Rad, *Wisdom in Israel*, 138ff. for a reading of ripe time in Ecclesiastes. When Milton cites Ecclesiastes in *Christian Doctrine* 1.4, "Of Predestination," to argue the freedom of the will, he does not read "The Preacher . . . wisest of all mortals" as a fatalist but as a theologian. "[Predestination is the] SPECIAL DEGREE . . . by which GOD, BEFORE THE FOUNDATIONS OF THE WORLD WERE LAID, HAD MERCY ON THE HUMAN RACE, ALTHOUGH IT WAS GOING TO FAIL OF ITS OWN ACCORD, AND, TO SHOW THE GLORY OF HIS MERCY, GRACE AND WISDOM, PREDESTINED TO ETERNAL SALVATION, ACCORDING TO HIS PURPOSE or plan IN CHRIST, THOSE WHO WOULD IN THE FUTURE BELIEVE AND CONTINUE IN THE FAITH" (*YP* 6:168). Milton quotes Ecclesiastes 9.11, "*but time and chance happen to them all*" to show that "[t]hose passages of scripture which do not scruple to use the words 'fortune' or 'chance,' imply nothing derogatory to divine providence by such expressions, but merely rule out the possibility of any human causation" (*YP* 6:329).

to know the times or the seasons, which the Father hath put into his own power," to which the last line of the Son's reply also alludes, before he drily reminds Satan:

> Know'st thou not that my rising is thy fall,
> And my promotion will be thy destruction?
> (3.201–2).

Jesus' couplet is a tissue of biblical wisdom materials that resonate throughout *Paradise Regained*.[26] He refers to the rising of the morning star, the epithet Milton applied to him at the end of the soliloquy, "So spake our Morning Star then in his rise" (1.294). The epithet echoes Revelation 22.16, "I am the root and the offspring of David, *and* the bright and morning star," where Revelation makes an apocalyptic use of a wisdom song in Isaiah 11.1 announcing "a rod out of the stem of Jesse, and a Branch . . . out of his roots." John transfers the image of the rising star to Jesus, quelling its application to Lucifer in Isaiah 14.12, "How art thou fallen from heaven, O Lucifer, son of the morning!" repeated by Jesus in Luke 10.18, "I beheld Satan as lightning fall from heaven." Milton retained that image for the trope of dismissal in the angelic hymn that ends the poem:

> like an Autumnal Star
> Or Lightning thou shalt fall from Heav'n trod down
> Under his feet.
> (4.619–21)

The original wisdom passage that resurfaced in gospel and apocalypse thus makes its way into *Paradise Regained* together with its motifs of morning renewal and watchful trust. When Satan, however, gives form to his fatalism by reading Psalm 90.4, "For a thousand years in thy sight *are but* as yesterday when it is past," as an expression of inexorability, in "Long the decrees of Heav'n / Delay, for longest time to him is short" (1.55–56), he rejects both the wisdom lesson of the Psalm at verse 12, "So teach *us* to number our days, that we may apply *our* hearts unto wisdom," and the eschatological hint in verse 14, "O satisfy us early with thy mercy."[27]

Since all the temptations of the kingdoms of the world are temptations to false heroic action, all involve Satan's version of time as a se-

[26] Some of my identifications may be found in Schaar, *The Full Voic'd Quire Below*, 208–16; others in MacKellar, *Variorum* 4:83, 157.

[27] Psalm 90 is the only psalm attributed to Moses; the attribution probably signals the scribes' high regard for its wisdom teaching. Dahood, *The Anchor Bible: Psalms II: 51–100*, 17:332.

quence of opportune occasions; temporal power is seized at opportune moments. Satan acknowledges that a strategic waiting may perhaps be necessary, but he scarcely recognizes a waiting for God's epiphanic moment. For Jesus, his kingdom comes when time is ripe, "when my season comes to sit / On *David's* Throne" (4.146–47). What waiting Satan acknowledges as necessary, he likens to a gradually dawning light and to learning what may be taught by those "led by Nature's light": "These here revolve, or, as thou lik'st, at home, / Till time mature thee to a Kingdom's waight" (4.281–82). But to Jesus ripe time brings another sort of light than the gradual dawning of natural light. It brings the illumination praised in wisdom psalms. He rejects the worldly bright, for

> he who receives
> Light from above, from the fountain of light,
> No other doctrine needs.
> (4.288–90)

That view elides Psalm 27.1, "The Lord *is* my light and my salvation," and Psalm 36.9, "For with thee *is* the fountain of life: in thy light shall we see light," with Psalm 43.3, "O send out thy light and thy truth: let them lead me."

Satan's final words on opportune time, just before the tower episode, proverbially summarize his politics of the possible: "each act is rightliest done, / Not when it must, but when it may be best" (4.475–76). To the end he insists that time is made up of instances for calculation, not of moments directed by providence in which enlightened men obey God and await his will in trust. But Satan does not have the last word in the epic about the ripeness of time; the angels hymn the Son's heroic obedience, for the past it redeems and the future it promises:

> A fairer Paradise is founded now
> For *Adam* and his chosen Sons, whom thou
> A Saviour art come down to re-install.
> Where they shall dwell secure, when time shall be
> Of Tempter and Temptation without fear.
> (4.613–17)

The doctrine of the ripeness of time defers the return of Adam's sons to the fairer paradise restored to them by one greater man. That deferral, taking nothing from the heroism of witness or *martus*, represented in the Son's rejection of temptation and standing firm, gives to human history the freedom within which choices may have ethical significance. The value of the wisdom psalm to *Paradise Regained* lies in its adaptability to represent the witness to truth, attesting to divine providence at epiphanic moments. Milton wrote into the gospel narrative of *Paradise Regained* two of the dominant traits of wisdom song, witness and kairos. He was drawn to the use of that genre in the brief epic because of its pervasiveness in the New Testament. If for Milton's first audience the presence of wisdom psalms confirms or authorizes his meanings, for us it gives them a quality of toughness, resilience, shrewdness, and proverbial pith on the one hand and an abstract serenity, the moral equipoise of purposes long maturing, on the other. These are the rewards of listening for psalmic resonance, a confirmation of the moral power of poetry.

Hymn and Lament in Paradise Regained

The other two genres of psalms imitated in *Paradise Regained*, hymn and lament, Milton used more restrictedly; once again, the Book of Psalms was not his sole authority. The occasions for strong psalmic lyricism in *Paradise Regained* are few; when they did arise, Milton took as his primary models the songs composed in the New Testament themselves modeled on psalms, both those in the Psalter and those outside it. The first community of Jewish Christians not only continued the forms of worship to which they were accustomed, including psalms, they also preserved the traditions of psalmody by composing new songs after the old models.[28] Paul takes it for granted that psalms are appropriately introduced into Christian worship and advises, in Ephesians 5.19, "Speaking to yourselves in psalms and hymns and spiritual songs, singing and making melody in your heart to the Lord." Milton knew that psalms were not limited to the Book of Psalms; as Jesus remarked in *Paradise Regained*, "All our Law and Story [is] strew'd / With Hymns" (4.334–35). And he knew the four songs associated with the childhood of Jesus in Luke, apparently translated from Hebrew by him for his gospel—Mary's *Magnificat* (1.46–55), Zacharias's *Benedictus* (1.68–79), the angels' *Gloria* (2.14) and Simeon's *Nunc dimittis* (2.29–32) all have non-Psalter models behind them. They all contain numerous phrases from psalms and song, attuned to New Testament themes. Milton's adaptations of hymn and lament in *Paradise Regained* differ from those in *Paradise Lost* in that the brief epic takes Luke's new psalms as primary models, while *Paradise Lost* takes

[28] See Mowinckel, *The Psalms in Israel's Worship*, 2:122–25 and Oesterley, *A Fresh Approach to the Psalms*, 178ff.

its psalms from the Hebrew canon, the Book of Psalms. The imitations are similar in the two epics in being designed to afford the poet lyric multivocality.

Hence Milton composed two new psalmic hymns and assigned them to the angels. When God finished explaining to Gabriel the purposed testing of the Son, the angels "into Hymns / Burst forth" (1.169–70); when they had taken the Son from the pinnacle and fed him celestial food, then "Angelic Quires / Sung Heavenly Anthems of his victory" (4.593–94). Both hymns praise the Father and the Son for intervening in human affairs to help mankind.[29] Hymns in the Book of Psalms praise specific acts of God in history or praise his essential nature across the spectrum of his acts; they praise God for what he has done or what he is. Luke's psalms, however, are all kerygmatic:[30] the gospel proclaims God's redemptive act in Jesus; an individual or group perceives it and responds with praise. They always praise a single but extended intervention of God in history, the coming of Jesus; they identify stages in that coming and praise those moments of kairos in traditional phrases and tropes of Hebrew psalmody. All four of Luke's psalms are hymns, but Milton converts two into laments ending in trust, reserving the other two for angelic hymns; all are suffused with signs of their scriptural models.

Each of Luke's psalms is patterned on songs from outside the Book of Psalms. Mary's *Magnificat* is modeled upon Hannah's song of joy at God's relief of her barrenness by a son (1 Sam. 2.1–10); Zacharias's *Benedictus* is modeled on the psalms of deutero-Isaiah (especially Isa. 40.3–5); the angels' *Gloria*, on two songs from Daniel prophesying the coming of the Son of Man (Dan. 7.9–10, 13–14) and Simeon's *Nunc dimittis*, also on deutero-Isaiah (especially Isa. 52.10–11, 42.6, and 49.6). To those models Luke transfers hymn phrases from Psalms using a typical hymn structure[31]—an introduction declaring the intention to praise God, a development specifying the grounds of praise, a conclusion proclaiming benediction, prayer, or alleluia. He is particularly given to an abbreviated structure, in the abbreviation also imitating the structure of the four servant songs of deutero-Isaiah—42.1–4, 49.1–6, 50.4–11, and 52.13–53.12—songs extolling the Lord's chosen, marked by very brief introductions and conclusions. Luke's most classical

[29] MacKellar calls both angelic songs hymns and identifies the *gloria* at the Nativity as the source of the first. *Variorum*, 4:71–72, 246–52.

[30] See Westermann, *Praise and Lament in the Psalms*, 21–24 and 31–32.

[31] Very likely, Luke's psalms were themselves traditional in the early Christian community and not, as it were, freshly composed by him. Milton adapted Lukean psalms that were themselves adaptations.

hymn introductions appear in Mary's "My soul doth magnify the Lord" and Zacharias's "Blessed *be* the Lord God." Both signal the development by the conjunction "for," a common device in descriptive psalms of praise, "For he hath regarded the low estate of his handmaiden" and "for he hath visited and redeemed his people." Both lack conclusions, whereas the angelic *Gloria* lacks development and could be taken to be entirely conclusion, and Simeon's hymnal prayer is almost all conclusion, his development, "For mine eyes have seen thy salvation," being merely a recapitulation of the prose narrative preceding the hymn, "And it was revealed . . . that he should not see death, before he had seen the Lord's Christ."

In Luke's hymns Milton has available several interesting resources. First, because hymns respond to narrative or historical occasions, Milton can imitate two of Luke's hymns and give them to a choir of angels to extemporize on occasions identical to (the *Gloria*), or similar to (the *Benedictus*), those in Luke's gospel. More interestingly, he can convert the other two, the *Magnificat* and the *Nunc dimittis*, from joyous praise to grieved lament simply by offering the hymnic occasion as a joyful past moment recalled sadly in an anxious present. Second, because Luke praises the individual epiphanic moments of a single, providential sequence with both past and future significance, Milton can bend the two hymns toward a temporal center, giving them the literary functions of introduction and closure. Third, because Luke's hymns resonate with impassioned psalm motifs, a freight of intense but compressed emotion, Milton can by his own abbreviations and understatements create the effect for *Paradise Regained* of a disciplined and chastened surge of emotion, rather than a corporate, liturgical, polyphonic praise such as the angelic and human hymnody of *Paradise Lost* creates.

The first angelic hymn in *Paradise Regained* lacks both introduction and conclusion. It simply lists the topoi of praise ("and this the argument") which would have formed the hymn's development had Milton used direct rather than indirect discourse, the list reading:

> Victory and Triumph to the Son of God
> Now entring his great duel, not of arms,
> But to vanquish by wisdom hellish wiles.
> The Father knows the Son; therefore secure
> Ventures his filial Vertue, though untri'd,
> Against whate're may tempt, whate're seduce,
> Allure, or terrifie, or undermine.
> Be frustrate all ye stratagems of Hell,
> And devilish machinations come to nought.
> (1.173–81)

The topoi are three, each given one sentence: the Son's conquest of his foe by wisdom; God's serene trial of his Son; the impotence of evil. The first and last combine the themes of the *Benedictus* and *Gloria*. From the former comes the notion that a savior has been raised "to give knowledge of salvation unto his people," "to give light to them that sit in darkness," frustrating "the hand of all that hate us." From the latter, the triumph is peaceful. The second topic is proleptic of the struggle with Satan. The *Benedictus* lacks a conclusion, as does Milton's angelic psalm; Luke's *Gloria* displaces introduction and development into the narrative, as does Milton's. Milton's hymn, like both of Luke's, concentrates upon the moment in which God in heaven acts through a mortal Son.

The last hymn in *Paradise Regained* is a full-scale summary of epic heroism, praising an unparalleled victory. For it, Milton reaches behind Zacharias's and the angels' hymns to a psalm he thought implicated in both, Psalm 68.[32] His themes include the imaging of the Father in the Son, whether the Son be in heaven or on earth; the Son's manifestation of godlike power in resisting Satan; his restoration to Adam of a fairer, more heavenly paradise; the guarantee of Satan's ultimate defeat. The breaking of Satan's snares to release Adam's sons is the principal topic of Simeon's psalm, which takes its language from the formula for the manumission of a slave, "now lettest thou thy servant depart in peace, according to thy word," and contains an echo of Psalm 124.7, "the snare is broken, and we are escaped." But its ultimate model is Psalm 68, of which Zacharias's is a brief echo and the *Gloria* an even briefer.[33]

Psalm 68 is even now considered "textually and exegetically the most difficult and obscure of all the psalms."[34] In *Christian Doctrine*, Milton cautioned against quoting it to proclaim Christ's "supreme deity" and referred to "certain ellipses" in it.[35] That hypothesis of "el-

[32] In *Christian Doctrine* (*YP* 6:347), Milton linked them as proof texts: "[Angels] often appeared looking like soldiers: . . . Psal. lxviii.18: *they are twenty thousand of God's chariots*; Luke ii.13: *a multitude of the heavenly armies*."

[33] Zacharias echoes Psalm 68.6: "He bringeth out those which are bound with chains." It is quoted in Ephesians 4.1, 6–8: "I therefore, the prisoner of the Lord, beseech you. . . . *There is* . . . One God and Father of all, who *is* above all, and through all, and in you all. But unto every one of us is given grace according to the measure of the gift of Christ. Wherefore he saith, When he ascended up on high, he led captivity captive, and gave gifts unto men." The *Gloria* echoes Psalm 68.4, "extol him that rideth upon the heavens," and 68.30, "scatter thou the people *that* delight in war."

[34] See Dahood, *The Anchor Bible: Psalms II: 51–100*, 17:133; Anderson, *The New Century Bible Commentary: The Book of Psalms*, 1:481.

[35] "Passages quoted in the New Testament from the Old will have much less validity

lipses" corresponds to one current explanation of its difficulty, that it is an ode adorned for the sake of an educated audience with the opening lines of a number of previously existing songs. His use of it as a model for the last angelic chorus is clear but selective.

Milton's last hymn (4.596–635), like Psalm 68, is a triumphant ode, authorized by Lukean psalms and making the same claims Luke makes, but enriched by figures from Psalm 68. From the psalm comes the call to an angelic choir to praise a great victory,[36] giving Milton his narrative prefix and conclusion. It then treats the theme of salvation in a mixture of conquest and deliverance themes. From it comes Milton's order of topics and structure. The psalm opens with a celestial theophany, displaying God "that rideth upon the heavens" in the midst of his people. His epiphany is hailed, and he is praised both in heaven and on earth, "in his holy habitation" and "when thou didst march through the wilderness." From this opening comes Milton's first praise of the Son whether throned in heaven or wandering the wilderness.

Psalm 68 then praises the mighty God as the merciful father to the fatherless. Its second section describes a specific rescue as habitual, in such phrases as "he bringeth out those which are bound with chains," "thou didst confirm thine inheritance, when it was weary," and "*this is* the hill *which* God desireth to dwell in; yea, the Lord will dwell *in it* for ever" (vv. 6, 9, 16). From this section Milton derives the foundation of the fairer paradise where Adam's sons will dwell secure. The psalm then draws a contrast between the chorus of angels and rescued people joyfully welcoming God's advent and the kings of earthly armies scattering in flight from his majesty. This section colors the wounding of Satan in Milton's hymn.

---

if they are used to prove something different or something more than the writer who quoted them intended. In this category are Psal. lxviii.18–20: *twenty thousand of God's chariots* etc. *the Lord with them. Ascending on high*, etc. *you have received gifts for men*. Here (leaving aside the fact that there are certain ellipses, which interpreters venture to supply, in various ways, as they think fit), two people are mentioned, God and the Lord. This goes against those who try to make a case for Christ's supreme deity from a comparison of this passage with Eph. iv.5,8. Such a notion had never entered the apostle's head, and indeed his argument in iv.9 follows quite a different line: *what is it that he ascended, if it does not mean that he also descended first into the lowest parts of the earth?* Here the writer wished only to show that the Lord Jesus Christ, who was once dead and is now received into heaven, gave gifts to men which he had received from the Father." *YP* 6:250.

[36] Psalm 68.11: "The Lord gave the word: great *was* the company of those that published *it*." Verse 17: "The chariots of God *are* twenty thousand, *even* thousands of angels." Verse 25: "The singers went before, the players on instruments *followed* after." Verse 4: "extol him that rideth upon the heavens." Verse 19: "Blessed *be* the Lord, *who* daily loadeth us *with benefits*." Verse 34: "Ascribe ye strength unto God: his excellency *is* over Israel, and his strength *is* in the clouds."

Psalm 68 ends after the accomplishment of the people's liberation and the enemy's defeat with a call to the whole world to sing the advent of the God who rides on the clouds and to whom all power is ascribed: "lo, he doth send out his voice, *and that* a mighty voice," "his strength *is* in the clouds," "O God, *thou art* terrible out of thy holy places" (vv. 33, 34, 35). From this conclusion, Milton devises his own:

> hereafter learn with awe
> To dread the Son of God: he all unarm'd
> Shall chase thee with the terror of his voice
> . . . .
> Hail Son of the most High, heir of both worlds,
> Queller of Satan, on thy glorious work
> Now enter, and begin to save mankind.
> (4.625–27, 633–35)

Psalm 68 is perfectly congruent with the Lukean hymns; Milton echoes both in framing in lyrical praise the heroic conquest of devilish temptation by wisdom, giving full but restrained emotional value to the achievement, the function of hymnic psalm wherever it is found.

The literary function of lament in *Paradise Regained* is the expression of a human longing for a promised and necessary help with life. It is spoken by those closest to the Son who act as surrogates for Milton's readers. On the Son's fidelity their hopes hang. Psalmic lament expresses a number of sorrowing responses to experience: some look back to a time of distress, need, and failed promise, asking why the failure and how long the present misery; others penitently or anxiously recall misdeeds in grief; some complain or reproach God or the enemy, especially for the scorn or abuse endured by the abandoned; some bemoan physical pain or sickness, especially its disgrace. Whatever the sorrow lamented, the cast of characters includes a person or a people; God; numerous friends, enemies, kinsmen, and rulers. Hence, whether personally or collectively voiced, the lament always involves a social world; it is the genre most frequently found in Scripture.[37]

Much of the full roster of lament impulses and themes is useful to *Paradise Lost*, but, as might be anticipated, for *Paradise Regained* only a few are valuable. The Son is sinless, confident and trusting; no penitence, grief for sin, confession of wrongdoing is appropriate. The testing in the wilderness is solitary and exclusive to the hero; he makes nothing of his suffering, even his hunger, and others who might sorrow at it are absent. His betrayal is still to come; his followers need not

[37] See Weiser, *The Psalms*, 66, who reckons that almost one-third of all psalms are lament.

reproach themselves for it, although they appropriately remember the meaninglessness of their lives before he called them. But with a sure and economical touch, Milton functionally adapts lament to his poem. He uses it to foreground the Son's temptations against the emotions of the waiting world. Mary's feelings of grief and loss predict the Passion; the disciples' anguish and loneliness at Jesus' absence predict his death; their sorrowing at loss of hope reveals their need.

Old Testament lament directs its expressions of grief so as to secure compassion or exact it from God, who alone, it is felt, can both pity man and offer hope of redress. Although the New Testament claims that God's compassion has already been moved and the redress made, the faithful Christian is not always required to suppress lament.[38] The Gospels show Jesus compassionate toward suffering, and Milton attributes pity for Job and Socrates to him (3.95–99); Milton allows himself to express compassion at Jesus' suffering, too, in his exposure to the storm: "ill wast thou shrouded then, / O patient Son of God" (4.419–20). Nonetheless, instructed perhaps by the moral stoicism of Paul's epistles and determined to show victory and banish loss, Milton wrote only two laments into *Paradise Regained*, and he based those on Luke's hymns of praise and turned them toward trust at the end. His overall generic strategy was to place wisdom psalm at the core of the epic, to frame the Son's contest with Satan between two hymns, and to foreground it against lament that also praises, a strategy designed to reinforce the brilliant economy of the spiritual duel.

The first of Milton's two laments is the disciples'; Mary's immediately follows it. Taken together they present the human response to Jesus' absence, moving from doubt and fear to faith and hope. In the first, Andrew and Simon "Thir unexpected loss and plaints out breath'd" (2.29). Like Simeon, their "eyes beheld / Messiah certainly now come"; like him, they were sure "deliverance is at hand" (2.31–32, 35).[39] They are now alone, and in distress they interweave griefs characteristic of lament, that God or chance is the cause of their trouble and that it will go on and on to "prolong / Our expectation" (2.41–42). They ask God to send the Messiah to free them from a sacrilegious enemy in lines that transfer a reproach from lament psalms:[40]

[38] Nonetheless, as Richard Baxter's *Breviate Life* of his wife Margaret shows, a pressure was felt among seventeenth-century nonconformists to show joy as the mark of sanctification or grace.

[39] Luke 2.30–31: "For mine eyes have seen thy salvation, Which thou hast prepared before the face of all people"; 2.26: "And it was revealed unto him by the Holy Ghost, that he should not see death, before he had seen the Lord's Christ."

[40] *Variorum* 4:107 and Sims, *The Bible in Milton's Epics*, 275 both suggest Psalm 2.2.

> Send thy Messiah forth, *the time is come*;
> Behold the Kings of the Earth how they oppress
> Thy chosen, to what highth thir pow'r unjust
> They have exalted, and behind them cast
> All fear of thee, arise and vindicate
> Thy Glory, free thy people from thir yoke.
> (2.43–48; my emphasis)

The combination of prayer and censure of ungodly oppressors is common to lament; the prayer itself, full of lament phrases.[41]

Milton makes use of the entire Simeon episode in Luke, both Simeon's warning to Mary, "Behold, this *child* is set for the fall and rising again of many in Israel . . . (Yea, a sword shall pierce through thy own soul also)" (2.34–35), and the *Nunc dimittis*. Milton's disciples move through fear into trust—"But let us wait; thus far he hath perform'd"—and then hope and confidence: "Soon we shall see our hope, our joy return" (2.49, 57). That conclusion in which sorrow modulates into thanksgiving is typical of psalmic lament.[42] The disciples' communal lament traces a course from sorrow and fear to trust and hope that not only foregrounds the Son's human ordeal against the people's great need but also gives his audience a channel for their own responses. It shadows the gospel anxiety and confidence in any Christian's experience and places the long temptation of the kingdoms of the world, next to follow in the poem, in a concrete historical setting of political uncertainty and early messianic expectation.

Mary's interior monologue or soliloquy of lament casts her joyous praise of God in a remembered past and brings Simeon's foreboding, "(Yea, a sword shall pierce through thy own soul also)," forward to the present moment. To the Son, Mary's account of the annunciation was strengthening; alone, her recollection is sorrowful. Her opening theme is the very pastness of the event: "O what avails me *now* that honour high. . . . While I to sorrows am no less advanc't" (2.66, 69, my emphasis). As she ponders the course of Jesus' life, the birth, the flight into Egypt, the childhood "Private, unactive, calm, contemplative" (2.81), and the baptism reported to her, she recalls Simeon's prediction of trouble, "My Exaltation to Afflictions high" (2.92). Her patient re-

But Psalms 5.10, 10.3, 14.1 and 4, 28.5, 36.1, 52.7, 54.3, 55.19, 73.27, 86.14, 119.85, and 119.139 all handle the enemies as sacrilegious in a similar way.

[41] See Psalms 44, 74, and 80; see also Psalms 10.12 and 12.1.

[42] MacKellar, *Variorum* 4:107, identifies Psalm 55.22, "Cast thy burden upon the Lord, and he shall sustain thee," but the strategy and phrasing can be found throughout the genre, as in Psalms 6.9, 22.21, 28.7, 41.11, 54.7, 55.22, 61.3, 69.35, 71.21, 86.17, and 102.13.

fusal to pity her own lot gives way to an anxiety about his current absence, which she allays by thoughts of his earlier absence to teach in the temple on "His Father's business" (2.99). She expresses her renewed trust:

> But I to wait with patience am inur'd;
> My heart hath been a store-house long of things
> And sayings laid up, portending strange events.
> (2.102–4)

The soliloquy is proleptic, but she ends "with thoughts / Meekly compos'd" (2.107–8) into trust.

The scene dramatizes Luke's remark that "Mary kept all these things, and pondered *them* in her heart" (Luke 2.19) but shapes Mary's emotional course to run from a past trust through sorrowing reminiscence to renewed trust by drawing on the emotional pattern in psalms of personal lament. Psalms 6, 22, and 102, among others, could supply a model, but Psalms 27 and 40 are especially interesting possibilities. Both are mixed-genre psalms of lament and thanksgiving, commencing in trust and ending in trust but plumbing lament in a central aria of remembered sorrow. Milton used Psalm 27 in *Christian Doctrine* once as a proof text for "CONFIDENCE . . . in God, as an effect of love" and "HOPE in God . . . that we await confidently the fulfilment of his promises," and again as a proof text of "FORTITUDE . . . when we repel evils or stand against them unafraid."[43] He cited Psalm 40 in conjunction with the angel's conversation with Mary in Luke 1.35 as showing the manner of Jesus' conception, and he used it as proof text for his reflections on Christ's priestly function and on "alacrity . . . when we do good readily" and "CONTENTMENT . . . which makes a man . . . accept what seems to him to be divine providence."[44] In *Paradise Regained* the Son's test is not treated as the Son's ordeal, and if Mary gives expression for Milton's audience to an appropriately controlled grief, it is nonetheless noticeable that Mary especially controls sorrow and converts lament into trust, that she is allowed little proleptic mourning, and that she speedily withdraws her thoughts from the sword in her own heart.[45] Milton's Satan, however, is given a romanticized bib-

[43] *YP* 6:657, 659, 738.

[44] *YP* 6:428, 434, 654, and 728.

[45] See Curran, "*Paradise Regained*: The Implications of Epic," 220, for a suggestive comment on the kind of sadness that *Paradise Regained* lacks: "The numerous attempts to define what is wanting in *Paradise Regained* that earlier epics possess have always boldly missed the point. What the poem lacks is not encyclopedic scope, but the im-

lical lament and passionately projects himself into a lyrical longing for escape, solace, succor, and loving care. When Milton is stern against the sobbing voice of self-concern, he does not thereby deform psalmic lament by his emphasis but reads it with fidelity to his sources, not coldly.

The structure of lament moves through a predictable schedule—an address and introductory petition or expression of the motive for lament, the lamentation proper, the confession of trust, the renewed prayer, the vow of praise.[46] As mixed-genre laments, both Psalms 27 and 40 establish a secure trust at the outset—"The Lord *is* my light and my salvation; whom shall I fear?" in the former, "I waited patiently for the Lord; and he inclined unto me, and heard my cry" in the latter—and then both recall the threats to that posture. The speech prefix to Mary's lament likewise shows trust, and trust threatened:

> Within her brest, though calm; her brest though pure,
> Motherly cares and fears got head, and rais'd
> Some troubl'd thoughts, which she in sighs thus clad.
> (2.63–65)

Mary speaks when her Son is absent and "tydings of him none" (2.62). The occasion and motives for lament are just as explicit in Psalm 27, where the sorrower in danger and longing only to "dwell in the house of the Lord all the days of my life" has been abandoned by his family, "When my father and my mother forsake me, then the Lord will take me up" (27.4, 10), and in Psalm 40, where a dutiful servant of God who preached "righteousness in the great congregation" recalls how his heart failed him at the "innumerable evils" and "mine iniquities" (40.9, 12). Mary thinks of events apparently at odds with God's promise—the unprotected birthplace, the flight from danger, the unheralded return, the unpropitious withdrawal from the world; both psalms detail encirclement by enemies, their derision, the psalmist's sense of abandonment. Then Mary expresses trust and refuses to protest her fate "nor will repine" in a midlament assertion like those of the two psalms. Mary steadies her renewed concern by remembering Jesus' earlier absence. Her resolution in fortitude, "But I to wait with patience am inur'd," is the moral equivalent of the lament's recollection, vow, and prayer. In Psalm 27, recollection of trust takes the form

---

mense sadness of the traditional epic, even of *Paradise Lost*. Spare, compressed, restrained—paradoxically *Paradise Regained* celebrates the simple, absolute value of life."

[46] On lament structure see Westermann, *Praise and Lament in the Psalms*, 265 and Mowinckel, *The Psalms in Israel's Worship*, 2:9–11. See also Lewalski, Paradise Lost *and the Rhetoric of Literary Forms*, 97–105, on the coalescence of soliloquy and lament.

"*I had fainted*, unless I had believed to see the goodness of the Lord in the land of the living" (v. 13) and in Psalm 40, "But I *am* poor and needy; *yet* the Lord thinketh upon me" (v. 17). Both psalms make a lament vow, in Psalm 27, "therefore will I offer in his tabernacle sacrifices of joy" (v. 6) and in Psalm 40, "I have not hid thy righteousness within my heart; I have declared thy faithfulness and thy salvation" (v. 10). Both conclude with prayer: "Wait on the Lord" and "make no tarrying, O my God." Mary describes her own state of mind; her trustful self-knowledge and constancy stand in the position of vow and prayer, as arising from them. The circumstances of lament, the formulations of prayer and trust, the conclusions in patience, the vows and prayers—all these constitutive elements differ in detail in every lament, but their structure and order are constant and are the model for Mary's lament. It is in the ethical nature of its vow that sorrow be controlled.

At the opposite remove is Satan's stagy pseudo-lament asking the Son to shelter him from God (3.209–22). Like a penitential psalm, his lament confesses error and crime; unlike a penitential psalm, his confession is without remorse. Like a penitential psalm, it entreats the end of suffering: unlike one, it aims at "ultimate repose," not holy awe. Like a psalmic lament, his petitions are for succor:

> to that gentle brow
> Willingly I could flye, and hope thy raign,
> From that placid aspect and meek regard,
> Rather then aggravate my evil state,
> Would stand between me and thy Fathers ire,
> (Whose ire I dread more then the fire of Hell)
> (3.215–20)

Unlike a psalmic lament, the rescue he prays for is not by, but against, God, the shelter not under his wing but from his wrath. No vow of praise or trust concludes it. Editors have seen in his canny request for mercy an allusion to Isaiah 25.4–5, "For thou hast been a . . . shadow from the heat, . . . *even* the heat with the shadow of a cloud." But the formula hide me, shelter me, shade me is the commonest petition in personal lament.[47] What Satan omits from lament clarifies its inner nature; no contrast could be greater than that between the operatic performance Milton writes for him and the quietness of human distress

[47] See Psalms 3.3, 5.12, 6.4, 7.1, 17.8 "hide me under the shadow of thy wings"; 18.11, 22.18, 27.5, 32.6, 35.17, 38.22, 40.13, 44.26, 51.1, 54.1, 55.8, 57.1 "in the shadow of thy wings will I make my refuge"; 69.18, 71.20, 94.22, 102.19, 140.7, and 143.9 "I flee unto thee to hide me."

overcome in those he writes for the disciples and for Mary. Theirs prompt a sense of the needfulness of the Son's victory; his is floridly self-serving. The lyric genres of New Testament psalmody have been put by Milton to uses in which an acute formal analysis serves a strong sense of literary decorum. Wisdom song is inscribed in the very mimesis of the brief epic, angelic hymn surrounds the Son's victory with praise, lament directs and qualifies the emotions of the audience of that victory.

INTERCHAPTER

"*Sion*'s songs, to all true tasts excelling"

MILTON'S ENGAGEMENT with the psalms as preeminent instances of the poetry of the Bible, poetry capable of recapture in English versification, began early, persisted through his public career, and came to fruition in his two epic poems. As early as *The Reason of Church Government* he had written that psalms, "not in their divine argument alone, but in the very critical art of composition may be easily made appear over all the kinds of Lyrick poesy, to be incomparable." When he then desired a multivocality in *Paradise Lost* that would enable him to "[teach] over the whole book of sanctity and virtu through all the instances of example with . . . delight," he turned to the "frequent songs throughout the law and prophets" and adapted them to the voices and occasions of a spectrum of individual speakers.[1] At the time of the composition of *Paradise Regained*, he turned again directly to "our Psalms with artful terms inscrib'd" "to all true tasts excelling" (4.334, 346) to shape a poetry of intellectual debate, producing an English versification of markedly greater plainness of style than that he had reconciled with Psalms in *Paradise Lost*. Because of the very intensity and dedication of Milton's earlier psalm study, he came to the composition of epic, whether diffuse or brief, already thoroughly primed to adapt the relevant features of Hebrew versification to differing expressive needs. Milton had, before the composition of either epic, translated two groups of psalms, aiming at two separate ends. First, seeking fidelity to psalm meaning and style, he had translated Psalms 80–88 in April 1648, using only the psalm tunes of common measure; second, seeking the reproduction of psalm poesis in a variety of metrical patterns, he had translated Psalms 1–8 in August 1653.[2] His understanding of psalm poesis, gained from both these periods of psalm study, affected the distinctive registration of Hebrew verse in the two epic modes. Milton did not learn how to be biblical by imitating Psalms in *Paradise Lost* and then apply his findings with greater compression and consistency to *Paradise Regained*; he learned by direct study of Psalms to understand the Hebrew medium as a parallelistic medium incorporating rhetorical, poetic, and prosodic figures. Al-

[1] *YP* 1:816, 817, 816.

[2] See *Variorum*, 2:991–1006, for the circumstances and dates of the translations.

though Milton could and did read psalms in Hebrew, his translations are geared not to transpose Hebrew metrics into English but to make English accentual syllabic verse feel metrically psalmlike. A similar prosodic ethnocentrism is involved in his adapting classical quantitative verse to English accentual syllabic verse, as in his giving *Lycidas* a Greek strophic irregularity by domesticating some of the effects of Pindaric odes and tragic chorus rather than by seeking to reproduce the strophes themselves, if that were possible.[3] What he found admirable and poetically of supreme beauty in Hebrew poetry was available to him for imitation not only in the epics but also in *Samson Agonistes*; he had already taken advantage of psalms as models in a variety of brief early religious poems. In conformity, therefore, with my plan to move from the more single and simple use of biblical models for the genres and themes in *Paradise Regained* to the more complex, varied, and multiform use in *Paradise Lost*, I will describe first Milton's incorporation of psalm versification in the brief epic and turn then to the effects of psalms on the diffuse epic. I use Milton's translations of Psalms 1–8 in conjunction with *Paradise Regained* and reserve his translations of Psalms 80–88 for *Paradise Lost*, the moods and themes of the two groups suggesting that match.

In *Paradise Regained* Milton seeks to reconstitute psalmic parallelism through schemes of rhetorical placement in order to offer its pith and plainness as the chief aesthetic pleasure of that kind of reduplication. The sensitive ear is trained to hear the continuous play of mind in judicious reechoings and hence reconsiderations or readjustments of meaning. The reader is to admire justice of expression, to recognize and approve shrewdness and discipline of speech as it triumphs over any impulse toward "lincked sweetness long drawn out" ("L'Allegro," 140) and to delight in the edge that the natural idioms of educated seventeenth-century speech tersely display. But parallelism in itself may be promoted as well by other means than rhetorical placement and lead to other aesthetic pleasures than the delightfulness of approving the natural strength of unadorned exactitude. When Milton wrote into *Paradise Lost* his adaptations of the medium of the psalms, he did so no less aware of the importance of parallelism as an aspect of Hebrew poetry than in the later poem; he simply offered as supremely beautiful a biblical parallelism achieved by a variety of poetical means and made suitable to a variety of speakers, under the laws of decorum.

Biblical parallelism may be defined as the kind of dynamic repetition

[3] See Weismiller, "Studies of Verse Form in the Minor English Poems," in *Variorum*, 2:1057–74, and "Versification," in *A Milton Encyclopedia*, 8:118–35.

in which, as Herder put it, "two [parallel] members strengthen, heighten, empower each other."[4] Milton's awareness of parallelism as a compositional principle was grounded and is self-evident in his handling of psalm translations. In the literal translations of Psalms 80 through 88 into common measure, for example, Milton arranged all the materials not in the original but necessary for the meter of common measure to confirm the dynamic parallelisms of the Hebrew verses.[5] In *Paradise Lost*, he reconstitutes biblical parallelism by metaphors urging similarity and dissimilarity; by iterative images, themes, and motifs, whether hyperbolically or naturally conceived, along both geophysical and historical axes; by unfolding his thought in successive parallel waves of elevation, in imitation of what has been called *parallelismus membrorum*; and often by capping and reining in his extensive parallelisms by the finalities involved in such wordplay as paronomasia, or punning.

Milton perceived Hebrew rhythm as free enough so that in translation he could render it in a range of modern meters. He chose to write *Paradise Regained* in a verse marked by a good deal of end-stopping and by the attenuation of the long involved periods, complex inversions, and verse paragraphs of *Paradise Lost*. To adopt parallelism as his principal poetic means of creating pithy plainstyle involved a complementary decision to use a linear unit compatible with psalm structure to create the sense of disputation, of debate rather than oration, of irony rather than celebration, he thought suitable to his design. For *Paradise*

[4] See Kugel, *The Idea of Biblical Poetry*, 1–58 for a description of the parallelistic line, called by him the "seconding" sequence. See Alter, *The Art of Biblical Poetry*, 1–19 for a discussion of interlinear semantic parallelism. See also Preminger and Greenstein, *The Hebrew Bible in Literary Criticism*, 145–60. Herder is quoted in Alter, 11.

[5] For example, note Milton's additions to verse 2 of Psalm 85, given in italics:

2 Th'iniquity thou didst forgive
   That wrought thy people woe,
And all their Sin, *that did thee grieve*
   Hast hid *where none shall know*.

The Coverdale translation in the Book of Common Prayer reads "Thou hast forgiven the offence of thy people, and covered all their sins." The King James Version translates the verse as "Thou hast forgiven the iniquity of thy people, thou hast covered all their sin."

Translating into common measure, a quatrain with the stress pattern 4 3 4 3, Milton simply divides each of two bicola into two to make up four lines. Having divided the first line of the original into two lines, Milton's addition is made to supply a second semantic member to the second line. Similarly, having divided the second line of the original into two lines, Milton's two additions are made to supply a second member to each line. The procedure confirms his awareness both in the original Hebrew and in translation of the compositional principle of parallelism.

Lost, however, Milton adapted psalmic rhythm by creating alliterations and assonances across verse paragraphs, so that distant items are interrelated, while sound play and sound pattern develop: by emphasizing the parallelisms through distinctive balancing or echoing rhythms that take advantage of medial and terminal pauses in individual lines; and by combining regularity and freedom in the stress patterns within his individual lines and across his verse paragraphs. The pleasures of the ear in both these versions of psalmic virtuosity doubtless attracted Milton, but I think it probable, too, that he found in Psalms an assuagement of the pain of his blindness.

The extreme visibility of the metaphors of scriptural poetry must have solaced him, for the poetry of psalms has a natural concreteness: its mountains skip like rams and its harps hang on willows. It persistently defines by things that may be seen, as when God's people have the beasts of the field under their feet, are drawn up out of deep waters, fly the banner of God's name, take shelter under God's wing, fall into the pit they have themselves dug, are moth-eaten, or broken pottery, or like a bride dressed in cloth of gold. It makes even its moral or philosophical points through concrete objects, as when God touches a man, washes him, or blots his sins out of a book, or when a good man is a fruit-bearing vine or a flourishing tree, but a bad man has swords in his lips. It translates ideas into such physically present, colored things as green pastures, red wine, flaming arrows. To a man who once could see but can see no longer, this spectacular lucidity must have counted.

The rhythm of the psalms in any of the translations Milton would have used, whether English or Latin, is initially experienced as found in a single line, composed of either two or three internal parallelisms, each line freestanding without enjambment among lines. That single line rhythm containing either two or three units of stress and thought is then combined with one other such line as much as three-fourths of the time, and with two other such lines about one-third of the time to form a brief strophe. These couplet or tercet strophes of distich (bicola) or tristich (tricola) lines are then experienced as the normal unit of rhythmic organization. Since the psalmist is not constrained to repeat the rhythm of one strophe in the following strophe, in a whole psalm the strophes are normally read as free rhythmic counterpointings of each other. Occasionally the strophes seem organized into stanzas—quatrains appear in Psalms 18, 28, 39, and 40, for example; sestets in Psalms 19 and 25; a ten-line stanza of couplets in 38; a six-line stanza in Psalm 119.[6] The freedom and unpredictability of these rhythmical

[6] See Preminger and Greenstein, *The Hebrew Bible in Literary Criticism*, 227–30.

structures enables the epic poet to reconstruct some of their patterns and improvisatory effects in a verse organized not simply as thoughtful, terse debate but as long, rich, and complex verse paragraphs. In conformity with the general plan of this book, I will give the simpler uses first.

Biblical Parallelism in Paradise Regained

The Son and Satan oppose each other in *Paradise Regained* not only substantively but also stylistically, as many have noticed.[7] Satanic floridness is rebuked by the Son's plain style, is parodied by him so that its artifice is seen to cloak bluster or threat, and is meant to be regarded by the ideal reader like "varnish on a Harlots cheek" (4.344). Nonetheless, since Milton thought Hebrew poetry worthiest of imitation because the most beautiful and skillful poetry ever composed, he imitated it comprehensively too, without respect to speaker, as a fluent medium recognizably scriptural, a verse on which to play variations. In his protracted mythopoeic engagement with psalms, he did not simply attach some kinds to the Son as speaker and others to the devil; he did not merely render the Son's lines psalmically and the devil's ornately; he did not only give his actors a psalmic inflection and reserve for his narrator the idiom of the educated late-seventeenth-century speaker, though traces of all these distinctions can be found in the text. In *Paradise Regained* he imitated psalms generally throughout a narrative poem.

Well trained in analyzing Hebrew and classical poetry according to the schemes and tropes of classical rhetoric, Milton grasped the fundamental operation of compositional parallelism as the ground of Hebrew verse.[8] He had thought the revival of the rhetorical analysis of poetry as an organic art one of the special glories of Renaissance humanistic learning. And he read Hebrew poetry as susceptible to rhetorical analysis. He thought that Job and the Psalms contained the highest poetical achievement of Scripture. To see the superiority of the Psalms to pagan poetry as art and not simply thought was to discern its superior flexibility, variety, and purity in the very devices that Greek poetry learned from the Hebrew, Milton said through Jesus' praise of it in *Paradise Regained*. Although Hebrew poetry clearly dif-

[7] See Martz, "*Paradise Regained*: The Meditative Combat," 223–47; Laskowsky, "Miltonic Dialogue and the Principle of Antithesis in Book Three of *Paradise Regained*," 24–29; Steadman, "Milton's Rhetoric: Satan and the 'Unjust Discourse,' " 67–92; Elliott, "Milton's Biblical Style in *Paradise Regained*," 227–41.

[8] See Kugel, *The Idea of Biblical Poetry*; Alter, *The Art of Biblical Poetry*; and Berlin, *The Dynamics of Biblical Parallelism*.

fered from classical poetry and was to Milton's way of thinking more beautiful, it excelled as a texture of "artful terms" for which classical rhetoric had names, placed in arrangements classical rhetoric efficiently described. Perhaps Milton's rabbinic reading reinforced his sense of parallelism as definitive of Hebrew poetry. That commentators agreed that the Old Testament was inspired truth, of which every word, phrase, or arrangement was significant, would tend to reinforce his sense that parallelism involves more than a taste for reduplication. Rabbinic midrash says the point of parallelism is complementarity and not repetition;[9] Milton's practice as a translator reveals his agreement.

The parallelism of Psalm 5.3, for example, has a chiastic form: "My voice shalt thou hear in the morning, O Lord; in the morning will I direct *my prayer* unto thee, and will look up." Milton translates that verse so as to retain the crossing parallelism:

> Jehovah thou my early voyce
> Shalt in the morning hear;
> Ith'morning I to thee with choyce
> Will rank my Prayers, and watch till thou appear.
> (5–8)

The psalm repeats the formula "in the morning" in each hemistich, establishing a relationship between the two halves; Milton retains its ploche. The psalm does not focus on the same actor in each half, but shifts from God hearing to the speaker praying; Milton's word order actually emphasizes the distinction. The psalm artfully extends the length of the second hemistich, by specifying two actions, to pray and to wait, surprising the reader who anticipates parison with isocolon; Milton similarly elaborates: where trimeter is anticipated in the quatrain, he uses pentameter. The psalm begins as though simply reversing a repetition—my voice you hear in the morning; in the morning I lift my voice. In the event, the second hemistich both augments the thought and adds personality to the speaker. The verse now says, in the morning you hear my voice; in the morning I pray to you and furthermore, I watch for your response. Milton translates the verse, that is, so as to preserve parallelism, preserve the rhetorical scheme and its variation from a repeating base, and preserve the distinctiveness of the parts by which the idea was developed.[10]

[9] Kugel, *The Idea of Biblical Poetry*, chap. 1.

[10] Ploche is the repetition of a word or phrase. The verse is an epanados or statement expanded by repetitions of terms. Parison is a repetition of phrases or clauses of equal length; isocolon is the placement of such repetition as a parallelistic structure. Definitions of rhetorical terms will follow Lanham, *A Handlist of Rhetorical Terms*.

To identify parallelism as the essential principle of biblical poetry is to recognize not only its variation through figures of balance, repetition, and antithesis but also its counterpoint, suspension, or deferral, later to be reasserted as the commanding rhythm of the line. Schemes suppressing parallelism include amplification and brevity. Of course the identification of some sort of binary process in biblical poesis and its counterpointing is possible for readers unskilled in classical rhetoric. A modern close reader would pick up the figures reinforcing or varying parallelism, and would identify the pattern of noun-verb-object / noun-verb-object and its chiastic version noun-verb-object / object-verb-noun whether or not they would call the first anaphora or the second antimetabole. Milton was not innocent of training in poetic theory, however. When he imitated Hebrew poetry, imitating the schemes and figures of classical rhetoric as he saw them working in Hebrew poetry, he wrote as a Renaissance Englishman defining the biblical in classical terms. Figures of juxtaposition, balance, and equilibrium became his means of imitating Hebrew poetry; they "pleased [his] ear" and "delight[ed his] private hours / With Music" (*PR* 4.331–32). That the strongest effect of Hebrew parallelism in the Psalms is pungency and cogency in expression suited his conception of "profit and delight" within a brief epic by enacting the laconic and decisive.

In *Paradise Regained*, Milton's imitation of the poetry of Psalms is not primarily lexical, although many verbal echoes have been noted.[11] Nor is it primarily metrical, and it is only partially figural. Milton's principal means of imitation are the structural tropes or schemes of psalmic parallelism. To cite but one simple example of his preference for psalm structures of parallelism over well-known translated psalm locutions, one might look for a moment at his version of Psalm 8.6–8. Psalm 8 is a hymn that glorifies God the creator, who has given man trusteeship over the works of his hands. It shows human beings the kind of achievement that suits them and the kind of moral behavior that is acceptable to God: because God wills for men the scope they should desire for themselves, Psalm 8 tells us, manly rebellion or ambition is folly, while pious reverence for nature is truly heroic. By implication Nimrod and Absalom are unheroic, David and the Son truly heroic. In *Paradise Regained*, Psalm 8 is at issue between Satan and the Son because of that ideal role it identifies. The psalm tells us that human beings were not meant to establish their humanity in opposition to fate or nemesis; they were intended to live in pastoral and agricultural harmony with God and the land. To reject that intended role in

[11] See Sims, *The Bible in Milton's Epics*, 64–102.

rebellion against God results not in self-realization but in exile. Wilderness-and-exile is throughout the psalms the symbol of a moral and spiritual estate that men have made themselves. Exile-and-wilderness figures man's sense of alienation as both of his own making (hence suffused with remorse) and as unnatural to him and meaningless (hence suffused with guilt and religious longing).[12] Many psalms depict moments of individual anguish arising from feelings both of loss, abandonment, remorse, guilt and the like, and of being watched by an offended God. The desert is the perfect locus for these feelings; its dangers and its resistance to sheepherding and gardening combine with its eerie featurelessness to make an uncanny place where God may show himself and where man, reenacting the scene that haunts him, may put off his self-destructive rebellion and accept a nobler role. Psalm 8 tells the reader that God neither made nor desires wilderness; he made a pastoral world for man and willed glory for him there.

Psalm 8.6–8 details the good world God made for men:

> Thou madest him to have dominion over the works of thy hands; thou hast put all *things* under his feet:
> All sheep and oxen, yea, and the beasts of the field;
> The fowl of the air, and the fish of the sea, *and whatsoever* passeth through the paths of the seas.

When Milton translated the *oves et boves* of the Latin Junius-Tremellius Bible, he retained the hendiadys and discarded the homoioptoton of the Latin, disliking its jingle; he substituted his own phrasing "flocks and herds" for the "sheep and oxen" of both the King James Version and the Coverdale.[13]

[12] See Schneidau, *Sacred Discontent: The Bible and Western Tradition*, 129ff. and 279ff.

[13] Hendiadys is the expression of a single idea by two nouns connected by "and"—"domestic farm animals" here expressed by "sheep and oxen." Homoioptoton is rhyme of two or more words with like case endings—"*oves et boves*"; homoioteleuton is simply rhyme, e.g., "ox and flocks." By the time he wrote his epics, Milton thoroughly disliked homoioteleuton or all rhyme, and not simply homoioptoton. Even when, earlier, he translated psalms "into Metre" he avoided the jingles of homoioptoton. Thus the Latin *benedixisti*, *avertisti*, and *remisisti* in Psalm 84.2, translated in the King James Version as longeth, fainteth, and crieth out, becomes:

> My Soul *doth long* and almost *die*
> Thy Courts O Lord to see,
> My heart and flesh aloud *do crie*,
> O living God, for thee.
> (5–8, my emphasis)

Milton may have preferred "flocks and herds" to "sheep and oxen" because they are exclusively English words, were Shakespeare's choice before him, and had also the sanction of the King James Version in other places, as in Leviticus 27.32.

O're the works of thy hand thou mad'st him Lord,
Thou hast put all under his lordly feet,
All Flocks, and Herds, by thy commanding word,
All beasts that in the field or forrest meet.
(17–20)

Milton never echoed from the King James Version the phrase "sheep and oxen," but he frequently echoed the Psalm in his own phrase. In *Paradise Lost* he described the wanton destruction of God's creation in wartime, tragically recalling the psalm:

One way a Band select from forage drives
A herd of Beeves, faire Oxen and faire Kine
From a fat Meddow ground; or fleecy Flock,
Ewes and thir bleating Lambs over the Plaine,
Thir Bootie.
(11.646–50)

That suspended sentence, unified by crossing the alliterations of band-beeves-bleating-bootie with those of forage-fair-fat-fleecy-flock, and by the half-rhymes *band* and *lambs*, *oxen* and *flock*, instances the grand style of *Paradise Lost*. Both in that poem and in *Paradise Regained* Milton offers in place of lexical reminders of the King James Version his own hendiadys "flocks and herds" as a signal that the creator's care for man is at issue and Psalm 8 is on his mind.

His own locution appears, for example, in the catalogue of God's gifts lost to him, in the proem in Book III of *Paradise Lost*:

Thus with the Year
Seasons return, but not to me returns
Day, or the sweet approach of Ev'n or Morn,
Or sight of vernal bloom, or Summers Rose,
Or flocks, or herds, or human face divine.
(3.40–44)

Milton recalls the gifts of nature lost with his eyesight, to turn them toward a prayer for the gift of inner light; the blankness of his exile can be removed by a theophany in his wilderness.[14] The dyadic "flocks or herds" reappears in the poet's description of Noah's worship in *Paradise Lost*, where dominion over nature is piously expressed in conformity with the ethos of Psalm 8:

[14] The oxymoron of "human face divine" is constructed as a form of parallelism. So also was the polyptoton in Milton's original translation, "Thou mad'st him *Lord* . . . put all under his *lordly* feet" (my emphasis).

> Labouring the soile, and reaping plenteous crop,
> Corn wine and oyle; and from the herd or flock,
> Oft sacrificing Bullock, Lamb, or Kid.
> (12.18–20)

Here the phrase is caught up in a richly inventive texture of parallelisms: "Labouring the soile" and "reaping plenteous crop" in parison and anticipating the complementary "sacrificing"; "corn wine and oyle" in parison with "Bullock, Lamb, or Kid." The harvest is shown in a line and a half-line of verse balanced by the sacrifice in a half-line and a line of verse, while the dyad of participle and noun in the former completed by three nouns is reversed by a dyad of nouns in the latter completed by a participle and three nouns. The phrase that signals the presence of Psalm 8 is seconded by a parallelistic practice like that of Psalm 8. Finally, it appears in the description of the "Fair Champain" under the Son's feet in Book III of *Paradise Regained*, when Satan places him on a "Mountain high" to tempt him with "the Monarchies of the Earth" (3.252, 246). Satan's *coup de théâtre* contrasts with God's gift of the created world to mankind, like that recalled in Psalm 8:

> Fertil of corn the glebe, of oyl and wine,
> With herds the pastures throng'd, with flocks the hills.
> (3.259–60)

Those lines Milton also very simply decorates with the increments of psalmic parallelism.

Psalm 3, too, bears importantly on *Paradise Regained*, was translated by Milton in a metrical form he thought suited it, and may illustrate the way he uses parallelism to suggest that the Bible was written in a rhythmically imitable style even within the conventions of English metrics.[15] In Psalm 3, the psalmist in distress cries to God for help against his enemies. The subtitle, "A Psalm of David, when he fled from Absalom his son," retrospectively attaches it to an occasion when David "passed over the brook Kidron . . . *toward the way of the wilderness*" (2 Sam. 15.23; my emphasis), rebellious Absalom having seized his kingdom. It reads in the King James Version:

> Lord, how are they increased that trouble me! many *are* they that rise up against me.

[15] See Lewalski, *Protestant Poetics and the Seventeenth-Century Religious Lyric*, 39–41; Kugel, *The Idea of Biblical Poetry*, 70–73, 127–30, 156–63, and 233–66; and Baroway, "The Hebrew Hexameter," 66–91, for metrical theories of biblical poetry. The rhythm of extended parallelism, sometimes called "thought rhyme," is in *Paradise Regained* naturally shorter than in *Paradise Lost*, but is still the operative principle.

> Many *there be* which say of my soul, *There is* no help for him in God. Selah.
>
> But thou, O Lord, *art* a shield for me; my glory, and the lifter up of mine head.
>
> I cried unto the Lord with my voice, and he heard me out of his holy hill. Selah.
>
> I laid me down and slept; I awaked; for the Lord sustained me.
>
> I will not be afraid of ten thousands of people, that have set *themselves* against me round about.
>
> Arise, O Lord; save me, O my God: for thou hast smitten all mine enemies *upon* the cheek bone; thou hast broken the teeth of the ungodly.
>
> Salvation *belongeth* unto the Lord: thy blessing *is* upon thy people. Selah.

When Milton cited the psalm in *Christian Doctrine*, he read in it that moral insight comes from suffering and repentance, noted that divinely regulated punishment is often an instrumental cause of repentance,[16] and took the last verse as a public prayer, exemplifying fortitude. The tractate shows Milton's interpretation of the psalm—God tests a man and enlightens him so that he becomes trustful, pious, and courageous; for that God is to be praised. Milton quotes in the Latin three verses from the psalm: 3.3, "*quam multi dicunt de anima mea, non est ulla salus isti in Deo plane!*"; 3.7, "*non timebo a myriadibus populi, quas circum disposuerint metatores contra me*"; and 3.9, "*super populum tuum sit benedictio tua maxime.*"[17] Milton's moral interpretation of the psalm is perfectly faithful to a literal single sense, but when he echoes it in *Paradise Regained* he reads it not simply as a good doctrinal exegete but also as a poet. He refers it to the Son's night of hunger in the wilderness and dramatizes the unexplained experience in the psalm that causes a change of mood from lament to trust between verses 4 and 5, reconstituting the morning prayer in Psalm 3 to account for the sequence "I

[16] "REPENTANCE . . . IS THE GIFT OF GOD BY VIRTUE OF WHICH THE REGENERATE MAN, SEEING WITH SORROW THAT HE HAS OFFENDED GOD BY HIS SINS, DETESTS AND AVOIDS THEM AND, THROUGH A SENSE OF THE DIVINE MERCY, TURNS TO GOD WITH ALL HUMILITY, AND IS EAGER IN HIS HEART TO FOLLOW WHAT IS RIGHT" (*YP* 6:466). "God sets a limit to his punishment, in case we should be overwhelmed by it. What is more he gives us strength to overcome even those afflictions which, as sometimes happens, seem to us to exceed that limit. . . . We should not, then, make rash judgments about other people's afflictions . . . Psal. iii.3: *how many say of my soul, There is clearly no salvation for him in God*" (*YP* 6:469–70).

[17] *CE* 15:390; *CE* 17:248 and 17:96, my emphasis.

cried," "I laid me down and slept," "I awaked," "I will not be afraid [*non timebo*]," regardful of suggestions in the Latin he retranslates.

In the psalm, the worshiping singer addresses God in a present-tense erotema, "O Lord, how are they increased that trouble me."[18] He answers his own rhetorical question with the anaphora "Many are they . . . many there be," distinguishing the enemies who attack him from the acquaintances who dismiss his soul [*anima*] from God's concern so utterly that they apply to it the neuter pronoun *isti*, a reification whose force English loses. That part of the psalm closes with Selah. Selah, used seventy-one times in thirty-nine of the psalms, apparently signals a pause to be filled musically, perhaps by a sung response, a musical intermezzo while the congregation prays, or a musical signal like a trumpet call, at which the congregation pays God homage.[19] The pause permits pity at the lament to develop.

In verse three, the psalmist resumes, still in the present tense, as his faith in God protests against his acquaintances' dismissive certainty. God is his protection (shield), his source of personal value (glory), the restorer of his identity (who lifts up his head). The phrases are given in auxesis;[20] to the psalmist, his safety is important, his honor more important, and his identity the most important of God's gifts. At verse four he changes tense from the present to the imperfect, so that his current reliance on God is seen as habitual to him: whenever he prayed or cried, God answered or heard. In effect, by the change of tense, the psalmist changes his implied audience and also his style. He addresses not God but a congregation, prompted in the second Selah to feel awe. In verse five, the speaker adopts the past tense to refer to a single night now passed. He awakens in a new confident state of mind, shown by a shift into the future tense, *non timebo*. The implication of a decisive experience during the night conveyed by those shifts of tense is so strong that some commentators have proposed "an oracle revealed to one sleeping in the temple."[21] Milton supplies the missing event in *Paradise Regained* when he attributes the Son's change of feeling to a kerygma experienced as a dream. The remainder of the psalm identifies the speaker's enemies with God's enemies, asking that God render his powerless as he renders his own powerless, like lions whose teeth are

[18] Erotema, rhetorical question, is the figure Augustine thought the most moving and powerful of psalm formulas, according to Cassiodorus, who used this psalm to instance it.

[19] See Weiser, *The Psalms*, 22; and Mowinckel, *The Psalms in Israel's Worship*, 2:211.

[20] Auxesis or climax is a mounting by degrees through phrases of increasing weight in parallel construction.

[21] Weiser, *The Psalms*, 118, note 1.

blunted into harmlessness. That trope of the blunting of lions' teeth, so familiar in Psalms, Milton passes over. The psalm closes with a dyadic sententia: "Salvation *belongeth* unto the Lord: thy blessing *is* upon thy people," the last Selah allowing for moral satisfaction.

In Milton's translation, lament and prayer are intertwined in a full passionate declamation, with few internal demiclosures, even more lightly punctuated than the light Miltonic norm as Milton creates a strong forward rhythmical pulse.[22] His translation reads:

Lord how many are my foes
How many those
That in arms against me rise
Many are they
That of my life distrustfully thus say,
No help for him in God there lies.
But thou Lord art my shield my glory,
Thee through my story
Th'exalter of my head I count;
Aloud I cry'd
Unto Jehovah, he full soon reply'd
And heard me from his holy mount.
I lay and slept, I wak'd again,
For my sustain
Was the Lord. Of many millions
The populous rout
I fear not though incamping round about
They pitch against me their Pavillions.
Rise Lord, save me my God for thou
Hast smote ere now
On the cheek-bone all my foes,
Of men abhor'd
Hast broke the teeth. This help was from the Lord
Thy blessing on thy people flows.

The interlacing rhyme and light punctuation do not occlude the division of David's recitative into four stanzas corresponding to the two verse units of the psalm, rhyming *aabccb*, with a stress pattern 4 2 4 2 5 4. The appearance of the poem on the printed page, however, disrupts our sense of the identity of each unit; the decorated opening letter *L* in the first stanza interferes with the beginnings of its other lines so that

[22] See Treip, *Milton's Punctuation and Changing English Usage, 1582–1676*, 68–69.

the first stanza does not look like the second, third, or fourth.[23] More importantly, while the pattern of stresses is identical in each stanza, the number of syllables is very different indeed, running 7 4 7 4 10 8 / 9 5 8 4 10 8 / 8 4 9 5 10 10 / 8 4 7 4 10 8. Unaccented or lightly accented syllables fall into a strong idiomatic speech stressing; the rhythmic structure of the verse sounds much more important than its metrical structure. Spoken English and the allowable variations in English prosody override a rigid stress metric. The Son in *Paradise Regained* explained his preference for Hebrew poetry in terms of its musicality:

> if I would delight my private hours
> With Music or with Poem, where so soon
> As in our native Language can I find
> That solace?
> (4.331–34)

The metrical translation of Psalm 3 emphasizes as its musical principle a counterpointed rhythm of natural stress over the rhythm of quantity or feet. Milton's willingness to translate eight Psalms in a wide variety of meters without imposing a traditional English one suggests that he thought Hebrew verse observed its own kind of ancient freedom, overruling the preference for any single English metrical practice. Like the verse of Pindar, that of David privileged rhythm over meter.[24] Thus Milton's version owes nothing to previous translations, although he adopts the same stanza form Sidney took from the Marot-Beza translations of the Latin psalter; what he feels himself bound to imitate is a rhetorical scheme emphasizing parallelism; what he considers he is free to vary is the kind of rhythm based on stress. For this psalm using Sidney's rhyme pattern Milton writes only two feminine rhymes, *glory / story* and *millions / Pavillions*, the first to subject the speaker to God's action but the second to belittle the enemy in a hyperbolical jingle; millions of pavilions are the reverse of terrifying. Sidney liked a careful admixture of masculine and feminine rhymes; they were not in his

[23] I cite here as elsewhere the Columbia edition for Milton's poetry. The only text for the psalm translations is that of the 1673 edition.

[24] This position was common in the Renaissance, popularized by Scaliger, who wrote: "the verses of Job and of Solomon are dipodies, or like two dimeters, but sometimes cut short and sometimes lengthened, however the meaning dictates. For meaning is governed by meter, but *rhythmus is governed by meaning, and for this reason a metrical line will never exceed its rule, but rhythmus* does exceed when the meaning so dictates. Therefore, it is so far from being the case that a Hexameter or Pentameter line may be found in the holy Bible, that their lines are composed not even of [a constant] *rhythmus*, but the *rhythmus* is now lengthened or shortened to express the meaning." Quoted in Kugel, *The Idea of Biblical Poetry*, 257.

French model, but William Ringler points out that he used them in more than a third of his stanzas.[25] His translation is parallelistic by virtue of couplet rhymings but does not strive for rhetorical patterning. By contrast Milton's translation locates the essence of biblical poetry in reinforced pithy parallelism within a natural accentual handling of stress among many unstressed syllables.

In Book II of *Paradise Regained*, Milton echoes the third Psalm to introduce the banquet temptation, significantly pairing it with Psalm 4. Jesus' situation is similar to that of David given in 2 Samuel 15.23 when, connived against by Absalom and his conspirators, "the king also himself passed over the brook Kidron . . . toward the way of the wilderness." At nightfall in the wilderness Satan "takes a chosen band / Of Spirits likest to himself in guile / To be at hand" (2.236–38). Those versicles describing Satan, a pattern of 5 10 4 syllables rhyming *aba*, encapsulate the measure of Milton's translation of Psalm 3 within a blank verse paragraph. The Son after forty days in the wilderness is conscious of hunger and solitude. He "laid him down" (261), and "there he slept" (263); during the night he dreamed of God's intervening in the wilderness on behalf of other hungering men, and in the morning he "lightly from his grassy Couch up rose" (282). He had dreamed of Elijah awakened from his hungry sleep in the wilderness to be fed, and of Daniel also nourished by God. The allusion to Psalm 3 in the Son's entrusting himself to sleep while surrounded by his enemies and missed by former friends, and to his awakening sustained by God, implies that the night's dream involved his being given spiritual nourishment in sleep by God. Spiritual feeding before sleep is the theme of Psalm 4, which Milton translated:

> Into my heart more joy
> And gladness thou hast put
> Then when a year of glut
> Their stores doth over-cloy
> And from their plenteous grounds
>   With vast increase their corn and wine abounds.
> In peace at once will I
> Both lay me down and sleep
> For thou alone dost keep
> Me safe where ere I lie
> As in a rocky Cell
>   Thou Lord alone in safety mak'st me dwell.
> (31–42)

[25] *The Poems of Sir Philip Sidney*, 507. See also Freer, *Music for a King*, chap. 2.

Milton attributes Jesus' change of mood based on Psalm 3 to a dream vision based on Psalm 4. Satan interprets his dream. He reminds Jesus of God's goodness to the hungry in the wilderness, adding the stories of Ishmael and of Moses' people to the Son's dream of Elijah, and he ends: "Of thee these forty days none hath regard, / Forty and more deserted here indeed" (2.315–16). The Son questions the false logic, "what conclud'st thou hence?" before responding in a pithy contrastive parallelism: "They all had need, I as thou seest have none" (2.318).

Milton recounts the Son's dream in the third person as a narrator's summary of events while the subject sleeps:

> Him thought, he by the Brook of *Cherith* stood
> And saw the Ravens with their horny beaks
> Food to *Elijah* bringing Even and Morn,
> Though ravenous, taught to abstain from what they brought.
> (2.266–69)

He does not enter the sleeper's consciousness, and he glosses the dream in advance as wish-fulfillment, "as appetite is wont to dream" (2.264). In the dream "Ravens . . . Though ravenous" (enallage) are "taught to abstain from what they brought" (chiastic rhyme) but the Son imagines not abstaining, "with *Elijah* he partook . . . [and] as a guest with *Daniel*" (2.277–78). And in the summary, Milton conceals artfully metrical effects in plainstyle blank verse: the straightforward four-line description, in three pentameters and one casual hexameter concealing the rhymes *thought, taught, brought*, and half-rhymes *brook, stood, food.* Milton then presents the feeding of Elijah in a picture even more vivid and concise than that given in 1 Kings 19.5–8, by revising narrative toward psalmic pith. The King James Version reads:

> And as he lay and slept under a juniper tree, behold, then an angel touched him, and said unto him, Arise *and* eat. And he looked, and, behold, *there was* a cake baken on the coals, and a cruse of water at his head. And he did eat and drink, and laid him down again. And the angel of the Lord came again the second time, and touched him, and said, Arise *and* eat; because the journey *is* too great for thee. And he arose, and did eat and drink, and went in the strength of that meat forty days and forty nights unto Horeb the mount of God.

Milton uses less than half the words of that effective scenario, incorporating the curiously specific feeling of spacelessness and placelessness of dreams into his plain but rhetorically patterned account:

> He saw the Prophet also how he fled
> Into the Desert, and how there he slept
> Under a Juniper; then how awakt,
> He found his Supper on the coals prepar'd,
> And by the Angel was bid rise and eat,
> And eat the second time after repose,
> The strength whereof suffic'd him forty days.
> (2.270–76)

Among its metrical effects, one might notice the crossing slant rhymes in *Prophet, fled, Desert, slept*; the repetition of sounds in *Prophet, Juniper, Supper, prepar'd,* and *repose*; the anaphora of *how he fled, how there he slept, then how awakt*; and the ploche of *and eat, And eat.* Milton adopts the words *Juniper, coals, rise and eat, strength,* and *forty days* from his source and matches their linguistic register with *fled, Supper,* and *awakt.* He seems to have overlooked the most resonant phrase in the account—"because the journey *is* too great for thee"—but has reserved it.

To interpret the dream as wish-fulfillment would be to understand that the Son hopes to be granted God's aid in the present just as men of faith were granted it in the past. But the salvation theology Milton derives from Psalm 3 makes another point: God appears to the faithful man and sustains him by his presence wherever he sleeps, under whatever threat he may feel. The Son wore out the night between hunger and hope, resignation and faith. Milton glosses his awakening as disappointed hope:

> As lightly from his grassy Couch up rose
> Our Saviour, and found all was but a dream,
> Fasting he went to sleep, and fasting wak'd.
> (2.282–84)

Disappointed hope is what Satan provocatively underscored in the episode: a voice invited Elijah to eat, but only an unfulfilled dream came to the Son. Then Milton secures closure with a reversion to the most resonant line from Kings. Elijah was fed "because the journey *is* too great for thee." The Son's case is different: "They all had need, I as thou seest have none." Whether on grassy couch in the wilderness or in rocky cell in exile, the Father fulfills his promise, hence the Son's trust. The Son's reply is markedly parallelistic in construction, alliteration, and near-rhyme. The psalm is present in the episode for it is apt to theme and occasion; once evoked, its parallelisms are consistently imitated as scriptural effects.

Finally, Milton's stylistic echoing of psalms is not primarily a matter of imagery. The relative metaphorical plainness of *Paradise Regained* has been frequently remarked. Critics have noticed images of light and dark, wilderness and pastoral life, and tasting and eating. A few similes resembling some in *Paradise Lost* have been noted, as have Scripture-based key words that function in *Paradise Lost* and *Paradise Regained* both metaphorically and conceptually—such nouns as *hand, sheep, head, root, wilderness, dark* or such verbs as *stand, fall,* and *feed* having the force of both referents and similitudes. Milton's is a poetry not even as metaphorical as psalm poetry; psalms authorize a richer imagery than *Paradise Regained* uses. One has only to consider, for example, the density of psalm-based imagery in metaphysical religious poetry in contrast to the figural simplicity of Milton's to see that Milton turns to psalms not for metaphoric enrichment so much as for rhetorical variety within conceptual clarity. One psalm image, the growing tree, does have force in *Paradise Regained,* however, and may register Milton's metaphorical restraint there.

Of the few psalm-based images to be found in *Paradise Regained,* readers will readily recall the concluding images of the victorious Son fed by "Fruits fetcht from the tree of life," the Son who has "supplanted *Adam*" by his sinless obedience (4.589, 607). Milton uses a complex of images of "tree," "fruit," "plant," and "leaf" to designate moral cultivation in opposition to the wilderness motif in *Paradise Regained.* Milton's translation of Psalm 1 exploits that image cluster:

> Bless'd is the man who hath not walk'd astray
> In counsel of the wicked, and ith'way
> Of sinners hath not stood, and in the seat
> Of scorners hath not sate. But in the great
> *Jehovahs* Law is ever his delight,
> And in his Law he studies day and night.
> He shall be as a tree which planted grows
> By watry streams, and in his season knows
> To yield his fruit, and his leaf shall not fall,
> And what he takes in hand shall prosper all.
> Not so the wicked, but as chaff which fann'd
> The wind drives, so the wicked shall not stand
> In judgment, or abide their tryal then,
> Nor sinners in th'assembly of just men.
> For the Lord knows th'upright way of the just,
> And the way of bad men to ruine must.

Modeling his diction on the Coverdale and King James Psalms, Milton's principal aim is to preserve the poetical parallelism of his text.

He has, for example, like the psalmist, contained the three elements of verse 1 in one sentence, reversing the structure of the first clause in the isocolon of the second and third clauses, preserving identical verb tenses "hath not walk'd," "hath not stood," "hath not sate," and identically structured prepositional phrases "in the counsel of the wicked," "ith'way / Of sinners," and "in the seat / Of scorners," and slowing the rhythm of his lines by substituting polysyndeton for the asyndeton of the King James Version.[26] Milton's sentences exactly match the number and structure of the verses of the King James Version. The second verse of the King James Version achieves parallelism by antimetabole, Milton by isocolon; contrariwise, the fourth verse of the King James Version uses the parison "are not . . . but are," Milton, the antimetabole "not so the wicked . . . so the wicked shall not." Milton converts the phrase "the chaff which the wind driveth away" into two quasi-rhymes across the line "as *chaff* which *fann'd* / The *wind drives*," his decoration promoting another parallelism. Milton's third sentence is very close to that of the King James Version, save that his rhyme word is an addition. He writes of the tree "which planted grows . . . and in his season *knows* / To yield his fruit," in an ethical attribution of free will not part of the more naturalistic botany of "bringeth forth his fruit in his season." He ends the paraphrase with a similar effect, created by the archaic use of *must* as a verb of impersonal necessity in "the way of bad men to ruine must."[27] The phrase carries with it a sense of unwilling necessity in the case of the bad man which balances the sense of conscious choice in the good tree.

Whenever Psalm 1 is evoked in *Paradise Regained*, the seasonable and voluntary fruitfulness of the good, a fruitfulness arising from wisdom, is stressed. In *Christian Doctrine* Milton cited Psalm 1 on three occasions. He used verse 6, "*Jehovah knows the way of the just*," to explain the works of grace; he used verse 2 to recommend "alacrity . . . the virtue we display when we do good readily and of our own free will"; and he read verse 1 to discountenance any "association with the wicked."[28] Milton's interpretation of the psalm in the tractate informs his allusion to it in *Paradise Regained*. It is echoed when the Son's promptitude and alacrity are shown, the Father's knowledge and approval of the Son are hymned, and the Son's rejection of friendship or association with the wicked is complete. No Milton annotator has as-

[26] Polysyndeton is the use of a conjunction between sequential clauses; asyndeton is its omission.

[27] Satan uses the verb similarly in a similar case in *Paradise Lost* 9.168–70: "But what will not Ambition and Revenge / Descend to? who aspires must down as low / As high he soard."

[28] *YP* 6:182, 654, 751.

sociated the psalm with any passage of *Paradise Lost*;[29] and only one early reference to it has been noted in *Paradise Regained*, when the Son remembers his dedication to the Law: "[I] Made it my whole *delight*, and in it *grew* / To such perfection . . ." (1.208–9, emphasis added) in words reminiscent of the paraphrase. Nonetheless the psalm is recalled by Milton at the climax of the poem; analysis of it may show why it appears there.

In the psalm and in Milton's translation, three stages of wickedness are ordered in auxesis; the three stages are repeated in the climactic arrangement of Satan's behavior to the Son, although it would strain the evidence to imply an intended structural echo in the poem. The psalm praises the man who refuses to walk in the council of the wicked, to stand in the way of sinners, and to sit in the seat of the scorner; Satan takes counsel from his peers, masses them against the Son, and taunts him; his temptations invite the Son to hear oracles, to banquet with and to worship the devil.[30] In verse 2, God's law, the fruit of which is right behavior, is described as delightful. The elucidating metaphor follows: the godly man fully and naturally living God's will is like a flourishing tree planted by a watercourse bearing seasonable fruit and unwithered leaves; the wicked man is like fruitless chaff. Although the psalm is not quoted in the New Testament, the metaphor of the good tree, seed or fruit appears there.[31] The chaff metaphor is repeated in other psalms, though not any Milton translated,[32] and echoed in Matthew 3.12: "he will . . . gather his wheat into the garner; but he will burn up the chaff with unquenchable fire." In verse 5 the conclusive "therefore" of the King James Version or "so" of Milton's translation, the distinguishing rational mark of wisdom psalms, follows from the two analogies: the futility of a rootless life will be

[29] It influenced, however, the likening of fallen angels to autumnal leaves in Vallombrosa and sedge scattered by winds (1.302–12), Raphael's teaching Adam of God's hierarchical creation by the tree metaphor (5.469–90), and the description of the angels in heaven walking by living streams among the trees of life (3.354–59). The psalm's metaphorical source is Genesis 2.8–9, 15: "And the Lord God planted a garden eastward in Eden; and there he put the man whom he had formed. And out of the ground made the Lord God to grow every tree that is pleasant to the sight, and good for food; . . . And the Lord God took the man, and put him into the garden of Eden to dress it and to keep it."

[30] See Cullen, *The Infernal Triad*, 99–124.

[31] See, for a few examples only, Matthew 7.17: "Even so every good tree bringeth forth good fruit; but a corrupt tree bringeth forth evil fruit"; or see Luke in the parables, for example, of the fig tree (21.29ff.) and of the mustard seed (13.18ff.).

[32] For example, Psalm 35.5: "Let them be as chaff before the wind."

exposed to God's judgment, for God cares only for the responsibly good.

Milton introduces the metaphor of Psalm 1 only in the last stages of *Paradise Regained.* The Son rejects Satan's offers of alliance with Rome by claiming eternal kingship on the model of two of Daniel's prophecies, the flourishing tree and the stone that shattered the monarchic icon (4.146–151). Satan at once makes his conditional offer of "The Kingdoms of the world" "if thou wilt fall down, / And worship me as thy superior Lord." (4.166–67). Heretofore Milton has referred to the Son's testing in terms of the ripeness of time and the urgency of occasion, deliberately refraining from the metaphor of the season of fruitfulness, save for the line in which the Son chooses to await God's will, "He in whose hand *all times and seasons* roul" (3.187, emphasis added), epitomizing the conciseness of Hebrew parallelism in a hendiadys. But when Milton comes to the storm and tower temptation in Book IV, the issue is joined between the Son and Satan in terms of the metaphorical materials of Psalm 1.

Before the storm Satan first grimly predicts that the Son will rue his rejection of assistance "Now at . . . thy *season*" (4.380; emphasis added) and then after it calls the storm the ominous result of missing "The perfect season offer'd with my aid" (4.468). Milton differentiates the metaphorical flourishing tree from the real trees that in the storm "Bow'd their Stiff necks, loaden with stormy blasts":

> And now the Sun with more effectual beams
> Had chear'd the face of Earth, and dry'd the wet
> From drooping plant, or dropping tree; the birds
> Who all things now behold more fresh and green,
> After a night of storm so ruinous,
> Clear'd up their choicest notes in bush and spray
> To gratulate the sweet return of morn.
> (4.432–38)

That description is poetic in all the ways we have been noticing, parallelism providing Milton with rhetorical models even where no psalm is called upon.[33] It makes use of the lightest of twin prosopopoeias (the Sun cheered: the birds cleared), prosopopoeia so light as to withdraw metaphor in the very continuing of the thought, so that the Sun metaphorically cheers but naturally dries and the birds metaphorically "gratulate" a morning that naturally returns. The passage understates

[33] See Lewalski, *Milton's Brief Epic*, 349–55.

with several litotes[34]: the sun has here only "effectual beams" and not the golden, radiant, arch-chimic, full-blazing, clear, fiery, or orient beams of *Paradise Lost*; the birds' notes are here only "choicest" and not tuneful, joyous, orderly, early, gay, or melodious; the coercive storm is here only a "night . . . so ruinous" and not dark, wild, railing, or ever-threatening. The descriptive single sentence is held together by line-end near-rhymes (fresh, green, bush, spray), medial full- or half-rhymes (cheer'd, clear'd; night, note; wet, sweet), and alliterations (dry'd, dropping, drooping; beams, birds, behold, buds; more, morn). The sentence is binary; its second half, augmentative: the sun arises, the birds respond.

Having sustained the storm that buffeted real trees and could not blow them away like chaff, the Son without recourse to any power save the strength of his trust stands on the pinnacle of the temple, and Satan falls. The narrator then draws on the metaphorical resources of Psalm 1 for an angelic hymn, after which the brief epic briefly concludes in a final glance at the psalm. The narrator works toward the psalm figure by proposing and canceling two classical figures. He offers two similes for Satan's fall: Satan falls "as when Earths Son Antaeus" was defeated by Hercules holding him aloft, and he casts himself down "as that *Theban* Monster" the Sphinx cast herself from the acropolis in Thebes into the river when Oedipus rightly answered her riddle. But Satan's fall is greater than those heroic falls, as the Son's deeds are greater than those of Hercules and Oedipus. His standing establishes the new heroism, reconceptualized and saluted with a biblical metaphor. The Son's refusal to call upon angels and his trustful standing are what at the outset of the poem the narrator named "deeds / Above Heroic, . . . Worthy t'have not remain'd so long unsung" (1.14–15, 17). As Satan falls in the final episode, the narrator continues,

[angels] upbore [the Son]
As on a floating couch through the blithe Air,
Then in a flowry valley set him down
On a green bank, and set before him spred
A table of Celestial Food, Divine,
Ambrosial, Fruits fetcht from the tree of life.
(4.584–89)

The fictionality in the metaphor of the Son's transportation by angels, the peculiar flamboyance of their moving him as though on a magic carpet–spread chaise, ends with the plainstyle phrase "Fruits fetcht

[34] Prosopopoeia is personification; litotes is understatement that intensifies.

from the tree of life." Then the globe of angels hymns his achievement in an anthem of victory, where *supplanted* Adam, a tree uprooted, is reinstalled by the Son:

> now thou hast aveng'd
> Supplanted *Adam*, and by vanquishing
> Temptation, hast regain'd lost Paradise
> . . . .
> A fairer Paradise is founded now
> For *Adam* and his chosen Sons, whom thou
> A Saviour art come down to re-install.
> (4.606–9, 613–15)

Their hymn completed, the angels "Brought [him] on his way with joy" (4.638), the way of the good man in Psalm 1.

In short, as in this example, where *Paradise Regained* is metaphorical, its imagery replaces classical allusion with psalmic; but throughout the poem Milton imitates Hebrew poetry by means other than scriptural metaphor. The wisdom emphasis of Psalm 1 and its devices of parallelism are reproduced in the sequence of the tempest, the temptation on the tower, and the hymn as the primary yield of Milton's rhetorical analysis and translation of that psalm; its figurative value to him is checked by a stronger moral interest. "Tree" and "way" are exceedingly common figures in Milton, but they are not always figures at all. "Way" has that very slightly metaphorical force in *Paradise Regained* in such places as "my way must lie / Through many a hard assay" (1.263–64) or "to guide Nations in the way of truth" (2.473) or "brought [him] on his way with joy" (4.638); "tree" has even more restricted metaphorical force. Both very often have none.

The poetry Milton created in *Paradise Regained* is biblical by virtue of its imitation of psalm parallelism. Although musical, lexical, and metaphorical psalm inspiration can be seen in it, a Hebraic texture is achieved principally by the use of rhetorical schemes of balance and repetition with variation. In Book II of *Paradise Regained*, for a final example in which Milton now draws on one of the other group of psalms he translated, Psalms 80–88,[35] Milton gives Mary an interior monologue during which she ponders the events of Jesus' life and expresses her fears for him. Her meditation is very simply phrased; recollecting from Luke the Magnificat, it draws especially on Psalm 86.16, "save the son of thine handmaid." Mary's version of psalm la-

[35] See Boddy, "Milton's Translation of Psalms 80–88," 1–9 and Hunter, "Milton Translates the Psalms," 485–94.

ment fulfills the expectations of that genre. Her chief poetic resources are harmonious reduplications. She begins:

> O what avails me now that honour high
> To have conceiv'd of God, or that salute
> Hale highly favour'd, among women blest;
> While I to sorrows am no less advanc't,
> And fears as eminent, above the lot
> Of other women, by the birth I bore,
> In such a season born when scarce a Shed
> Could be obtain'd to shelter him or me
> From the bleak air.
> (2.66–74)

She first doubles "that honour" and "that salute," balancing a line and a half for the honor with a half-line and a line for the salute, and recalling the "honour *high*" in the salute "hale *highly* favour'd" (emphasis added). She next doubles "sorrows advanct" and "fears eminent," before she recollects her first sorrow, the danger to which the son of the handmaiden was exposed at birth. Psalm 86 is a lament by the servant of God which turns to thanksgiving when the servant, the son of God's handmaid, remembers how God "hast delivered my soul from the lowest hell" in the past and will again.[36] Milton translated verses 15–16 in common measure:

> But thou Lord art the God most mild
> Readiest thy grace to shew,
> Slow to be angry, and *art stil'd*
> Most mercifull, most true.
> O turn to me *thy face at length*,
> And me have mercy on,
> Unto thy servant give thy strength,
> And save thy hand-maids Son.
> (53–60)

In the second sentence, he adds "*thy face*" to the translation of the King James Version to strengthen the grammatical parallelism in the chias-

[36] The important verses (15–16) read:

> But thou, O Lord, *art* a God full of compassion, and gracious, longsuffering, and plenteous in mercy and truth.
> O turn unto me, and have mercy upon me; give thy strength unto thy servant, and save the son of thine handmaid.

It is similar to Psalm 116, a song of gratitude remembering God's help when the psalmist was ill, verse 16 reading, "O Lord, truly I *am* thy servant; I *am* thy servant, *and* the son of thine handmaid: thou hast loosed my bonds."

mus "turn to me *thy face*" and "unto thy servant give thy strength." The parallelism in this psalm source for Mary's lament, strengthened in his translation, informs the lament in *Paradise Regained.* Her finest and subtlest lines, however, lament her eminence among women "by the *birth I bore,* / In such a *season born,*" and complete the alliterations on *s* and *b*—"when *s*carce a *S*hed / Could *b*e o*b*tain'd to *s*helter him or me / From the *b*leak air."

At the end of Mary's meditation, a similar gravity results from a similar parallel balancing of rhetorical figures:

> But where delays he now? some great intent
> Conceals him: when twelve years he scarce had seen,
> I lost him, but so found, as well I saw
> He could not lose himself; but went about
> His Father's business; what he meant I mus'd,
> Since understand; much more his absence now
> Thus long to some great purpose he obscures.
> But I to wait with patience am inur'd;
> My heart hath been a store-house long of things
> And sayings laid up, portending strange events.
> (2.95–104)

She answers the opening rhetorical question just as neatly as she framed it: "where delays he / intent conceals him." Her next sentence is binary in conception and proudly reassured in feeling. Thus the first clause contains the striking sequence "I lost . . . but so found . . . He could not lose." A quotation from the New Testament is the fulcrum on which Mary's past assurance and present reassurance rests. In the New Testament account of Jesus' youth in Luke, the Son went to the temple, "and Joseph and his mother knew not *of it.*" Luke continues:

> And when they saw him, they were amazed: and his mother said unto him, Son, why hast thou thus dealt with us? behold, thy father and I have sought thee sorrowing. And he said unto them, How is it that ye sought me? wist ye not that I must be about my Father's business? And they understood not the saying which he spake unto them. And he went down with them, and came to Nazareth, and was subject unto them: but his mother kept all these sayings in her heart. (2.48–51)

Luke's narrative skill created the play on *father,* where Mary means Joseph and Jesus means God.[37] Milton's narrative skill converts Luke's

[37] Luke's account offers a midrash of Psalm 27.4, 10, "One *thing* have I desired of the Lord, that will I seek after; that I may dwell in the house of the Lord all the days of my

dialogue into interior monologue, unifying it with the half rhymes "not lose" / "I mus'd" and "obscures" / "inur'd," not to mention such lighter echoes as "delays" / "sayings," "great" / "wait," and "purpose," / "store-house," / "portending," echoes imitative of the quality of her musing. He concludes it with Mary's silence and wonder, given in the common psalmic metaphor "heart" / "store-house."[38] Her soliloquy uses only one other metaphor, likewise taken from Luke and ultimately from Psalms, when she recalls Simeon's prophecy of her grief and loss, "that through my very Soul / A sword shall pierce" (2.90–91).[39]

In Mary's soliloquy the heart-piercing sword is just as consciously introspective as Milton's practice in the whole passage is consciously a reserved plainstyle. One has only to recall Crashaw's "The Flaming Heart," for example, or indeed many Counter-Reformation instances of the iconography of the dart-pierced heart to measure the reserve, sensuous restraint, and biblical plainness in Milton's version.[40] In *Paradise Regained*, Mary's soliloquy links mother and son spiritually while they are separated physically; she meditates upon the Son whose life has been "contemplative" but whose future will contain "trouble," joining his condition to her own, who had "honour high" but is to be "soul . . . pierced." Her soliloquy is not exceptional in its metaphorical restraint and parallelistic precision; it is representative of Milton's imitation of psalm poetry.

Finally, it remains only to show that plainstyle parallelism in *Paradise*

---

life, to behold the beauty of the Lord, and to inquire in his temple. . . . When my father and my mother forsake me, then the Lord will take me up," combined with Psalm 68.5–6, "A father of the fatherless, and a judge of the widows, *is* God in his holy habitation. God setteth the solitary in families."

[38] E.g., Psalms 25.17; 40.8, 10; 64.6; 119.11; 119.32.

[39] Simeon warned Mary, "(Yea, a sword shall pierce through thy own soul also,) that the thoughts of many hearts may be revealed" (Luke 2.35). Hebrews explains the metaphor in 4.12: "For the word of God *is* quick, and powerful, and sharper than any two-edged sword, piercing even to the dividing asunder of soul and spirit, and of the joints and marrow, and *is* a discerner of the thoughts and intents of the heart." Revelation rephrases it "and out of his mouth went a sharp two-edged sword" (Rev. 1.16). Psalm 149.6 is the source of the figure: "*Let* the high *praises* of God *be* in their mouth, and a two-edged sword in their hand." The verse, which has been bathetically imitated in "Praise the Lord and pass the ammunition," was cited by Milton in *Christian Doctrine* to prove "There is no reason why war should be any less lawful now than it was in the time of the Jews." *YP* 6:803.

See Weiser, *The Psalms*, 839. Some have argued that the "two-handed engine at the door" in "Lycidas" is the word of God, that two-edged sword that pierces the soul in these places.

[40] *The Complete Poetry of Richard Crashaw*, 61–65, see ll. 35–36.

Regained is not restricted to Mary, the Son, and the narrator, but extends even to Satan, notwithstanding the stylistic differences between his speech and the Son's that arise from their moral opposition and their hermeneutic dissimilarity. Flexible stylistic applicability is central to psalm parallelism itself. It is a versatile medium used in psalms by every sort of speaker from wise to naive, good to wicked, young to aged, common to kingly. Defiant kings and guilty commoners, a maiden in a marriage song, a nation in defeat resort to it. Furthermore, the parallelism of relatively short sentences formed from two or three equivalent clauses is not only given to every kind of speaker for all sorts of audiences, but also to every kind of discourse. Historical fact and apprehensive rumor are conveyed in identically parallelistic mode in psalms, as are indirect discourse and quoted speech, iterative questions and redoubled imperatives, collective expressions of profound grief and moralistic saws, rules of conduct and liturgies of praise.[41]

This all-encompassing parallelism reinforces succinctness of expression by a reduplication that moves discourse forward rather than simply saying the same thing twice. It pleases by displaying the mind's power to relate parts to parts, to see similarity or difference and rapidly or emphatically encapsulate it. Decisive or preemptive pithiness is by no means unsuited to Satan's posture in *Paradise Regained*, nor does Milton fail to cast his speeches in the prevailing parallelistic plainstyle of the poem. Satan uses parallelisms when he shapes his persistently attacking discourse on the models of psalm genres, but he also uses them when he is not imitating psalm genres. Milton devised one repeated mode in Satan's speech in imitation not of a psalm genre but of a subgenre of classical drama, the dialogic summary or metabasis.[42]

Milton gives Satan linking summaries or transitional speeches at the end of each temptation. Each is sardonic and calculated whatever the occasion and with whatever degree of mounting strain the poet colors it. Thus Milton introduces the first of such summaries with little inflection and the metabasis briefly but provocatively looks back at the temptation to turn stones into bread and forward to the temptation to banquet with devils (2.300–306). That temptation over, another metabasis follows, again neutrally introduced, again provocatively and

[41] For example, one might note the invariant parallelism of wicked kings in 2.3, a guilty commoner in 6.1; history in 106.9, paranoia in 10.8; indirect discourse in 36.1, direct quotation in 35.21; iterative questions in 22.1, redoubled imperatives in 4.4–5; national grief in 137.1, autobiographical complacency in 37.25; rules of conduct in 82.3, liturgies of praise in 104.2–3.

[42] Metabasis is a brief statement of what has been said and what will follow, a linking summary, or transition.

evenly phrased (2.404–11). In introducing successive temptations, the narrator intensifies the sense of Satan's strain, representing him "as mute confounded what to say" (3.2), then "Perplex'd and troubl'd at his bad success" (4.1), "with fear abasht" (4.195), "Quite at a loss . . . with stern brow" (4.366–67), and finally "swoln with rage" (4.499). Not equally arresting, all the metabases are functional, governed by decorum of character, and unmistakably Satanic.

One summary within the sequence of temptations that moves from wealth to glory may illustrate Satan's manipulation of the poetical medium in imitation of biblical parallelistic verse. Satan congratulates the Son:

> I see thou know'st what is of use to know,
> What best to say canst say, to do canst do;
> Thy actions to thy words accord, thy words
> To thy large heart give utterance due, thy heart
> Conteins of good, wise, just, the perfect shape.
> Should Kings and Nations from thy mouth consult,
> Thy Counsel would be as the Oracle
> *Urim* and *Thummim*, those oraculous gems
> On *Aaron*'s breast: or tongue of Seers old
> Infallible; or wert thou sought to deeds
> That might require th'array of war, thy skill
> Of conduct would be such, that all the world
> Could not sustain thy Prowess, or subsist
> In battel, though against thy few in arms.
> These God-like Vertues wherefore dost thou hide?
> (3.7–21)

The summary is a masterpiece of rhetorical patterning in which dyads and triads vary a consistently parallelistic placement. The triad of infinitives "to know," "to say," "to do" in the first two lines is reversed in the parallel triad of nouns "thy actions," "thy words," "thy heart" and rearranged in the parallel triad of adjectives "good," "wise," "just"; each element in the triad is then compressed dyadically "thou know'st what is of use to know," "what best to say canst say," "to do canst do," and consistently recast in a further dyadic form "thy actions to thy words," "thy words / To thy . . . heart," and "thy heart" "the . . . shape." By so much repetition in antimetabole Satan means to create an impression of the Son's platitudinous country ethic.

Having set forth three propositions and ironized them all, Satan expands two of them—the Son's probable ability to speak wise words of counsel and his probable power to engage in heroic action in battle, from the second of which comes the momentum forward to the next temptation of military alliance with earthly kingdoms. But when Satan reduces the triad of virtue to two parts, he throws into relief a further complication in his initial parallelism. We now read it as a general truth, "thou know'st what is of use to know," followed by two concrete defining instances of that truth: "what best to say canst say, to do canst do." Line two, that is, is a merismatic explanation of line one; merismus, dividing the whole into its two extreme or absolute parts, is a common psalmic figure, intended to create intellectual pleasure in the discovery that one contains two or two becomes one.[43] Satan then develops the virtue of wise-speaking in four and a half lines to include prophecy; and the virtue of military heroism in an equal four and a half lines to specify triumph over superior numbers.

Both these neatly balanced explanations are full of ironies. First, the Son has rebuked Satan for claiming oracular powers and has proclaimed "Oracles are ceast," for he is God's "living Oracle" and all "pious Hearts" contain "an inward Oracle" (1.456, 460, 463). When Satan recalls that Aaron had oracular powers, he belittles the Son's claim to be the "living Oracle," since his is provisional ("*should* Kings and Nations from thy mouth consult") and deflates Aaron's antique claim to consult "the Oracle / *Urim* and *Thummim*" by phrasing it grotesquely: "Oracle . . . oraculous gems." Second, Satan's praise of the Son's probable ("wert thou sought") force in battle even when outnumbered is absurdly hyperbolic; the Son is not outnumbered but utterly alone, the opening for Satan's temptation to alliances.

Finally, Satan's merismatic line "What best to say canst say, to do canst do" is redeemed by the Son and stripped of all its patronizing. Jesus corrects that parallelism to conclude the verbal sparring over glory and gives it his own stamp:

> who best
> Can suffer, best can do; best reign, who first
> Well hath obey'd.
> (3.194–96)

Both Satan and the Son speak here in psalmic parallelism. Behind Satan's words are such formulas as those in Psalm 37.30, "The mouth of the righteous speaketh wisdom, and his tongue talketh of judgment." The characteristic patience of the Son and his intuition of all that his messianic role will require of him reformulate the significance of Psalm 37 in a truth at the furthest possible remove from Satan's pro-

[43] See Dahood, *The Anchor Bible: Psalms III: 101–150*, 17a:xiv and xxxi.

vocative worldliness. But when the Son highlights from Psalm 37 its adjuration to "Trust in the Lord, and do good" as the theme of his own parallelism, he does not parody Satan in reformulating him. The unmistakable force of the Son's retort relies for its conclusive pith on the very rhetorical devices of parallelism to which Satan had recourse.[44] In *Paradise Regained*, the Hebrew verse medium is constantly imitated through parallelism and that parallelism is as readily adaptable to Satan as to Jesus, Mary, or the narrator.

Parallelism in Paradise Lost

In the more densely figured epic *Paradise Lost*, Milton's imitation of scriptural parallelism places metaphor, iterative imagery, and psalmic motifs within large binary structures. This figural procedure, local at first, quickly develops into a thematic architecture of similarities and contrasts. To illustrate the various kinds of parallelism in *Paradise Lost*, I work with the second group of psalms Milton himself translated, Psalms 80–88, when he particularly sought fidelity to the words of the original Hebrew while casting them into common measure. I begin with local effects in a few early ones; but Milton also made compositional use of iterative motifs within waves of increasing elevation, by attending to key words and themes appearing in parallelism across a group of psalms, and to illustrate grand style parallelism, I next examine the subgroup Psalms 80–83. Finally, to show how Milton echoes the parallelism of rhetorical placement by sound parallelisms in *Paradise Lost*, I use the subgroup Psalms 84–88. To illustrate his parallelistic metaphorical structuring after psalm models in *Paradise Lost*, in designs far ampler than those of *Paradise Regained*, I now refer the first psalm in the group to the beginning of Book V. Milton echoes Psalm 80, a psalm urging God to awaken and shine his face on mankind, when Adam awakens Eve and hears her dream of levitation to the forbidden tree during the night that has just ended.

Psalm 80 confines its metaphors within one overarching allegory, an allegory of the vine of God's people. Brought from Egypt by God, it was first tended by God and protected by hedges so that it grew to take deep root and fill the land, sending boughs to the seas and branches to the rivers. Then God broke down the hedges and turned away his face.

[44] Even the line spoken by Jesus after the storm, sometimes mistakenly dismissed as the worst single line in the poem because of its unidiomatic Latin word order, "Mee worse than wet thou find'st not," owes no more to Milton's Latinity than to his Hebraism (4.486). It seeks, that is, to secure equivalence on either side of the caesura, to make for a firm clinch by the "wet . . . not" half-rhyme, and to achieve pith in parallelism.

Passersby plucked from it; beasts raided it; it burned. If God were to turn again, his people would be saved. The central contrast between the prosperity and the ravaging of the vine is reinforced by the structure of the psalm, a four-part lament, each section closed by a recurrent refrain, "Cause thy face to shine; and we shall be saved, O Lord God of Hosts." The allegory of the vine is developed between the second refrain at verse 7 and the closing refrain of 19, across a variant at 14, the psalmist first attempting to awaken a sleeping God from his dwelling between the cherubim and then lamenting the people's woes (vv. 1–6).

The two motives—awake from sleep, and tend the vine—introduce Milton's narrative of Eve's dream. Adam awakens Eve to the profusion of created nature and their plant tending:

> Awake
> My fairest, my espous'd, my latest found,
> Heav'ns last best gift, my ever new delight,
> Awake, the morning shines, and the fresh field
> Calls us, we lose the prime, to mark how spring
> Our tended Plants.
> (5.17–22)

Between the two whispers "awake," come two lines of endearment in envelope structure very common in Psalms and found in the refrains of verses 3 and 7 of Psalm 80, "Turn us again, O God, and cause thy face to shine; and we shall be saved," where the phrases "turn us again" and "we shall be saved" are to be read as logically linked, as meaning the same thing. The sleeping God is less clearly represented in Psalm 80 than in the companion Psalm 44.23–24: "Awake, why sleepest thou, O Lord? arise, cast *us* not off for ever. Wherefore hidest thou thy face . . . ?" But Psalms 44 and 80 mean the same thing, and many editors believe them to have been composed by the same poet.[45] Thus roused, Eve awakens and tells Adam her dream:

> methought
> Close at mine ear one call'd me forth to walk
> With gentle voice, I thought it thine; it said,
> Why sleepst thou *Eve*? now is the pleasant time,
> The cool, the silent, save where silence yields
> To the night-warbling Bird, that now awake
> Tunes sweetest his love-labor'd song; now reignes
> Full Orb'd the Moon, and with more pleasing light

[45] Dahood, *The Anchor Bible: Psalms II: 51–100*, 17:255.

Shadowie sets off the face of things; in vain,
If none regard; Heav'n wakes with all his eyes,
Whom to behold but thee, Natures desire,
In whose sight all things joy, with ravishment
Attracted by thy beauty still to gaze.
I rose as at thy call, but found thee not.
(5.35–48)

The ten lines between the call to awaken and the awakening are themselves full of parallel structures of paired concepts from the sound of the love-labor'd song and the light of the full orb'd moon to the doubling formula: heaven wakes, still to gaze. Adam woke Eve to a bright, flourishing, spring day; Satan, in a voice she thought Adam's, appears in a dream to waken her to a moonlit world. Adam proposed to take his bride to fields of plants; Satan flatters a solitary beauty and takes her to the tree of forbidden fruit.

Milton contrasted two awakenings, one by a protective loving being, one by an enemy "squat like a Toad" (4.800). The second awakening introduces a dream flight to the "fair Plant . . . with fruit surcharg'd" (5.58). Milton now imitates in Satan's myth of the tree the metaphorical and allegorical practices of the psalmist in the vine allegory. The psalmist describes how God tended the vine (Ps. 80.8–14):

> Thou hast brought a vine out of Egypt: thou hast cast out the heathen, and planted it.
>
> Thou preparedst *room* before it, and didst cause it to take deep root, and it filled the land.
>
> The hills were covered with the shadow of it, and the boughs thereof *were like* the goodly cedars.
>
> She sent out her boughs unto the sea, and her branches unto the river.
>
> Why hast thou *then* broken down her hedges, so that all they which pass by the way do pluck her?
>
> The boar out of the wood doth waste it, and the wild beast of the field doth devour it.
>
> Return, we beseech thee, O God of hosts: look down from heaven, and behold, and visit this vine.

The vine in the allegory, with branches big as cedar boughs, is not only a horticultural but a moral and political entity. The responsibility for its ruin is deflected first from God's people onto God and then to the enemies of the people, ravaging beasts; but the prayer "return, we beseech thee, O God" means the same thing as the prayer "turn us again,

O God": at root, the problem is the falling away of the people. Satan treats the tree in the garden, however, as magical; he celebrates its mysterious power:

> O Fruit Divine,
> Sweet of thy self, but much more sweet thus cropt,
> Forbidd'n here, it seems, as onely fit
> For Gods, yet able to make Gods of Men.
> (5.67–70)

He promises Eve that if she eats it, she will fly among the Gods. His words contain "resemblances . . . Of our last Eevnings talk," when Raphael likened the great chain of being to a growing tree (5.114–15). The difference between the false progress Satan promises from his tree and the true moral evolution Raphael likens to the growth of the tree represents a distinction in the interpretation of metaphor, a distinction about what can be read as parallel to what. Milton treats metaphor psalmically, linking a literal or historical vehicle to a philosophical or moral tenor; Satan treats, or pretends to treat, metaphor sacramentally, revealing an identity between an outer visible vehicle, the tree, and its inner essence, the power to deify.

Psalm 80.5 uses the metaphor of God's giving his people food and drink of tears, formulated in semantic parallelism: "Thou feedest them with the bread of tears; and givest them tears to drink in great measure." But it has a historical referent too: the present is contrasted with the time when God fed his people manna in the desert and found fresh water for them. This overt doubling that contains an underlying shadow doubling is so common to psalmic metaphor that a psalm is only completely read when its historical burden is manifest. When Milton juxtaposes Raphael's metaphor likening moral growth to botanical with Satan's pretense of identity between eating and ascending, he interprets the relationships among two contrasting forms of perception, each essentially dualistic. Of course not only psalm metaphors reveal both the binary nature of perception itself, and the further binary nature of typology; that kind of figuralism is everywhere in Scripture. But Psalms certainly exhibits it, and Milton certainly imitates it.

Psalm 80 also supplies iterative images or motives across the narrative texture of the poem. If Adam with Eve would look to their "tended Plants," they would grow to become a vine "to take deep root . . . and . . . [fill] the land"; when they pluck and eat the fruit of the tree that is only an arbitrary sign of obedience and not a material mystery, they turn from God, who turns from them, and they are cast out from the garden. But God's mercy renews them, their prayers in penitence become "first fruits on Earth . . . From [God's] implanted Grace in Man" (11.22–23). The prayers fly up "Dimentionless through Heav'nly dores" (11.17). In the modifier "dimentionless," Milton typically takes care to turn an image that if taken literally would suggest a miracle, into an imaginatively phrased idea. A real judgment seat where God sits between the cherubim is spiritually reachable by prayers, not magically or miraculously reachable.[46]

Psalms 80 through 88 were thought to present something of a unified group in Milton's day.[47] George Wither noted, for example, that Protestants interpreted them as treating "the estate of the Church, and Commonwealth of the *Messias*" "[in] Politicall, Ecclesiasticall, and Oeconomicke Orders."[48] The first four are psalms of judgment, recording God's displeasure with his chosen people, their longing for Sion, and their prayers for renewed grace "in the time of trouble." As a group, each comments on other members in a pattern of cross-psalm inclusion and iteration. Milton cited all but two in *Christian Doctrine*.

Psalm 80, then, treats the plight of Israel as a geopolitical entity through the moral parable of the vine. Psalm 81 has two parts: it opens with a call to worship according to the historical covenant God made with Joseph; it then turns by way of the prophetic formula "I *am* the Lord thy God, which brought thee out of the land of Egypt" to a history of God's dealings with Israel. Its most powerful organizing idea is an epiphany of God, offering renewal of covenant, an idea conveyed across a historical axis. In Psalm 82 God "standeth in the congregation of the mighty" and judges all other gods, pronouncing death upon them for their unjust and immoral rule: "I have said, Ye *are* gods; and all of you *are* children of the most High. But ye shall die like men, and fall like one of the princes" (vv. 6–7). Here the psalmist presents history mythologically, in a story of celestial life in which God assigns responsibility to minor gods for subkingdoms of creation, and punishes their misrule.[49] Milton adapted Psalm 82, the prophetic liturgy

[46] See Budick, "Milton and the Scene of Interpretation: From Typology toward Midrash," 211. See also Budick, *The Dividing Muse*, 48–69.

[47] Modern critics divide the group into two parts—Psalms 79–83, attributed to Asaph, all using Elohim for God; and Psalms 84–89, attributed variously to the sons of Korah (save for the Davidic Psalm 86), using Yahweh for God.

[48] See Fixler, *Milton and the Kingdoms of God*, 143–44; see also Collette, "Milton's Psalm Translations: Petition and Praise," 243–59.

[49] Psalm 83 is God's imprecations upon the enemies of Israel, using a conventional cursing formula; Milton did not cite it in *Christian Doctrine*, even when dealing with the propriety of the curse itself. Nor did he use it in *Paradise Lost*, perhaps on the grounds of decorum, as suiting neither his God nor his angels.

of the Lord's judgment on pagan gods, for the roll call of the fallen angels,[50] taking from it "the congregation of the mighty" and "the gods" that "walk on in darkness" to become the "pitchy cloud" of "Godlike shapes and forms / Excelling human, Princely Dignities, / And Powers that earst in Heaven sat on Thrones" (1.340, 358–60). But Milton also made compositional use of iterative motifs within waves of increasing elevation, by attending to key words appearing in parallelism across the subgroup Psalms 80–83.

Taken as a subgroup, Psalms 80–83 treat the themes of epiphany, promise, covenant, and judgment. They do so in terms of history and of cosmology, in both temporal and spatial contexts. They translate the abstract concepts of epiphany, promise, covenant, and judgment into the synecdoches of God's face (80.3), God's hand (80.15, 17; 81.14), the people's hearing or seeing (81.8, 11; 82.5), and God's voice (83.1). The same concepts become the metaphors of the sun shining (80.3, 7, 19), being fed (81.10, 16), planting the vine (80.8–16), and burning with fire (80.16; 83.14). These iterative images play an important role in the last of the three great epiphanic scenes of celestial life in *Paradise Lost*—the first occurring in Book III after Christ offers to die for man, the second occurring in Book VII before Christ goes out to create the visible universe, the last occurring in Book XI. That last epiphanic scene of celestial life is really a double scene, one part located at the place of judgment on earth where Adam and Eve pray in penitence and the other part located at God's judgment seat in heaven, where Christ directs God's attention to their prayers. That double scene shows both Milton's handling of iterative imagery and waves of elevation, his versions of *parallelismus membrorum*.

Book X closes with a strangely reduplicated account, giving first Adam's proposal to Eve that they confess their faults and then, in identical words, the narrator's report of their making that confession. Adam tells Eve:

> What better can we do, then to the place
> Repairing where he judg'd us, prostrate fall
> Before him reverent, and there confess
> Humbly our faults, and pardon beg, with tears

[50] Milton interprets the psalm in *Christian Doctrine* as referring to judges and magistrates not fallen angels or pagan national gods, but twice cites the psalm in the context of a discussion of angels. Recent scholarship identifies the gods with national gods of various peoples of the world who have been demoted to become Yahweh's servants. Anderson notes that heavenly assemblies are mentioned in the Old Testament at 1 Kings 22.19–22, Job 1.6, 12, 2.1–6; Psalms 29.1, 58.1, 103.20ff., 148.2; and Dan. 7.9ff. and 10:13, 20 ff., *The New Century Bible Commentary: The Book of Psalms*, 2:592–95.

> Watering the ground, and with our sighs the Air
> Frequenting, sent from hearts contrite, in sign
> Of sorrow unfeign'd, and humiliation meek.
> (10.1086–92)

Book X ends with those words reduplicated by the narrator:

> they forthwith to the place
> Repairing where he judg'd them prostrate fell
> Before him reverent, and both confess'd
> Humbly thir faults, and pardon beg'd, with tears
> Watering the ground, and with thir sighs the Air
> Frequenting, sent from hearts contrite, in sign
> Of sorrow unfeign'd, and humiliation meek.
> (10.1098–1104)

When Book XI commences, with Adam and Eve having arrived at the judgment seat, the narrator lifts them to their feet—"Thus they in lowliest plight repentant stood / Praying" (1–2)—and traces the upward course of their prayers to the "Mercie-seat above." The Son presents the prayers to the Father with intercessory words; the Father gracefully accepts them. The Son then calls together all the "Sons of Light." The Father proclaims to them what he has just agreed with the Son. And in the final wave of parallelism, he then charges Michael to take the action that apparently not only rules against the hopes of the contrite prayers of Adam and Eve, but may seem to withdraw concessions earlier won by Christ the intercessor. This whole narrative course—from Adam's proposal to Eve and the narrator's repetition of his words in summary, to God's triple explanation of his judgment to the Son, all the angels, and Michael—is a full-scale imitation of *parallelismus membrorum*, not just within a line, a strophe, or a stanza, but in large units of thought arranged in waves of repetition.

Several observations ought to be made about the structures of psalm parallelisms. First, parallelism perceives difference as well as similarity, and contrast is one of its effects. Parallelism becomes an interesting poetic device, indeed, when obvious parallelism is avoided in favor of parallelism with some sort of intellectual bite, or when understanding is delayed just appreciably enough to make for a tension between parallel elements. In Psalm 82.6–7, for instance, the reader is given a verse in which similarity is clear and the parallelism obvious, and then a verse still parallelistic but in unexpected contrast: "I have said, Ye *are* gods; and all of you *are* children of the most High. But ye shall die like men, and fall like one of the princes." The laconic contrast of meaning in parallelistic structure is telling.

Second, contiguous lines of parallelism intrinsically prompt the reader to find relationship between them; as Roman Jakobson puts it, "anything sequent is a simile."[51] In Psalm 81.10, for example, the psalmist represents God as speaking, "I *am* the Lord thy God, which brought thee out of the land of Egypt: open thy mouth wide, and I will fill it." Here the contiguity may suggest two complementary readings of epiphany and covenant in polysemous verse: God declares his nature, and he covenants with his people. Milton is interested in the possibilities of juxtapositional contrast, similarity, and interrelationship—his human beings (Adam and Eve, the narrator) refer to the "place of judgment," then God directly over that place is found in heaven on "the Mercie-seat above." The parallelisms of similarity and contrast in the scene show Milton making a complementary effort to justify both the ways of God to man and the ways of man to God.

Finally, Milton adapts the psalmic device of merismus to epic by making it the basis of persistently encyclopedic epic similes. Merismus is the trope of inclusion that suggests a totality by enumerating its parts. In Psalm 80.1–2, God's omnipresence is conveyed first by dividing his cosmos into earth ("Israel") and heaven ("*between* the cherubims") and then by dividing earth into three parts that make an everywhere, "Ephraim and Benjamin and Manasseh."

Like the fourfold thematic concepts of Psalms 80–83 (epiphany, promise, covenant, and judgment) or the four iterative images (God's face and God's hand, man's ear and man's voice), or the parallel synecdoches (sun, bread-and-wine, vine, fire), Milton's long scene too treats the four themes of God's epiphany, the promise in the protevangelium, the Son's covenanted intercession, and the judgment of expulsion. It too involves the four iterative parallelistic images of softened hearts, the seat in heaven between the cherubim, the tending of vine and tree or fruit and seed, and the altar where God is worshiped and may be found. Recalling the promise, with "hearts contrite" Adam and Eve not only pray for forgiveness, they anticipate by prayer a life "sustain'd / By him with many comforts." The Father seemed to promise as much when he sent his Son, "Mans Friend . . . [and] his design'd / Both Ransom and Redeemer voluntarie" (10.60–61), to judge them; and the Son, too, thought God "appeas'd" when he transmitted man's prayers "mixing intercession sweet" (10.226, 228).

[51] "Linguistics and Poetics," in *Style in Language*, ed. T. Sebeok, 350–77. (Cambridge: M.I.T. Press, 1960), 370, quoted in Berlin, *The Dynamics of Biblical Parallelism*, 100.

Adam, at first doubtful if "Prayers / Could alter high Decrees," also thought God would "turn / From his displeasure" (10.952–53, 1093–94). The next scene begins to spell out what intercession and redemption mean, and to point the parallels between the judgment and mercy seats.

Before the mercy-seat is a "Golden Altar" on which can be seen the noncorporeal "dimentionless" prayers of Adam and Eve, fumed with incense by the intercessor. The Son approves the "first fruit" prayers in the golden censer over "those . . . all the Trees / Of Paradise could have produc't" (11.27–29).[52] By composing in these broad bands of concept and image, Milton creates the greatest possible interest and anticipation in seeing God's reactions to the intercession, the more so when the Son frames it so that it includes a thorny parenthesis of his devising on the subject of mankind's doom, "(which I / To mitigate thus plead, not to reverse)" (11.40–41). But the reader of psalms has, of course, made his own parenthetical reservations too, anticipating that the judgment-seat and mercy-seat may be parallels in contrast, not similarity. Man's softened heart will soon need to steel itself: the first of the Father's mitigations of doom is the redefinition of death from punishment into "final remedie"; the second, the conversion of expulsion from Paradise into a further epiphany: God reveals himself a God indifferent to place, who may be found outside Eden.

In the last scene of the parallelistic psalm-based drama of epiphany, promise, judgment, and covenant, Michael begins to teach Adam the mitigations—"supernal Grace contending / With sinfulness of Men" (11.359–60). When Adam laments the "many grateful Altars" he was going to build in Paradise and "thereon / Offer sweet smelling Gumms and Fruits and Flours," Michael quickly gives the lesson, "surmise not then / His presence to these narrow bounds confin'd" (11.326–27, 340–41). With that, he begins to set forth by typical scenes the lessons of history. At every stage of the process, Milton, by repeating the four concepts from Psalms 80–83 together with their prominent tropes, encourages us to recollect those Psalms. But he is using means typical of a psalmic sequence, built of smaller parallelistic effects, to create pressure upon the reader to interrelate and interpret complex parallelism, offering the rewards of tensional richness and gradual illumination common to psalmic parallelism.

[52] The preference for prayerful fruit over literal fruit is like the preference for an upright heart over burnt offering in Psalms 40.6, "Sacrifice and offering thou didst not desire; mine ears hast thou opened," and 51.17, "The sacrifices of God *are* a broken spirit: a broken and a contrite heart, O God, thou wilt not despise."

Psalm Rhythms in Paradise Lost

Milton's adaptation of psalm rhythm is the practice of building sound and word patterns to reinforce rhetorical and semantic parallelism. Since he read the Psalms in Hebrew, Latin, the Coverdale English translation, the King James Version, and a plethora of English metrical translations, his imitative composition does not depend on the individual sounds of words peculiar to one foreign language or to any one English translation but on the practice of freely creating rhythmical correspondences to parallelism. There is no incongruity, therefore, in referring to translated sound echoes, where Hebrew sounds themselves are by no means represented in the English. As the most acute musician in English poetry, Milton transposes sound patterns from one tongue to another as easily and quickly as any musician transposes them from one key to another, one instrument to another, one scale to another. Furthermore, sound patterns that Milton translated in common measure he transposes just as securely into blank verse. His rhythmic adaptations are of practices common to psalms and their translations. I turn to his translations of Psalms 84–88 to illustrate those adaptations in *Paradise Lost.*

If the *principles* of Hebrew prosody were not agreed upon or even understood from Bede through the English Renaissance[53] (they are no more unanimously interpreted today than then),[54] Milton was nonetheless certain of the *existence* of poetry in the Bible and that it was better composed than any other kind of "lyrick Poesy" (*YP* 1:816). In

[53] Kugel, *The Idea of Biblical Poetry*, 169, 205–26, 244–46.

[54] Alter, *The Art of Biblical Poetry*, adopts the analysis of Benjamin Hrushovski, in "Prosody, Hebrew," *Encyclopaedia Judaica*, 1200–1202, especially his definition of " 'a free rhythm,' " " 'a rhythm based on a cluster of changing principles,' " its freedom " 'clearly confined within the limits of its poetics,' " the limits numerically fixed so that " 'by rule no two stresses are permitted to follow each other. . . . each stress dominates a group of two, three, or four syllables; there are two, three, or four such groups in a verset; and two, three or four parallel versets in a sentence.' " Hrushovski quoted in Alter, *The Art of Biblical Poetry*, 8.

Berlin, *The Dynamics of Biblical Parallelism*, considers that "phonologic similarity or equivalence promotes the perception of semantic equivalence" and "similarity in syntactic or semantic structure foregrounds phonologic similarity" (112); she identifies "sound pairs" or rhyme to argue that "sound must also be considered an aspect of parallelism" (125), and concludes, "The occurrence in contiguous lines of equivalent or contrasting sounds is the phonologic aspect of parallelism" (125).

Kugel, *The Idea of Biblical Poetry*, having noted "[p]resent-day metrical theory . . . proceeds . . . by looking at the conventions of our own poetry and seeking equivalents in the Bible" (250), rejects the whole idea of metricality in the Bible to conclude "*parallelism is the only meter of biblical poetry*" (301). No consensus along this range of opinion has established itself.

Paradise Regained he preferred the poetry of the psalms to that of the ancients with respect to its figures and tropes and commended its purity; in the note to *Paradise Lost*, entitled "The Verse," he preferred "*English* Heroic Verse without Rime, as that of *Homer* in *Greek,* and of *Virgil* in *Latin*" to the rhymed verse of "some famous modern Poets" and considered rhyme "as a thing of it self, to all judicious ears, triveal and of no true musical delight; which consists onely in apt Numbers, fit quantity of Syllables, and the sense variously drawn out from one Verse into another, not in the jingling sound of like endings." He thought his own unrhymed practice "an example set, the first in *English*, of ancient liberty recover'd to Heroic Poem from the troublesom and modern bondage of Rimeing."[55] In the preface to *Samson Agonistes*, Milton indicated that, however wholeheartedly he followed "the antient manner . . . and still in use among the *Italians*" "in the modelling" of his tragedy rather than "what among us passes for best," he would not attempt to reproduce Greek choral measures in his own choruses.[56] Rather he attempted there to reproduce lines various and irregular in length, based upon shifting stresses or accents varying from three to five per line, very occasionally rhyming, a rhythmic practice imitated from Psalms. With respect to the measure of *Paradise Lost*, Milton once again reads through the classical writers whom he admires back to the previous excellences of Hebrew verse; when he says his verse is without rhyme like that of Homer and Virgil because the old classical practice is freer and more beautiful than the modern "jingling sound of like endings," he suggests that the imitation of scriptural rhythm is also a liberation.

In *Christian Doctrine* Milton cited three psalms from the subgroup Psalms 84–88. He cited Psalm 84.12 on "CONFIDENCE, which is placed entirely in God, as an effect of love and a constituent of internal worship,"[57] having translated it in common measure in 1648:

> Lord *God* of Hoasts *that raign'st on high*,
> That man is *truly* blest,
> Who *only* on thee doth relie,
> And in thee only rest.
> (45–48)

The psalm contains as a refrain three versions of that verse, a benediction on the man who dwells in the house of the Lord God of Hosts.

[55] *CE* 2:6.

[56] Kermode long ago argued that in writing odes for the chorus in *Samson Agonistes* Milton "decided to provide it with non-Parnassian imitations of '*Sion*'s songs, to all true tasts excelling' " ("*Samson Agonistes* and Hebrew Prosody," 61).

[57] *YP* 6:657–58.

He cited Psalm 86.4–5 as proving that God is numerically one whether given a plural name (Elohim) or a singular (Adonai) and that his external worship includes the petition for lawful things.[58] The psalm is noteworthy for the range of words it uses to address God. And he cited Psalm 88 as a morning prayer confirming that death consumes the entire man, body and soul, and linked it with the Book of Job.[59]

Taken as a group these psalms are generically complex, although all are personal laments. In Psalm 84 a lamenting pilgrim on his way to the temple in Jerusalem sings a canticle of longing for Sion with which he mingles a prayer for rain and for his king. In Psalm 86 the lamenting singer is himself the king who addresses his God in a sustained supplication—opening and closing with a hymn to God's magnanimity. In Psalm 88 the lamenting singer, a desolate man isolated from all others by a mortal illness, makes an unrelieved strophic exploration of his despair. Previous editors and commentators on *Paradise Lost* have found a few lexical echoes to the translations in the King James Version.[60] But at the hinge of Books XI and XII in *Paradise Lost*, stands the episode of the Flood, by which Adam is taught subjects of importance to the whole group 80–88—epiphany, promise, covenant, and judgment—and during his education, Adam first laments at human history and then takes heart. Milton puts into the Flood episode phonological parallelisms that echo or reinforce the figural and semantic parallelisms by which he adapts psalm poetry to epic purposes. He takes the patterns for his sound paralleling from among Psalms 84–88 and uses those patterns in treating the matter of the Flood.

The episode of the Flood is represented in three binarily conceived moments—the deluge and Adam's tears, the change of the Mount of Paradise into an arid island and the recession of the waters from around the Ark, and finally the appearance of the rainbow and Adam's change of mood. (These might be represented as A and A′; B and B′; C and C′.) Sound patterns parallel and enforce the lessons attached to each pair—after the first watery pair, the lesson of the one just man; be-

[58] His citation in Carey's translation reads: "*to you, O Lord, I lift up my soul. For you, Lord, are good and forgiving, and full of kindness to all who invoke you.*" *YP* 6:669.

[59] See *YP* 6:401, where Milton brings together on the subject of death Gen. 37.35 and 42.36; Job 3.12–18, 10.21, 14.11 and 13, 17.12, 14, and 15; and Psalms 6.5, 88.11–13, 105.17, 39.14, and 146.2.

[60] These amount to an echo in 3.141, "Divine compassion visibly appeerd," of 86.15, "But thou, O Lord, *art* a God full of compassion," and an echo in 3.231, "Comes unprevented, unimplor'd, unsought," of 88.13, "and in the morning shall my prayer prevent thee," both suggested by Sims. Verity thought that Milton, in describing Eden's fruit as hanging "amiable" at 4.250, was inspired by 84.1, "How amiable *are* thy tabernacles, O Lord of hosts!" See Verity, ed., *Paradise Lost*, 459.

tween the two scenes of drying off, the lesson of God's omnipresence; and finally after the last pair showing the rainbow and Adam's relief pair, Michael's final double lesson of covenant and the second stock. The last lesson is first given and then summarized when Milton leaves Book XI and crosses to Book XII. (This pattern might be represented as A A′ lesson; B lesson B′; C C′ lesson lesson′.)

That pattern or structure of development is the structure of the treatment of the refrain in the three strophes of Psalm 84. The full refrain of the psalm reads, "O Lord of hosts, my King, and my God. Blessed *are* they that dwell in thy house" (vv. 3–4). It appears first at the end of a binarily conceived, three-verse expression of the pilgrim's longing for Temple worship and closes off that strophe before the sign Selah. The refrain is then divided into two reversed halves, "Blessed *is* the man whose strength *is* in thee" (v. 5) and "O Lord God of hosts, hear my prayer: give ear, O God of Jacob. Selah" (v. 8). The first reversed half opens the middle, binarily conceived strophe that the second closes before the second sign Selah. A curt version then ends the last binarily conceived strophe, "O Lord of hosts, blessed *is* the man that trusteth in thee." Each strophe uses such rhythmical or rhetorically doubling devices as may be illustrated in the first:

> How amiable *are* thy tabernacles, O Lord of hosts!
> My soul longeth, yea, even fainteth for the courts of the Lord: my heart and my flesh crieth out for the living God.
> Yea, the sparrow hath found an house, and the swallow a nest for herself, where she may lay her young, *even* thine altars, O Lord of hosts, my King, and my God.
> Blessed *are* they that dwell in thy house: they will be still praising thee. Selah.
> (vv. 1–4)

Verse two varies its parallelism chiastically, shifting from single subject (my soul) and doubled verb (longeth, yea, even fainteth) to double subject (my heart and my flesh) single verb (crieth out) by an enallage which suspends the object (the courts of the Lord) between the two members and then duplicates it with a synonym (the living God). Verse three likewise varies its parallelism: the worshiper compares his joy and security in the temple and its altars to the sparrow at home and the swallow nesting, the second image twice the length of the first.

Although the patterned intricacy of Psalm 84 is present in the Noah narrative because Milton is imitating biblical verse skillfully in varied parallelisms, there is a justice and special relevance in echoing a rain prayer in a deluge narrative. In the second strophe the pilgrim's refreshment by faith is compared to a rain shower, which he prays God, the raingiver, to send the pools he passes in the valley of Baca. In *Paradise Lost,* Milton turned to the antithetical situation of a deluge drowning the unfaithful.

The first of the double scenes of the rain and the tears of Adam Milton describes in one continuous sixteen-line sentence, composed of nine complex clauses, describing the south wind driving clouds together, the hills supplying vapor, the sky hanging like a ceiling, the rain rushing down until the earth was covered, the ark floating free, tilting over the waves that covered all the buildings with all their pomp, sea covering the sea, sea monsters inhabiting underwater palaces, and all mankind embarked in one little boat. The passage is based on parallelism with a little syntactic variation. It reads:

> Meanwhile the Southwind rose, and with black
> wings
> Wide hovering, all the Clouds together drove
> From under Heav'n; the Hills to their supplie
> Vapour, and Exhalation dusk and moist,
> Sent up amain; and now the thick'nd Skie
> Like a dark Ceeling stood; down rush'd the Rain
> Impetuous, and continu'd till the Earth
> No more was seen; the floating Vessel swum
> Uplifted; and secure with beaked prow
> Rode tilting o're the Waves, all dwellings else
> Flood overwhelmd, and them with all thir pomp
> Deep under water rould; Sea cover'd Sea,
> Sea without shoar; and in thir Palaces
> Where luxurie late reign'd, Sea-monsters whelp'd
> And stabl'd; of Mankind, so numerous late,
> All left, in one small bottom swum imbark't.
> (11.738–53)

Parallelism is apparent in the unvaried grammatical structure, given variety at midpoint in a change of subject within a complex independent clause (the vessel rode over the waves, the flood rolled the buildings under water). In the strongest mimetic rhythm of the passage, the ark rocks on top of the waves but beneath the waters one swell rolls pomp away; echoing the change in rhythm is the hesitation step of an internal rhyme *aba*: *rode, overwhelmd, rould.*

Although the entire passage is continuously binary, Milton freely composes each clause, or even line, from either two or three members for variety. Indeed under a pentameter beat Milton begins with four lines in triple rhythm—each line divided, that is, into three units by light caesuras—and ends the group with an enjambment ([1] meanwhile / the-southwind-rose / with-her-black-wings; [2] wide-hovering / all-the-clouds / together-drove; [3] from-under-heaven / the-hills / to-their-supply; [4] vapour / and exhalation / dusk and moist; [5] sent up / amain). The triple formulations are qualified by a redoubling sound system the essential components of which are the continuous contrast between the blowing *w* and *h* sounds of wind, wings, wide, hovering, heaven, hills, exhalation and the muffled thunder of *b*, *cl*, and *d* sounds in black, clouds, drove, and dusk. Finally, the passage ends with a powerfully restrained depiction of the underwater life of a submerged landscape over which swims the ark holding the eight remaining human beings. The expansive seascape reveals a triple repetition; *sea* covering *sea*, *sea* without shore; *sea*-monsters beneath in a palatial life, whelp'd and stabl'd. The pun of the stabled sea monsters neatly clinches the passage.[61] The actual closure in the last line depends on the interchange of pure and slant-rhyme (all / small; late / left) yielding to the mimesis of the sound and swing of the boat iambically rocking from *s* to *b* ("in one small bottom swum imbark't").

Adam's tears and his subsequent lament are also conveyed by such devices as the psalms abundantly provide:

> Depopulation; thee another Floud,
> Of tears and sorrow a Floud thee also drown'd,
> And sunk thee as thy Sons.
> (11.756–58)

The antimetabole of thee-another-flood / a-flood-thee-also, which allows of-tears-and-sorrow to hover grammatically attachable to either phrase, is contained within the alliteration in depopulation / drowned; and closure is supplied by the sound echo of sunk / sons. Both the envelope structure and the hovering apposition occur in Psalm 84. The flood as described by the narrator is then balanced by Michael's description.

Michael's didacticism has introduced and now divides two episodes of Earth's gradual drying. He begins by indicating to Adam mankind's own responsibility for its sufferings, as proven by God's rescue of "The one just Man alive" (11.818). He then summarizes the Deluge in an uninterrupted single sentence, complementing that of the narrator. As represented by Michael, the Deluge is not a moral response by God

[61] Fowler, *The Poems of Milton*, has identified the paronomasia: " 'stabled': Punning between 'lived as in a stable' and 'stuck in the mud.' " 1020.

the rainmaker to dishonest man, replacing human with fish population in a sunken palace, but a meteorological event dislodging the "Mount / Of Paradise," by permission of the reasonable God of natural causes:

> all the Cataracts
> Of Heav'n set open on the Earth shall powre
> Raine day and night, all fountaines of the Deep
> Broke up, shall heave the Ocean to usurp
> Beyond all bounds, till inundation rise
> Above the highest Hills: then shall this Mount
> Of Paradise by might of waves be moovd
> Out of his place, pushd by the horned floud,
> With all his verdure spoil'd, and Trees adrift
> Down the great River to the op'ning Gulf,
> And there take root an Iland salt and bare,
> The haunt of Seales and Orcs, and Sea-mews clang.
> (11.824–35)

Having drawn the moral that God attributes no sanctity to place "if none be thither brought / By Men" (11.837), Michael shows Adam the gradual drying off of the earth, this picture once more drawn by the narrator. Michael, however, describes the removal of the highest point in Eden to become a salt marsh island through parallelistic tropes for which Psalm 86 affords patterns; there are no scriptural precedents but a plethora of secular precedents for the matching scene of drying.

In Psalm 86, the psalmist represents himself as the spokesman for God's people in exile and asks God to intervene miraculously with a sign of his favor, "a token for good; that they which hate me may see." Tripartite in form, its central section praises God's magnanimity:

> Among the gods *there is* none like unto thee, O Lord; neither *are there any works* like unto thy works.
> All nations whom thou hast made shall come and worship before thee, O Lord; and shall glorify thy name.
> For thou *art* great, and doest wondrous things: thou *art* God alone.
> Teach me thy way, O Lord; I will walk in thy truth: unite my heart to fear thy name.
> I will praise thee, O Lord my God, with all my heart: and I will glorify thy name for evermore.
> (vv. 8–12)

The passage is unified by its stress in the middle verse on the wondrous works of God. Not only God's own people, but surrounding pagan nations ("All nations whom thou hast made") see in God's mercy to one individual, David the king, powers remarkable enough to turn them to "worship." This part of the psalm unmistakably recalls part of the hymn of Moses and the children of Israel in Exodus 15.11, "Who *is* like unto thee, O Lord, among the gods? who *is* like thee, glorious in holiness, fearful *in* praises, doing wonders?" In the Exodus hymn God's wonders include power over water: "with the blast of thy nostrils the waters were gathered together, the floods stood upright as an heap" and "Thou didst blow with thy wind, the sea covered [the enemies]; they sank as lead in the mighty waters" (vv. 8, 10). Michael emphasizes not the miraculous token but the natural causes of the Flood: not the rain alone, though cataract-like in density, but its effect in breaking through earth's crust to tap underground sources produced sufficient water to inundate high mountains; not God's hand but a surging wave wrenched loose the Mount of Paradise. Michael's moral is that human beings not God assign miraculous significances to naturally explicable events.

In contrastive parallelism Michael then invites Adam to behold "what further shall ensue," completing the story of the drying off of the earth:

> He lookd, and saw the Ark hull on the floud,
> Which now abated, for the Clouds were fled,
> Drivn by a keen North-winde, that blowing drie
> Wrinkl'd the face of Deluge, as decai'd;
> And the cleer Sun on his wide watrie Glass
> Gaz'd hot, and of the fresh Wave largely drew,
> As after thirst, which made thir flowing shrink
> From standing lake to tripping ebbe, that stole
> With soft foot towards the deep, who now had stopt
> His Sluces, as the Heav'n his windows shut.
> (11.840–49)

In contrast to Michael's discourse, this passage is contrived in an insistently "poetical" manner: anything personifiable is personified (cloud, deluge, sun, sea, ebb); and image fancifully succeeds image (the image of the sun looking at his hot face in the mirroring glass of the waters, for example, slides directly into the image of the sun drinking from the water glass of a wave). So artificial is the passage that analogies have been sought and found in works of secular literature (the *Arcadia*, *Davideis*, the *Metamorphoses*), not Scripture.[62] The drying

[62] See Fowler, *The Poems of Milton*, 1024, for the parallels to Sidney, Cowley, and

process is conspicuously poetical in order that attention be drawn to it as decorative rather than functional. When Milton translated Psalm 86, by an obvious parallelistic alliteration in reverse order he elided "glorious works" with "wonders great," underplaying the psalmic sense of the miraculous and turning it toward the natural, just as Michael's flood stresses the meteorological. The King James phrase "Show me a token for good," he rendered "Some sign of good to me afford"; God is to take a natural vehicle and give it a moral tenor. Milton's translation accepts typological reading in using the technical word *sign* as the historical counterpart of the literal.

In the last pair of scenes in the Noah episode, the narrator first modulates through a series of intermediate "signs"—the raven, the dove, the olive leaf—and arrives at the rainbow. The sign means, we are told, both epiphany and covenant, "Betok'ning peace from God, and Cov'nant new" (11.867). The final scene of the last diptych represents Adam's change of mood; in balance with his earlier tears is shown his quick-minded present disavowal of them. The crux of his revival reads thus:

> Farr less I now lament for one whole World
> Of wicked Sons destroyd, then I rejoyce
> For one Man found so perfet and so just,
> That God voutsafes to raise another World
> From him, and all his anger to forget.
> (11.874–78)

Once more a recollection of Psalm 86 shows the value of the tripartite structure that is itself fundamentally double. The hymn to God's magnanimity at the center of Psalm 86 divides a royal lament, which manifests trust in the promise of God to sustain his people, for in the past he has sustained their king "thy servant" and "the son of thine handmaid." David prays because he remembers, "Great is thy mercy toward me" and knows that God's mercy to him, the kingly servant, will bring "all the nations" to prostrate themselves before him. That assurance reveals not only the kingship of the psalmist but also the intellectual grounds of the parallelism within Psalm 86 and likewise between Psalm 86 and Milton's Noah episode. To be merciful to a chosen vice-gerent is by that mercy to elect a nation; the proper interpretation of the Noah episode is the same as that of the Moses episode before it and the Abraham after it; Adam is now on the threshold of

Ovid; see Sims, *The Bible in Milton's Epics*, 270, suggesting a parallel to Proverbs 25.23, "The north wind driveth away rain."

comprehending the protevangelium, of fully knowing what is meant by the woman's seed that will bruise the serpent's head. Adam's words highlight the triad "one whole World / Of wicked Sons," "one Man found so perfet," and "another World / From him," and put at its center the dyad in half-rhyme, destroyd / rejoyce. A sign has indeed been given of a covenantal moment: the past has been revisited and judged, the future is to go forward under a new dispensation. Without access to revelation, our intelligent ancestor can go no further, and so he puts an intelligent query:

> But say, what mean those colourd streaks in Heavn,
> Distended as the Brow of God appeas'd,
> Or serve they as a flourie verge to binde
> The fluid skirts of that same watrie Cloud,
> Least it again dissolve and showr the Earth?
> (11.879–83)

The poeticality of his own form of expression turns his intelligent question into a query about how signs mean, as well as what the rainbow means—are signs affects, accompanying God's epiphanies, or are they efficient causes, the instruments of God's modifications of natural law? Michael's answer makes them rationally but arbitrarily chosen instruments of progressive revelation.

Michael's twice-framed explanation of the meaning of the sign follows, crossing from Book XI to Book XII. The rainbow is the sign that God has covenanted with mankind. He has covenanted, Michael explains once to end Book XI, not to blot out mankind, or to destroy the earth by flood. The covenant means, he explains again to open Book XII, the end of one World and the treatment of the population of the new world as a second stock of men. Adam is to learn more about what that engrafting means, or who the "seed of Woman" shall be by Michael's continuing discourse, in which the next case history is Abraham's. Milton has Michael change his mode of educating Adam, however, from dramatic representation to oral exposition. His, and our, understanding the method of the arbitrary sign allowed that shift in method.

Lest the drying of Adam's tears abruptly terminate the themes of judgment, however, the twin nadirs of the Noah episode—Adam's grief and Michael's reprehension—reflect the last of the psalms of the group, Psalm 88. Psalm 88 is chiefly interesting for two interrelated qualities: its unrelieved sorrow and its inclusive parallelisms. Thus Alter notes of verses 12 and 13, which he translates "Will Your steadfast care be told in the grave, / Your constancy in Perdition? // Will Your wonders be known in the darkness, / Your bounty in the land of oblivion?"

> In these two lines, as is quite typical, one set of matched terms remains stable, being a complementary series of linked concepts: steadfast care, constancy, wonders, bounty. The other set of matched terms, on the other hand, carries forward a progressive imaginative realization of death: from the familiar and localized 'grave' to . . . 'Perdition,' a poetic synonym that is quasi-mythic and grimly explicit about the fate of extinction the grave holds; then, to another everyday word, 'darkness,' which is, however, a sensory realization of the experience of death, and then to a second poetic term for the underworld, 'the land of oblivion,' which summarizes and generalizes the series, giving emphatic closure to the idea that death is a realm where human beings are utterly forgotten and extinct, and where there can be no question of God's greatness being recalled. We ought to note as well in passing that the parallelism is conspicuously interlinear (in fact, the line that precedes these two is also part of the pattern), another very frequent feature of sequences of lines, despite the claim some have made that a line of biblical poetry is semantically self-contained and prosodically end-stopped.[63]

Kugel quotes Theodore of Mopsuestia, one of the earliest to consider the working of Hebrew parallelism, who identified the merismus in the first verse: "By day I called, and at night I am before you" means "All day and night have I called out before you."[64] These figures of inclusion are matched by figures of sound echoing and metaphorical progression—Dahood notes the exceptional richness in the Hebrew chains of synonyms for the grave,[65] which Milton translated: "*deaths uncherful dore,*" "*dismal* pit," "*Deaths hideous house,*" "the lowest pit," "thickest darkness," "horrid deeps," "*loathsom bed,*" "perdition," and "*gloomy* land."

The unrelieved despair of the psalm is so much its point that some commentators attempt to shift its gloominess a little; some find the gloom qualified by the address "O Lord God of my salvation," Milton's "Lord God that dost me save and keep"; others argue that the

[63] *The Art of Biblical Poetry*, 14. The King James Version translates "Shall thy lovingkindness be declared in the grave? *or* thy faithfulness in destruction? Shall thy wonders be known in the dark? and thy righteousness in the land of forgetfulness?" (AV Ps. 88.11–12)

[64] Kugel, *The Idea of Biblical Poetry*, 156–57.

[65] Dahood, *The Anchor Bible: Psalms II: 51–100*, 17:302–7.

conclusion or some verses have been lost.[66] Those who fail to lighten it often rebuke the psalmist, usually by comparing the psalm to the Book of Job and then preferring Job who attempts to answer the problem of suffering untouched in the psalm. Nevertheless, the despairing psalmist is also a godly man, although his lament contains no trust or comfort but fades into silence. His deepest grief is the knowledge that behind his afflictions—chronic ill-health, fear of death, loneliness and alienation—lies God's wrath and hatred directed against him. Milton translated the repetition of God's affliction of death upon him as a wave, flood, or breakers over his head. The lament, Milton understood in his translation, did not find death a mercy God shaped for man, but a deluge of anger and punishment by which he sunk him. The presence of the psalm in the Noah episode can be no more effaced or cheerfully forgotten than the despair it embodies can be emptied out of it: both lyrical expressions of hopelessly acknowledged darkness belong to human experience. They are necessarily expressed and give tragic force to loss.

Milton echoes a number of devices from Psalm 88: sound progressions, key word and metaphorical patterns, rhetorical schemes enhancing parallelism. In two places in the Noah episode Psalm 88 darkens the text so that Adam's grieving response to the Flood stands out as necessary and indelible. His despair is not dissipated by an authoritative interpretation given by Michael; in fact Michael restates the darkness. Adam will not be dismissed with consolation if left to his own interpretive devices, nor will terror be hid from him. His lament is not that God unjustly makes the innocent go to the wall, it is that everything without exception comes to ruin:

> I had hope
> When violence was ceas't, and Warr on Earth,
> All would have then gon well, peace would have crownd
> With length of happy dayes the race of man;
> But I was farr deceav'd; for now I see
> Peace to corrupt no less then Warr to waste.
> (11.779–84)

Adam's lament cannot be forgotten, although he does not continue it but rather commences to rejoice in the new human race from Noah's line, for Michael endorses it in his official interpretation. Michael teaches the doctrine of the one just man from the angelic point of view,

[66] See Anderson, *The New Century Bible Commentary*, 2:622–30.

but Milton does not forbear to put into Michael's lesson a lament matching Adam's:

> th'Earth shall bear
> More then anough, that temperance may be tri'd:
> So all shall turn degenerate, all deprav'd,
> Justice and Temperance, Truth and Faith forgot;
> One Man except, the onely Son of light
> In a dark Age, against example good,
> Against allurement, custom, and a World
> Offended; fearless of reproach and scorn,
> Or violence, hee of thir wicked wayes
> Shall them admonish, and before them set
> The paths of righteousness, how much more safe,
> And full of peace, denouncing wrauth to come
> On thir impenitence; and shall returne
> Of them derided, but of God observd
> The one just Man alive.
> (11.804–18)

In this passage, to be sure, as in the whole typological burden of progressive revelation in the last two books, the act of examining a world "devote to universal rack" is extolled as patience, just as suffering for it is called heroic martyrdom. But Milton is not writing simply of a moment of history; there is an undercurrent of contemporary reference in Adam's lament and in Michael's steely repetition of the judgment of the Flood. Milton shaped both places so that his own times could not fail to find the tragic within the note of merciful judgment: human beings are again and again given the freedom to shape their histories to an acceptable pattern, and their failures overwhelmingly require the response of execration. But the human sorrow remains unrelieved. Both Adam's lament and Michael's judgment are constitutive elements in the dark ground over which the rainbow is made a typological sign. The artificial and secular poeticism in parts of the whole Noah episode may now be refigured, then, as a will to comfort the reader; Milton's biblical echoing, as a resolution to write forward to the close of his great epic in double mood. To refuse to hide all terror is to think and write like a psalmist; to show that that is the case requires attention to parallelism and rhythm, the resources Milton admired.

PART II

Paradise Lost

THREE

"Smit with the love of sacred Song"

Psalm Genres

MILTON'S USE of psalm genre in *Paradise Lost* is not only prior to that in *Paradise Regained*, but richer. This richness owes something to the greater sweep of *Paradise Lost*, a sweep that allows him both to exploit all the literary capacities of those genres prominent in *Paradise Regained*—hymns, laments, and wisdom songs—and to deploy the three genres not significant in the briefer epic: prophetic psalms, blessing psalms, and thanksgiving psalms.

Hymns are sung across *Paradise Lost* not only by angelic choirs, praising both God's nature and his specific acts, but also by the human pair, extemporizing occasional forms of praise in their worship during all the liturgical hours of a day. Milton grounds them on his reading of hymnal psalms as describing God's deeds and qualities and appropriate both at canonical hours of worship and at seasonal celebrations of God's greatness unfolding through history. His Puritan dislike of fixed forms of worship, however, is usually clear when human beings invent hymns. Either Adam himself claims spontaneity to begin or end a hymn or the narrator draws attention to God's preference for extemporized song.

Laments are spoken across the epic not only by the human sufferers in penitence but also by the poet, the Son, and even God himself. Milton grounds them on his reading of lament as expressing grief for human sin and mortality by each witness to it. Of God's capacity to feel emotion and to sorrow, God being perhaps the most unexpected of the mourners, Milton wrote in *Christian Doctrine*:[1]

> On the question of what is or what is not suitable for God, let us ask for no more dependable authority than God himself. . . . If *he grieved in his heart* Gen. vi.6, and if, similarly, *his soul was grieved*, Judges x.16, let us believe that he did feel grief. For those states of mind which are good in a good man, and count as virtues, are holy in God.

[1] *YP* 6:134–35.

Wisdom song in *Paradise Lost* enters disputation or dialogue between Satan and various unfallen and fallen angels—Abdiel and Uriel or Belial and Beelzebub—and thoughtful conversation between the angelic visitors and Adam, or even Adam and Eve. Yet while *Paradise Lost* makes a more prominent use of hymn and laments than *Paradise Regained*, its use of wisdom song is more restrained, perhaps surprising readers who find the epic overfull of preaching and teaching. Nonetheless, in *Paradise Lost* dramatic or lyric speech overrides the enumeration, proverb, and generalized self-representation of wisdom song. Exceptionally, however, the last two books owe a good deal to it. The last two books of *Paradise Lost* are most like *Paradise Regained*, of course, so the similar use of wisdom materials is not surprising. Both are composed of dialogue between an angel (Satan or Michael) and a human being (Adam or Jesus); both conversations produce human education or enlightenment.

As well as those three psalm genres singled out later in *Paradise Regained*, Milton imitates three others in *Paradise Lost*. First, he makes the prophetic psalm the model for the proems, lyrically meditating on the power of poetry, on his own poetical intuitions, and on the godly inspirations that authorize his poetry. Second, he uses blessing psalms to respond quickly to, or briefly predict, the scripturally historic events of his plot. *Paradise Lost* surveys a historical sweep incomparably richer than that of *Paradise Regained*, tracing not only "the track Divine" (11.354) of God's acts but the faltering steps of men and fallen angels; the opportunity for benediction and imprecation is correspondingly much greater. Yet Milton modifies the genre by strikingly limiting the curse. Third, he treats thanksgiving not as an independent genre but as a mode naturally linking itself at crucial moments to other psalm genres. Hence thanksgiving instances the power of psalms as a lyric mode to communicate process or change of feeling within a sustained epic. Psalms contribute in *Paradise Lost*, therefore, not simply to variety and multivocality, or to plot foregrounding, but to narrative or psychological fluidity.

In *Paradise Regained*, Milton places Christ at the historical moment in which the old covenant gives way to the new; hence he makes particular use of New Testament psalms and of genres widely quoted or imitated in the New Testament. In *Paradise Lost* the Book of Psalms is Milton's primary authority, but the distinction between Old and New Testament psalmody is scarcely worth making, so little does the decorum of the epic highlight it. *Paradise Lost* treats all time, from man's first disobedience to one greater man's obedience; it does not center that sweep of history on a moment of fulfillment, or emphasize kairos over history. Not even in Michael's account of the transient world and the race of time does the distinctiveness of the gospel era pit the New Testament against the Old. A progressive revelation is shown to Adam, each stage of which has value not only in itself but in its role within an arc of enlightenment.[2]

Finally, in addition to the local effects of lyrical intensification, two overarching literary consequences of Milton's psalm adaptations are prominent in *Paradise Regained*—the securing of harmonious and varied multivocality on the one hand, the emphasis provided in foregrounding epiphanic moments on the other. These two strategies were developed first in *Paradise Lost* and carried over into *Paradise Regained.* One other literary result of generic adaptation in *Paradise Lost* deserves a preliminary word, however, and that is what I will call lyrical simultaneity, the personal expression of continuous worship. The large mimetic scope afforded Milton in *Paradise Lost* only partly explains the richer presence of psalm genres in *Paradise Lost.* Just as important is Milton's awareness of the interconnections among psalm genres as acts of worship. Milton not only draws on lyric at affective points in the narrative mode of *Paradise Lost,* both to vary and to structure it, he also shapes the epic itself into a mode of worship. He conceives of the whole poem, which he calls "my Song," as an act of praise for the special audience of God and his worshipers, not simply for the "fit audience though few" of his own time or "after ages." His conversion of an extended narrative into an offered lyric has for Milton the authority of David's Book of Psalms read not as an anthology of moments of worship but as an oblation. The intention to subsume narrative poetry into lyric controls the nature of Milton's individual adaptations.

Throughout *Paradise Lost* Milton refers to his poem diversely as *story, words, adventure, deeds, performance, verse,* and *process of speech.* These characterizations point toward sequence, duration, variety, completeness, drama; they point to Milton's narrative, dramatic, and encyclopedic intentions.[3] He also uses another group of words to refer

[2] In *Christian Doctrine,* Milton wrote that the Old Testament prefigures and proves the New, that the New is more liberating and doctrinally superior to the Old, but that the Old is textually more reliable and incorrupt than the New, and that personal interpretation of both testaments is the responsibility of each human being, aided by the spirit within him (*YP* 6:521–23, 576, 587–89). The effect is to diminish the wish to distinguish between them.

[3] See Grose, *Milton's Epic Process,* 9, 12, 18; Lawry, *The Shadow of Heaven,* 130–83; Steadman, *Epic and Tragic Structure in Paradise Lost,* chaps. 2 and 8; my introduction to Book VIII of *Paradise Lost,* 40–48; and Miner, "The Reign of Narrative in *Paradise Lost,*" 3–25.

to it, a group including *song*, *flight*, and *harp*. These point toward unity and synchronicity. The deep structure resulting from the rage for order is the lyric. Milton's love of the Book of Psalms as the clearest biblical form of the focusing of a poet's desire for intense expressive utterance shows him how to lift epic into the undisturbed song of pure consent without impairing his intention to justify God's ways to men. Psalms too narrate, but their narrative impulse is controlled by a constant desire to worship; lyric governs their mode and unifies them as looking toward God as much as toward men. When Milton envisages his poem not as a public or civic act but as a religious act, a further usefulness of the admixture of psalm genres into a book of worship in the control and unity of epic becomes apparent.

The Prophetic Psalm and Milton's Proems

Milton adapts the proem, the first literary genre one encounters in *Paradise Lost*, from the prophetic psalm. Prophetic psalms enclose a response from God to the psalmist's prayers. The response is given in God's words, though sometimes in indirect discourse or summary. Hence the psalmist sees himself as a channel of influence; he has a message from God that he will in turn communicate to the people. The signature of the prophetic psalm is the oracular message responding to significant questions posed by the psalmist, questions like those commonly found in the books of the prophets. When Milton treated the prophetic psalm in *Christian Doctrine*, he distinguished the superstitious and illicit claims of self-appointed soothsayers from the reasoned teaching of seers. The value of the genre to him stems from those two attributes: the prophetic message from God, and the thoughtful questions of the seer that prompted it.[4]

Prophetic psalms work through a predictable generic schedule. The psalmist and his world are troubled, or emerging from trouble.[5] In that dark time, God emerges from or speaks from his secret and holy dwelling place.[6] The theophany is sketched briefly or fully, and God

[4] See Introduction above, pp. 15–18. Prophetic psalms giving God's oracular words include Psalms 2, 12, 50, 60, 75, 81, 82, 85, 91, 95, 102, 108, and 110. The royal hymn and thanksgiving Psalm 18 and the royal Psalm 89 are also sources of inspiration for the proems. Royal songs attached by commentary to David at this or that moment in his life may be transferred by a poet to moments in his own life felt to be similar.

[5] The prophetic moments include, for example, times when "the heathen rage" (2.1), "the faithful fail" (12.1), "all the foundations of the earth are out of course" (82.5), or "as *in* the day of temptation in the wilderness" (95.8).

[6] For example, "upon my holy hill of Zion" (2.6), "in the secret place of thunder"

then speaks.[7] His oracle declares his absolute sovereignty and power over man and creation (Psalms 2, 110), his preservation of the oppressed and the good (12, 91, 102), his righteousness and hatred of evil (18, 81), his mercy to his people and those who are merciful (18, 89), his preference for inner holiness over burnt offerings (50), his contempt for rebellious nations (2, 60, 81, 108), his coming in judgment (75, 95), the union of mercy and truth with righteousness and peace in his salvation (89), and his giving of the law and his promise of the Messiah (2, 89, 110). The oracles are strikingly like the messages of the prophets. Prophetic psalms call on hymn to develop the themes of praise, on lament to detail the dark historical moment, on petition to ask for God's answer to it; in response to God's words, they turn finally to thanksgiving or to benediction. They organize borrowed features into an independent genre.[8]

The proems in *Paradise Lost*, despite their variety, also exhibit a consistent shape.[9] All open invoking the aid of a person or spirit associated with God in secret holy places, lament the poet's historical or personal afflictions, pray for inspiration and purification, center that prayer on a desire to praise or justify God, vow obedient response to God's grace, speak of renewed confidence or hope for deliverance, and express thanksgiving and strengthened faith; finally, all acknowledge that regenerated vision is the moral precondition for the fulfillment of God's promises. These elements common to all the exordia are recognizably similar to the sequence of motifs in prophetic psalms; if the words of God are what stand out in the prophetic psalms, the acknowledgment that he heeds and receives such words stands out in Milton's four proems. The shape and form of the proems, as well as the inclusion of some invariant topoi is the result of Milton's critical and imag-

---

(81.7), "from the height of his sanctuary" (102.19), and "from the womb of the morning" (110.3).

[7] It is announced, for example, in "The Lord also thundered in the heavens, and the Highest gave his voice" (18.13), and "Thou spakest in vision to thy holy one" (89.19) and "The Lord said unto my Lord" (110.1).

[8] See Lieb, *Poetics of the Holy*, 140–70; Budick, *The Dividing Muse*, 51–56, 142–43; and MacCallum, *Milton and the Sons of God*, 82–91. All three discuss prophetic psalms without identifying the genre. The Geneva Bible frequently calls David "Prophet" in subtitles pointing to lament (Psalm 25, "The prophet . . . grieved"), hymn or thanksgiving (Psalm 8, "The Prophet considering the excellent liberalitie and fatherlie providence of God towards man . . . doeth not only give great thankes, but is astonished").

[9] On Milton's exordia see Samuel, *Dante and Milton*, 47–66, 292–94; Schindler, *Voice and Crisis: Invocation in Milton's Poetry*, chap. 3; Lewalski, Paradise Lost *and the Rhetoric of Literary Forms*, 25–54; and my own " 'To make the people fittest to chuse': How Milton Personified His Program for Poetry," 3–23.

inative grasp of prophetic psalms. He found in David the model for the kind of personal utterance he also saw in the prophets. The proems would not take their distinctive shape without Milton's awareness of Virgil, Ariosto, and Dante as predecessors in the mode; neither would they have their distinctive form without inspiration from the Book of Psalms.[10]

The first proem, introducing not only the first structural section but the entire epic, opens with a full invocation to God who has heretofore from Oreb or Sinai, at Sion's hill or Siloa's brook, inspired prophets and teachers. It recalls a dark and troubled time when death entered the world, but promises a time when one greater Man will restore mankind. God is invoked as creator, figured in a trope of mighty wings like that in the prophetic Psalm 91.1 and 4: "He that dwelleth in the secret place of the Most High shall abide under the shadow of the Almighty. . . . He shall cover thee with his feathers, and under his wings shalt thou trust." God's aid is sought for the enlightenment of the poet's darkness; from his sustaining grace will proceed the poet's confidence in his poetry. All those elements are familiar in prophetic psalms, and the first proem is a contexture of the common features of the genre.[11]

But if one particular prophetic psalm especially inspires the first exordium, it is Psalm 18, a psalm David is shown composing in 2 Samuel 22, before ascribing all his songs to the inspiration of God. Paul quoted it in Romans 15.9 as confirming the promise of the Messiah. Milton frequently cited it in *Christian Doctrine*. Its themes of loss, victory, the upright man, and the inspired singer recommended the psalm to Milton's invocational use. Psalm 18 is one of the great theophanic odes of the Book of Psalms, showing the destiny and responsiveness of the royal worshiper in a vast context of divine action. It opens with an introduction praising God (vv. 1–2), details the psalmist's dark hours of affliction (3–6), fully narrates God's theophany (7–15), depicts the king's deliverance by divine help (16–19), characterizes that deliverance as a personal vindication (20–31), recites the consequent triumphs of the loyal king over his enemies (31–45), and concludes with inspired praise of God. The spaciousness of the psalm, filling the created and uncreated cosmos from God's secret dwelling down to the darkness of death, is equaled by its temporal sweep, enclosing the personal history

[10] For the first proem (1.1–26) the index to *CE* suggests Psalm 28.2; Sims suggests 23.3, 2.6 (a prophetic psalm), and 28.2. For the second proem (3.1–55) Sims suggests 104.2, 14.2, and 102.18–19 (a prophetic psalm). For the third proem (7.1–50) Sims suggests 17.3. For the fourth proem (9.1–46) no psalmic source has been suggested.

[11] For example, Psalms 50.23, 75.1, 82.5, 85.9, 91.1ff., 102.18–19, 102.25, 110.3.

of the psalmist and his transformation from a terrified to a confident man, within a mighty sequence of God's delivering acts. The most comprehensive of the prophetic psalms, it is well suited to Milton's most comprehensive exordium.[12]

Like the proem, Psalm 18 opens with hymnal invocation, in a series of synonymous metaphors for God's strength and worth—"my rock, and my fortress . . . my buckler, and the horn of my salvation, *and* my high tower"—as the source of the psalmist's song. God's moral worth figured in height becomes in other psalms his dislike of burnt-offering and preference for clean heart, hands, and lips; of the same order is Milton's faith that God prefers before all temples "th'upright heart and pure" (1.18). The psalm then modulates into a lament in the time of trouble when "the sorrows of hell compassed me about." The lament strikingly shifts tense among future, present, imperfect, and perfect, so that the reality of the loss in the past persists in the present, while the redemption of the past predicts the future—"will call," "shall be saved," "compassed," "called," "heard . . . yea . . . did fly," "regarded," "wilt shew," "will enlighten." The bravura of tenses creates a sense of historical comprehensiveness. Milton produces a similar effect by a similar variation in the first proem—"Brought Death," "Restore . . . and regain," "didst inspire," "taught," "Rose," "Delight," "Invoke," "intends to soar," "dost prefer," "Wast present," "Illumine," "may assert."

Psalm 18 presents the theophany in considerable detail, creating a spatial sweep just as comprehensive as the earlier temporal scope—the Godhead descends hidden behind bright fire and dark clouds; he rides a cherub in the storm and speaks in thunder; his energy exposes the foundations of the world and the fountainheads of the sea. Milton's similar cosmic setting refers not to God's descent as a bird "upon the wings of the wind" but to creation as a bird that "Dove-like satst brooding on the vast Abyss" (1.21). After an account of God's particular regard for David, the psalm concludes with trust, confidence, thanksgiving and renewed praise, in phrases powerful over seventeenth-century Puritan experience,[13] and behind Milton's prayer,

[12] Psalm 28 is a brief version of Psalm 18. Editors have found verbal echoes of 28.2, "I lift up my hands toward thy holy oracle," in Milton's "fast by the oracle of God." "Thy holy oracle" refers to "the mercy seat of thy holy temple," the same concept in 18.6, "he heard my voice out of his temple."

[13] Compare 18.28–29:

For thou wilt light my candle: the Lord my God will enlighten my darkness.
For by thee I have run through a troop; and by my God have I leaped over a wall.

with Bunyan's *Grace Abounding to the Chief of Sinners*:

"What in me is dark / Illumin." At the end the psalmist gratefully sings "deliverance . . . and . . . mercy to his anointed, . . . and to his seed for evermore," the theme of Milton's "great Argument." The first proem, like the others, is modeled on the scenario and topoi of the prophetic genre in general, but the cosmic scope of prophetic Psalm 18 made it particularly appropriate for an introductory exordium.

The second proem opens with a new invocation to God under the image of light, laments the loss of the poet's eyesight, gives God the tribute of a constant yearning for inspired song even in darkness, prays for inner light and dedicates its compensatory higher vision to renewed poetry. Among its moving confessions, it praises the psalms it imitates:

> Yet not the more
> Cease I to wander where the Muses haunt
> Cleer spring, or shadie Grove, or Sunnie Hill,
> Smit with the love of sacred Song; but chief
> Thee *Sion* and the flowrie Brooks beneath
> That wash thy hallowd feet, and warbling flow,
> Nightly I visit.
> (3.26–32)

The reference to the flowery brooks that wash the feet of Mount Sion carries a latent allusion to the priestly office in Joshua 3.13–15, when "the ark of the Lord, the Lord of all the earth" was carried over Jordan into the promised land, and "the feet of the priests that bare the ark were dipped in the brim of the water, (for Jordan overfloweth all his banks all the time of harvest)," and to the agricultural festival historicized and reinterpreted as the Feast of Tabernacles in terms of Israel's sacred election.

The Feast of the Tabernacles, a time for the renewal of the covenant with Yahweh, involved ceremonies at which water from the springs of Siloa and Gihon was poured over the altar, to secure salvation from "the well of salvation." The waters symbolize God's blessing in the renewal of the year and the hearts of the faithful. The water rite at the Feast of Tabernacles anciently took place at dawn. As light renewed the day, water renewed the earth. Both hymns and prophetic psalms analogize the return of light and the waters of renewal; Psalm 36, a hymn, strikingly combines the two: "For with thee *is* the fountain of

---

I am for going on, and venturing my eternal state with Christ, whether I have comfort here or no; if God doth not come in, thought I, I will leap off the Ladder even blindfold into Eternitie, sink or swim, come heaven, come hell; Lord Jesus, if thou wilt catch me, do; if not, I will venture for thy Name. (103)

life: in thy light shall we see light" (v. 9). Milton's images of renewal, too, intermingle images of light and water when God's voice commanding light "as with a Mantle didst invest / The rising world of waters dark and deep, / Won from the void and formless infinite" (3.10–12).[14]

As the poet leaves the darkness of hell to enter the world of light, he draws on the lyrical expressions of release from the dominance of darkness found in a number of prophetic psalms.[15] But if one in particular inspires the second proem, it is Psalm 102, a psalm having the contrastive shape of that proem. Psalm 102, the fifth of the penitential psalms, encloses a glorification of God within lament and supplication, a dark ground to the hoped-for blessing, and contrasts the glory of God with the state of man. Following a brief invocation and prayer (1–2), the psalmist laments his condition in detail (3–11), God appears in a glorious theophany (12–13), the psalmist praises God's mercy and power (14–22), he then recalls his lament, and faithfully acknowledges his God (23–28).

Psalm 102 not only supplies the structure contrasting man's transience with God's glory used in the proem but incorporates many of the figures Milton used. The ascent-descent figure, "thou hast lifted me up, and cast me down," is preserved in reverse in Milton's lines, "Taught by the heav'nly Muse to venture down / The dark descent, and up to reascend." The trope of the psalmist as a lonely bird—"a pelican of the wilderness," "an owl of the desert," "a sparrow alone upon the housetop"—is refigured in Milton's nightingale, the "wakeful Bird" that sings "in shadiest Covert hid." The psalmist's sorrow imaged as darkness, "like a shadow that declineth," is accommodated to Milton's isolation in blindness. In both psalm and proem, God is invoked from the height of his sanctuary, regarding the earth from heaven; in both theophany elicits a vow of praise: the psalmist will write "for the generation to come: and the people which shall be created shall praise the Lord" (v. 18) and Milton will "tell / Of things invisible to mortal sight." While the value to Milton of Psalm 102 for the second proem is both figural and structural, his imitation shows an analytic grasp of the whole psalmic genre.

In the third proem, an invocation to Urania gives way to a lament in which Milton mourns the historical "evil dayes" on which he has

[14] Sims, *The Bible in Milton's Epics*, 261, suggests Psalm 104.2, "Who coverest *thyself* with light as *with* a garment."

[15] For example, Psalm 18.12, "At the brightness *that was* before him his thick clouds passed"; 50.2, 89.15, "they shall walk, O Lord, in the light of thy countenance"; and 110.3.

fallen, surrounded by enemies and alone save for the nightly visit of his muse. He prays for inspiration, fit audience, and protection from malignant contemporaries. His prayer is trustful, for Urania has previously led him into Heaven "an Earthlie Guest," yet he fears his isolation (7.14). The entire three-part skeleton—hymnal invocation, historical lament, prayer—and many of Milton's motifs are familiar from prophetic psalms. One oracular psalm, however, Psalm 89, suffices as evidence of Milton's indebtedness to the genre. Psalm 89 too treats in a tripartite form a time of national disaster when God's covenant has failed. First, in a hymnic section (1–18), God is surrounded by celestial beings in heaven and faithful people on earth, while the psalmist "make[s] known [his] faithfulness to all generations." In the second section (19–37), a theophany, God delivers an oracle of promises to David. The last section (38–51) laments his historical misfortunes as king and prays to God for deliverance. (The last verse is also a doxology to the third book of the Psalter.)

The third proem opens with Milton's representation of heaven; God lives with Urania and Wisdom, his personified celestial companions. The scene is like the opening hymn of Psalm 89, also picturing God among abstract personifications and believers making music, "mercy and truth shall go before thy face. Blessed *is* the people that know the joyful sound" (vv. 14–15). The second part of Psalm 89 records the covenant God gave David, followed by the national failures that make David suffer, at which "all his enemies . . . rejoice." For Milton too "savage clamor [has] dround / Both Harp and Voice"; like David, he is personally threatened "In darkness, and with dangers compast round" (7.36–37, 27). While Milton places the psalmist's experiences in a contemporary historical context, he also represents his own historical era not only by psalm echoes, but by classical as well. As the heavenly muse and the classical muse are contrasted, the former trusted and the latter dismissed as a fiction, so the fit few and the barbarous dissolutes of the Restoration are contrasted. The royal Davidic context of Psalm 89 makes it suitable for the historic force of the third proem, while the promise of being led by the voice of God is the signature of prophetic psalms in general.

The fourth and last proem considers a series of topics also derived from prophetic psalm—God's former friendship and present alienation from man, the admonition of a faithless people, the poet's solitary nightly listening to the prophetic voice, and the extolling of patience and martyrdom as heroic. Psalm 50, for example, contrasts God's former shining face with his judgmental voice, "thou thoughtest that I was altogether *such an one* as thyself: *but* I will reprove thee" (v. 21), that yet promises salvation. Prophetic psalms in general comfort the faithful in such formulas as "be not afraid," "I am with thee," "I shall deliver thee," "I am thy help," and "wait on the Lord." Milton's last and darkest proem, surveying God's tragic distance from his creatures, also promises that to some in every generation, he will make himself known; they will be sustained by his voice, just as the poet is sustained by his inspiration. Psalm 12.5, for example, unites the denunciation of vain and duplicitous speakers with the promise of mercy "For the oppression of the poor, for the sighing of the needy."

Treating inspiration, or the voice of God heard as an inner voice, then, Milton wrote proems in imitation of prophetic psalms. His imitations draw upon hymn and wisdom song and place their strategies within the imitation of prophetic psalms. The proems are spoken by a seer who knows scribal poems and a bard whose role includes teaching and witness; they are also spoken by a worshiping poet to whom hymn is a natural mode. The same speaker—now prophet, now sage, now worshiper—is heard in three other places in *Paradise Lost* which, while not taking the form of proem, involve self-representation that combines prophetic psalms with hymns. Each converts narrative verse into lyric, or introverts an encyclopedic universe of action into a human heart of obedient worship. Those three places are the warning that opens Book IV (vv. 1–8) and the two variations of hymnic address in Book III (412–39) and Book V (202–8).

Book IV opens with a warning interpolation by the narrator, prophesying and pitying:

> O FOR that warning voice, which he who saw
> Th'*Apocalyps*, heard cry in Heaven aloud,
> Then when the Dragon, put to second rout,
> Came furious down to be reveng'd on men,
> *Wo to the inhabitants on Earth!* that now,
> While time was, our first-Parents had bin warnd
> The coming of thir secret foe, and scap'd
> Haply so scap'd his mortal snare.
> (4.1–8)

The poet here writes from within his own era, outside the moment of the poem. The lines are not a prayer, for the petition is out of date; they are not lament, but echo Revelation. Milton does not endorse Revelation, for he has another vision of how God's mercy will ultimately function, a vision that revises both Revelation and Psalm 2.

Milton quotes Revelation 12.7–12, depicting a final war in heaven between Michael and the dragon Satan and ending when the good angels chase Satan out of heaven "into the earth" and a loud voice cries: "Therefore rejoice, *ye* heavens, and ye that dwell in them. Woe to the inhabiters of the earth and of the sea! for the devil is come down unto you, having great wrath, because he knoweth that he hath but a short time" (v. 12). That vision offers a Christian explanation of Job 1.7, "And the Lord said unto Satan, Whence comest thou? Then Satan answered the Lord, and said, From going to and fro in the earth, and from walking up and down in it," and of Daniel 12.1, "And at that time shall Michael stand up, the great prince which standeth for the children of thy people: and there shall be a time of trouble, such as never was since there was a nation . . . and at that time thy people shall be delivered, every one that shall be found written in the book." The passage in Revelation 12.7–12 follows and explains the messianic prophecy of "a man child, who was to rule all nations with a rod of iron," and Psalm 2 is the source of both the prophecy and the millenial violence of threatened doom. In it, God promises his begotten son "the uttermost parts of the earth *for* thy possession" and warns mankind of the son's power:

> Be wise now therefore, O ye kings: be instructed, ye judges of the earth.
> Serve the Lord with fear, and rejoice with trembling.
> Kiss the Son, lest he be angry, and ye perish *from* the way, when his wrath is kindled but a little.
> (vv. 10–12)

Speaking in his voice as narrator, Milton would like to warn his own dramatic characters of the vengeful approach of Satan, defeated by Christ in an empyreal war that brought complete victory in heaven and forecasts a final victory on earth. But he is inhibited not only by epic convention but by the thematic force of *Paradise Lost*. Milton denies that Satan's prophesied rout will take place in a duel through the local wounds of head or heel; he foretells it will result from a cure effected in the heart of each human being, the ultimate stage on which the action of *Paradise Lost* is played out (12.386–96). He repudiates John's gloss of Psalm 2 in the treatment of the war in heaven in Revelation. Instead he converts John's psalm-based militant heroism into patient obedience. That introversion owes a good deal to Paul's discussion of the old and new Adam in Romans, to Paul's treatment of both love and the Resurrection in 1 Corinthians, and to Hebrews's treatment of priesthood, all three of which draw on the prophetic Psalms 2, 18, 95, 102, and 110. The instinctive warning thus hangs proleptically at the opening of Book IV not as revealed prophecy but as revised prophecy.

The other two lyrical self-representations occur within two of the hymns Milton composed for *Paradise Lost.* In context, the voices we hear seem to belong to characters in the epic, once to the angelic choir, once to Adam and Eve; upon consideration, the voice is the poet's.[16] On the first occasion a "multitude of Angels" sings a "sacred Song," their first hymn and the first hymn in the poem. The dialogue in heaven ended, they praise Father and Son, ending:

> Hail Son of God, Saviour of Men, thy Name
> Shall be the copious matter of my Song
> Henceforth, and never shall my Harp thy praise
> Forget, nor from thy Fathers praise disjoine.
> (3.412–15)

Nice grammarians might point out how suitable the singular "my Song," "my Harp," is for unison chant; nice explicators, how suitable the praise from angels who have just heard the Father promise the Son that "All knees to thee shall bow." But the lines implicate the poet himself and recall his resolution in the second proem some three hundred lines earlier.

On the second occasion, Adam and Eve sing a *Benedicite omnia opera* after their morning discussion of Eve's dream. With "Unmeditated . . . prompt eloquence" they invite all creatures in the hierarchic order of their creation to join praise of the creator. Toward the close of their hymn, Milton unobtrusively changes the number of the pronoun they use from plural to singular:

> Witness if I be silent, Morn or Eeven,
> To Hill, or Valley, Fountain, or fresh shade
> Made vocal by my Song.
> (5.202–4)

As their hymn ends they revert to the first person plural:

> Hail universal Lord, be bounteous still
> To give us onely good.
> (5.205–6)

The pronominal shift makes Milton's claim to have himself received from the "Parent of good" the expressive gifts and illumination by which he speaks for mute creation.

[16] See Ferry, *Milton's Epic Voice*, 49–55, for a strong monovocal case, the voice being that of the poet throughout the epic; see Swaim, *Before and After the Fall*, 159–214, for the argument that distinctions are carefully made between two kinds of angelic discourse.

Taken together, the personal interventions dedicate "copious matter" to a continuous act of praise. They establish concord as a primary intention and relate that concord to worship by all creation. The resultant undissenting song of pure consent contains words the poet finds in Psalms. The psalmist in like manner promises new song, as in the prophetic Psalm 89, incorporating the praise of heavens, the sea, the earth, and the mountains. Psalmists too narrate, of course, the histories of Israel's victorious destiny; but they narrate under the dominance of lyric and govern narrative by lyrical impulses to express their experiences of God in song.

The Hymnal Psalm and Milton's Hymns

Hymning begins in heaven; there is none in hell. In Book III Milton summons the "Heav'nly Quire" and puts them on stage in silence. "The Sanctities of Heaven . . . thick as Starrs" receive in silence "Beatitude past utterance" from the divine presence. While God and the Son converse, they remain silent, first with "new joy ineffable," then in fear of death, and finally with wordless wonder. Then at God's command the angels are released from the mute immobility to which Milton repeatedly directs our attention:

> But all ye Gods,
> Adore him, who to compass all this dies,
> Adore the Son, and honour him as mee.
> (3.341–43)

A vignette of life in Heaven then introduces their hymn that ends with Milton's personal vow of ceaseless praise. The whole scene is closed with a sibilant half-rhyme as "they in Heav'n, above the starry Sphear, / Thir happie hours in joy and hymning spent" (3.416–17).

That representation of heavenly hymning is remarkable, not the least for its extraordinary painterly feeling,[17] but the abiding impression it gives is of timeless praise, with all its themes and topoi. When the angels begin to move and sing, a reader might anticipate the passage of angelic minutes, an hour, a forenoon, or a day in eternity. (If for theological reasons celestial beings inhabit the present tense, for grammatical reasons a narrative of past events may not.) But setting the stage for the angels' hymn, Milton does not describe a past event in adjusted past tenses. He creates a syntactically remarkable twenty-

[17] See Allen, *The Harmonious Vision*, 98–103; Frye, *Milton's Imagery and the Visual Arts*, 187–205; and Fowler, *The Poems of John Milton*, 580–85.

one line sentence in which the important image is the timeless amaranth that shades the fountain of life, presented at the center of a triple complex-compound structure with angelic movements and songs on either side. The sentence begins with the anticipated pluperfect:

> No sooner had th'Almighty ceas't, but all
> The multitude of Angels with a shout
> Loud as from numbers without number, sweet
> As from blest voices, uttering joy, Heav'n rung
> With Jubilee, and loud Hosanna's fill'd
> Th'eternal Regions.
> (3.344–49)

The reader expects to hear that when God had ceased, the angels began to adore. The angels, however, remain within an ablative parenthesis of apposition in the present progressive tense; heaven is the subject of the sentence; and the verb when it comes is not the imperfect indicative "Heav'n rang" but "Heav'n rung," an intransitive past participle without auxiliary and so of infinite duration, "Heav'n rung" and rung and rung with jubilee.[18] The substitution of an unexpected tense for an expected (enallage) is one of the hallmarks of psalmic hymn, often for the same reasons of temporal infinitude as Milton's. The grammatical indeterminacy of the passage has been faulted,[19] but its suspensions suggest God's timeless omnipresence, to which jubilee and hosanna are awed responses. Then Milton transfers agency to the choir of angels as "lowly reverent / Towards either Throne they bow" (3.349–50) in an eternal present, casting down their crowns in a moment so extended by a description of the figures on them that the crowns never reach the jasper pavement. The scene reveals how easily psalm and classical figure unite in Milton's art. If the angels wear coronets of gold by way of Revelation 4, John having found them in the hymn Psalms 8 and 103, their enchased pagan figure does not fade, for its flowers are refreshed in running waters, waters Milton refers to the hymn Psalm 36, "the river of thy pleasures" and "the fountain of life."[20] He completes the mise-en-scène by commenting on the angels, the spirits elect, at the threshold of their praise, "No voice exempt, no voice but

[18] Compare the hypothetical heroisms of Satan's duel with his son Death in Hell, "and now great deeds / Had been achiev'd, whereof all Hell had rung . . ." (2.722–23), where the pluperfect conditional expresses irony.

[19] Fowler, *The Poems of Milton*, 580, notes William Empson, *Some Versions of Pastoral*, 160, and Adams, *Ikon*, 106.

[20] See Fowler, *The Poems of Milton*, 581.

well could joine / Melodious part, such concord is in Heav'n" (3.370–71).

Three terms in that remarkable scene govern the angelic hymn that follows it and may introduce Miltonic hymnography: jubilee, hosanna, and spirits elect. Jubilee signifies exultation and joy from the metonymic *yobel*, or Hebrew ram's horn used as a trumpet; hosanna signifies celebrative praise in its Greek transliteration of a Hebrew imperative "save now" or "save, pray"; spirits elect signify those called to sing praise. The first two are psalm-derived words for liturgical worship; the third, a psalm-derived concept for the unity of worshipers in hymn. Many psalms are written about the singing of psalms, about their own expressive exultation. Of these, Psalms 47, 98, and 150 command joy in referring to the *yobel*; Psalm 118 commands hosanna in using the formula "save now"; and Psalms 33, 68, 97, and 148 exhort the spirits elect, in translation called saints or the righteous, to praise God. Milton imitates all of those Psalms—33, 47, 68, 97, 98, 118, 148, and 150—in his first angelic hymn.

The angels have two themes for two subjects of praise, God and the Son, creation and redemption, majesty and mercy, power and love. Their sacred song interweaves the two subjects in a three-part hymn. The first part (3.372–89) uses the pronouns *thee*, *thy*, and *thou* to praise both the Father invisible in light and the Son who as divine similitude makes him visible, devoting one sentence to the "Father . . . Omnipotent" and one to the "Begotten Son." The second part (3.390–410) ritually crosses and alternates *thou* and *he* in a mazy pattern of reference now to the Father and now to the Son in their complementary roles, now stressing their interaction. As the first part describes the natures and qualities of Father and Son in parallel attributions, the second part prophesies their actions along the lines laid down in their dialogue. The third section (3.410–15) vows perpetual praise of Father and Son, which Milton also promises.

The angels praise the Father's nature through the topoi of king, creator and invisible light; they praise the Son's through the topoi of divine similitude, transfused glory, and visible light. They praise the Father's thunderous might and charioted justice in the agency of the Son's quelling the fallen angels; they praise the Son's offer to die for man, as his response to the Father's mercy and pity, accompanying his justice. Milton is careful to avoid the smallest sense of opposition in his role differentiations. Almost all these topoi can be found in the hymns echoed in the mise-en-scène: the father in 47, 68, and 97; the creator in 33, 96, 148, and 150; excessive light in 97; vice-gerency in 33, 68, 98, and 118; God's mercy in 97 and 98; his love in 118, 147, and

149.[21] Milton's thematic clusters of psalmic proof texts in *Christian Doctrine*, when discussing God and the Son, brought together such topoi; his analysis of hymn as worship gave him the sense of its structure within which to organize those topics.

In structure, hymns begin with an invocation, the call to sing God's praise.[22] A development follows, specifying the grounds of praise in God's nature and action, often in parallel clauses beginning "for he," and adducing the psalmist's own experience of God. The conclusion follows, frequently as a repetition or return to the invocation. Psalm 147 exemplifies the normal structure and uses topoi found in the first hymn.

Psalm 147 has a tripartite structure, each new section at verses 7 and 12 being introduced by a variation of the invocation "Praise ye the Lord: for *it is* good to sing praises unto our God; for *it is* pleasant; *and* praise is comely" (v. 1). Milton's triple form unites two praise formulas in part one, "Thee Father first they sung" and "Thee next they sang of all Creation first," varies them at part two into "Thee only extoll'd, Son of thy Fathers might," and varies that at part three into the direct discourse "Hail Son of God." Milton secures closure by the personal vow that repeats the motif of joint or unified praise from the opening formula "never shall my Harp thy praise / Forget, nor from thy Fathers praise disjoine" (3.414–15).[23]

Although the structure of Psalm 147 is triple, its thematic material is double; all the thoughts of the psalmist circle around the two concepts of the power of God and his compassionate grace, manifest in creation and election. Part one argues God's pity, efficacious because

[21] To give but one example of each, kingship is praised in Psalm 97.1, "The Lord reigneth; let the earth rejoice"; Creation in 96.5, "the Lord made the heavens"; excess of light in 97.2, 4, "Clouds and darkness *are* round about him. . . . His lightnings enlightened the world"; power exercised through vice-gerency in 98.1, "his right hand, and his holy arm, hath gotten him the victory"; his mercy and love in 147.3, "He healeth the broken in heart, and bindeth up their wounds." Editors note only Psalm 85.10, "Mercy and truth are met together; righteousness and peace have kissed *each other*" echoed in the angels' hymn at "and end the strife / Of Mercy and Justice in thy face," although there is equal verbal echo in Psalm 89.14, "mercy and truth shall go before thy face" (3.406–7), and, more to the point, topical and structural allusions to numerous psalms are found in the hymn.

[22] See chapter 2 (" 'With Hymns, Our Psalms . . . our Hebrew Songs and Harps' ") above.

[23] Fowler, *The Poems of Milton*, 585, suggests an adaptation of the promise to resume the god's praise common in pagan hymn, echoing the end of Virgil's hymn to Hercules. Among the many psalmic hymns that end with such a promise is Psalm 145, "My mouth shall speak the praise of the Lord: and let all flesh bless his holy name for ever and ever."

of his power—he who summons stars and names them affords trustworthy help—and ends "Great *is* our Lord, and of great power: his understanding *is* infinite. The Lord lifteth up the meek: he casteth the wicked down to the ground" (vv. 5–6). Part two urges God's care of all creation, even "the young ravens which cry," and his preference for man's faith over his strength. In *Paradise Lost*, the angels' hymn emphasizes the Father "to pitie enclin'd" by using the phrase twice. Part three extols God's election of one people, "He hath not dealt so with any nation," while the angels close as well with the Son's "unexampl'd love."

The literary value of echoing the topics, themes and structures of hymn at this point in *Paradise Lost* lies in the power of the hymn to unify narrative and worship, reinforcing the contrast of the realms of light and darkness in the poem. Book III began with the proem invoking light as God's element, the element revisited by the poet guided through hellish darkness by the heavenly muse, and petitioning for inner light in order to "see and tell / Of things invisible to mortal sight" (3.54–55). Between that invocation and the first hymn, the Father and the Son in heavenly precincts found the way to save all willing persons. The angels praise lyrically what the dialogue showed dramatically; their hymn modulates into Milton's in a recollection of the invocation, providing a framework of devotion for the theological dialogue, unifying a central episode, and foregrounding the immediate shift to the contrasting figure of Satan, who struggles toward the sun, a light he detests. Finally, the first hymn commences a devotional strategy that develops across the entire epic, rendering each decisive action of Father or Son its own praise.

Milton wrote eleven hymns in *Paradise Lost*, some in direct and some in indirect discourse, all signaled by references to hosanna or halleluia (Hebrew *hallel*, "praise," plus *Jah*, "God"), to jubilee or to the elect singers. Angels sing twice in Book III: the choir of elect saints in the hymn I have just analyzed, and Uriel in a brief spontaneous hymn in the presence of Satan disguised as a "stripling Cherube" (3.702–21). In Book IV, Adam's first words in the poem are a hymn to God spoken to Eve, ending with the formula "But let us ever praise him" (4.411–39); Adam and Eve together praise God in a liturgical evensong, ending with gratitude "when we seek, as now, thy gift of sleep" (4.721–35). In Book V, they balance the evensong with a matins hymn (5.153–208). In Book VI, at the end of the War in Heaven, the angels, "all his Saints . . . With Jubilie," briefly hymn the Son's victory (6.882–92). Book VII celebrates creation with three hymns; first the angels hail the proposal to create the world with a brief gloria (7.182–91), then the angels greet the Son with a royal processional hymn on the twilight before the seventh day of creation (7.565–73), and finally on the sabbath itself the angels sing a hymn to Creation (7.602–32). In Book VIII, when Adam recalls his own creation for Raphael, he reports his haunting search for his maker in order to praise him, asking fellow creatures: "how may I know him, how adore, / From whom I have that thus I move and live" (8.280–81). In Book X, the last hymn of *Paradise Lost* is a short halleluia sung "loud . . . as the sound of Seas" by "the heav'nly Audience" when God prophesies the end of time (10.643–48). Editors have identified some of these songs as hymns and found some verbal echoes to various psalms in only five of them.[24] Milton's practice, however, is to imitate the common structure of psalmic hymn and ornament or develop it with common hymnic topoi, not simply to transpose one psalm for the sake of one lyric moment.

The introit of hymns is usually a second person plural exhortation to worship, sometimes includes psalmist and congregation in the first person plural, and occasionally is personal to the psalmist.[25] Milton adapts various introits to one angelic singer, the choir, the individual human being, and the human chorus. The introit sometimes addresses a specific audience, sometimes includes bystanders, and sometimes, as in Psalm 148.1–4, draws in all creation, "Praise ye the Lord from the heavens: praise him in the heights. Praise ye him, all his angels: praise ye him, all his hosts. Praise ye him, sun and moon: praise him, all ye stars of light. Praise him, ye heavens of heavens, and ye waters that *be* above the heavens." This variety in practice was not wasted on Milton seeking multivocality. Thus he patterns the angels' processional song of victory in Book VI on enthronement hymns such as Psalms 68 and 97, for which the audience is the victorious king, just as he patterns the human *benedicite omnia opera* on creation hymns where creation is both subject and audience, and patterns Adam's tentative hymn seeking his maker on pilgrim song. In the last, where Adam questions the highest being he sees "Thou Sun, . . . faire Light" about God his maker, Milton asks us to recall how the sun figured as blasphemous introit to Satan's soliloquy in Book IV:

> O thou that with surpassing Glory crownd,
> Look'st from thy sole Dominion like the God
> Of this new World; at whose sight all the Starrs

[24] For 3.372–415, Ps. 85.10; for 3.702–35, Ps. 111.2–4, 8; for 4.411–39, none; for 4.720–35, Pss. 148, 74.16–17, and 127.2; for 5.153–208, Pss. 2.6–7, 148, and 137.6, 104; for 6.882–93, none; for 7.182–91, none; for 7.565–74, Pss. 8.6, 24.7, and 8.4; for 7.601–32, Pss. 8.3, 8.6–7, and 146.1; for 8.272–81, none; for 10.643–48, none.

[25] For example, Psalm 33.1, "Rejoice in the Lord, O ye righteous," uses the common exhortative form; Psalm 95.1, "O come, let us sing unto the Lord," the inclusive form; Psalm 104.33, "I will sing unto the Lord as long as I live," the personal form.

> Hide thir diminisht heads; to thee I call,
> But with no friendly voice, and add thy name
> O Sun, to tell thee how I hate thy beams.
> (4.32–37)

Both Adam's and Satan's introits recall the pantheistic origins of hymn in nature salutations; Satan founded that paganism, but his reason causes Adam to redirect his attention from nature to her maker. Exhortation in psalmic hymn always contains the name and aspect of God to be praised, often specifying musical instruments and dance, such gestures as shouting, clapping, and skipping, and the time and place of the praise.[26] The length of the introit varies, most of Psalm 148 and the whole of 150 being taken up with it, as one might say the whole of Adam's pilgrim hymn is an introit searching its object.

The body or development of the hymn commences with the grounds on which praise is to be offered. All hymns praise God either as creator or ruler of history. Milton's first and last angelic hymns deal with God's plans to save mankind and so direct attention to Christ as the perfect hero; his human hymns praise creation; all the other angelic hymns treat now one, now the other topic. In the Psalter, hymns consider either God's qualities or his acts and are generated from repetitions, accretions, or dramatizations of praiseworthy attributes or works of providence or creation. Hymns describing his praiseworthy nature consist of a sentence or a series of short sentences of which God is the subject, enumerating his traits. Hymns declaring his deeds consist of a dramatic or narrative rendering of one sort of action.[27] Psalm 147 and the first angelic hymn balance enumeration and drama, praising God's many holy attributes but focusing on two, his power and mercy. Milton's purest creation hymn is the matins *benedicite omnia opera*, in which Adam and Eve exhort other created beings, each in his own sphere, to praise the Creator; his fullest is the angelic processional at Creation itself. Psalms 104 and 148 have been correctly identified as sources for the *benedicite*, but the creation hymns 8, 29, 46, and 114 are generically typical and supplied Milton with a good deal, to which he added from Genesis and Job.

Of course Milton relates the action praised to the special occasion

[26] Instruments and gesture like those given, for example, in Psalms 33.2, 147.7, 47.1, and 149.3 are variously transferred to Milton's hymns: harps are noted at 3.365, 5.151, 7.559, and 7.594; shouts and bowing, at 3.345 and 351; standing and listening at 3.711; palm waving and singing at 6.885–86; offering incense at 7.599; running and moving at 8.268; and loud singing at 10.642.

[27] The distinction between descriptive and declarative hymns is that made by Claus Westermann, *Praise and Lament in the Psalms*, 81–122.

for each of his hymns. The morning hymn, when the earth seems renewed to awakening man, for example, naturally suggests creation. But morning and evening hymns are liturgical as well as occasional; thus as Adam and Eve's matins song derives from the morning liturgy, it uses topoi from Psalm 19, itself a hymn combining praise of Creation with wisdom thoughts about the law. The angels, singing on each day of Creation, hymns Milton does not record, mark the end of their hexameral task by imitating creation hymns. Uriel's hymn, treating God's defense of order against chaos, imitates simpler enumerative psalms, like Psalm 29, praising God who divided earth from water, light from darkness. Only the angelic *gloria* imitates New Testament hymn, and only in introit.

Hymns close in a circling return to the exhortation, sometimes in the psalmist's vow always to worship in the same way or in his prayer that his song be always acceptable. The poet's intrusion into the *benedicite*, for example, with both vow and prayer, recalls the combination in the closure of Psalm 19. The literary work of the matins prayer of Adam and Eve, however, is to modulate from Eve's dream to the Father's charge to Raphael to warn the pair; as lyric, it foregrounds narrative.

Uriel's hymn before the stripling cherub, Satan in disguise, may provide a final instance of that kind of literary usefulness. Uriel praises order emerging from chaos and describes the organization of the heavens, the earth, and the stars at God's voice (3.702–21). Psalm 29 traverses similar thematic ground. Its introit instructs the mighty to glorify the Lord. The development expresses awe at the power of God's voice to order nature: "The voice of the Lord *is* upon the waters. . . . The voice of the Lord divideth the flames of fire" (vv. 3, 7). After a terse theophany, "The Lord sitteth upon the flood; yea, the Lord sitteth King for ever" (v. 10), the psalmist concludes that the power of the God of creation will bless his people with peace; similarly Uriel indicates to Satan how God has beneficently ordained light for Adam's Earth. Satan then resumes his errand of darkness. The literary use of Uriel's brief hymn is to throw into relief a strangely menacing sequence. Preceded by the narrator's warning that neither man nor angel can penetrate the disguises of hypocrisy, Uriel's noble praise of "all [God's] works" (3.702) and his special care for "Earth the seat of Man" (3.724) ends with Satan's departure, with a reverentially deceitful bow, on his way to ruin that orderly creation. Book III closes with the vertigo of his "steep flight in many an Aerie wheele," and when the poet resumes in his own era, eons after the fall Satan engineers, he laments his helplessness to prevent human woe: "O FOR that warning voice" (4.1).

The hymn affords Milton many occasions to vary the expressive voices heard in his long narrative; the settings for individual hymns provide occasions for foreshadowing and for more than emotional coloring; finally, the consistency and interrelationship among hymns unifies the epic as itself an act of worship.

Wisdom Psalms in Paradise Lost

That Milton considers himself not only bard or seer but also spokesman or teacher, the "interpreter & relater of the best and sagest things among mine own Citizens throughout this Iland,"[28] prompts him to frequent sententiae in imitation of wisdom song. These occur from the beginning of the epic (e.g., Milton's apothegmatic comment [1.690–92] on how naturally gold grows in hell's soil) to the end (e.g., Michael's observation [12.220–22] on how unnatural military training is to both noble and ignoble human beings). But wisdom song most richly influences the witness of Abdiel before and during the war in heaven. Wisdom psalms range between the proverbial expression of practical morality and the meditation on faithful witness by a suffering servant of the Lord; Abdiel's dialogue with Satan draws on both.

In conclave in Lucifer's camp, the proposition is debated that God the King is an arbitrary tyrant. Satan there does not so much misread psalms as he misappropriates Milton's own language of liberty in the prose to justify rebellion against God. Abdiel corrects him with right reading of both psalms and Milton. Milton sought no models for human institutions from revelations of celestial life and none for the human political state in the monarchic government of heaven. God's kingship presented to him no grounds for legitimating human kingship, the position of the Stuart ideologues. When Israel sought and was given monarchs in 1 Samuel 8.4–8, both Scripture and Milton thought its desire contemptible, degenerate, and contrary to God's progressively revealed will that human beings be free and mature. The debate between Lucifer and Abdiel interweaves scriptural and contemporary political language; but although the contest results in pseudo-libertarian wisdom proverbs by Satan and wise commonwealth corrections by the Servant of God (Abdiel is called by the etymology of his name at 6.29), it owes more to Milton's political experience than his generic

[28] *The Reason of Church Government, YP* 1:811–12.

experience of psalms.[29] His analysis of wisdom song gave him, however, Abdiel's role as witness to God's perfect justice and God's acknowledgment of him. The mild voice that greets Abdiel from golden cloud (6.28) as he returns to the Mount of God speaks the fullest wisdom psalm in the poem, announced both by the salutation "Servant of God" and the description of Abdiel's role as "the testimonie of Truth":

> Servant of God, well done, well hast thou fought
> The better fight, who single hast maintaind
> Against revolted multitudes the Cause
> Of Truth, in word mightier then they in Armes;
> And for the testimonie of Truth hast born
> Universal reproach, far worse to beare
> Then violence: for this was all thy care
> To stand approv'd in sight of God, though Worlds
> Judg'd thee perverse: the easier conquest now
> Remains thee, aided by this host of friends,
> Back on thy foes more glorious to return
> Then scornd thou didst depart, and to subdue
> By force, who reason for thir Law refuse,
> Right reason for thir Law, and for thir King
> *Messiah*, who by right of merit Reigns.
> (6.29–43)

Editors have properly noticed echoes of Psalm 62.7, "In God *is* my salvation and my glory: the rock of my strength, *and* my refuge, *is* in God" in its opening two lines, and of Psalm 69.7, "Because for thy sake I have borne reproach" at line 34.[30] Psalm 62, a wisdom song growing out of a song of trust, exhibits the normative morality and the counting device common in the genre: "God hath spoken once; twice have I heard this; that power *belongeth* unto God. Also unto thee, O Lord, *belongeth* mercy: for thou renderest to every man according to his work" (vv. 11–12). Psalm 69, a personal lament by a suffering servant, shows the afflicted psalmist persecuted in a religious cause ("the zeal of thine house hath eaten me up") and his witness resulting in his alienation ("I am become a stranger unto my brethren, and an alien unto my mother's children," "I became a proverb to them" [vv. 9, 8, 11]). Psalm 62, representing God as moral judge of human value, and Psalm 69, depicting the servant as witness to religious truth, are Milton's sources.

[29] See my essay "The Politics of *Paradise Lost*," in *Politics of Discourse*, ed. Kevin Sharpe and Steven N. Zwicker, 204–29.

[30] See Sims, *The Bible in Milton's Epics*, 265 and Fowler, *The Poems of Milton*, 731.

Milton used "testimony," the Puritan term of art for professing God and being acknowledged by him, on only three occasions in his poetry, once when the Father's voice at Jesus' baptism is called "the testimony of Heaven" in *Paradise Regained* (1.78), once in his literal translation of Psalm 81.5 on God's testimony to Joseph, and once now for Abdiel. He used the term "servant" also sparingly, in psalm translation and in concurrence with testimony. Both words spoken to Abdiel point to wisdom song. God hails Abdiel for maintaining the truth alone against many and for upholding it by force of reason. In the quintessential posture of wisdom song, Abdiel cared only for divine approval. In the wisdom tradition an enlightened agent without specific command or authority from God sees what is right in any given situation and acts on the rational basis of his knowledge of God and the universe. Psalm 37.5–6 instances the God-fearing rationality of the wisdom teacher and of Abdiel equally: "Commit thy way unto the Lord; trust also in him; and he shall bring *it* to pass. And he shall bring forth thy righteousness as the light, and thy judgment as the noonday" (vv. 5–6). The prophet knows God has sought him out and given him a special message, but the sage mediates a total attitude and culture; both act in the shadow of God. Abdiel reasons against Satan, taking right reason for his law; through it he discerns God's nature and Christ's merit. He refutes the worldly wisdom of Lucifer by rational argument based upon his total experience. His message is not prophecy, though some have seen prophecy in it; it is wisdom.[31] The truth he teaches about God's nature is reciprocally acknowledged by the Father.

The value to *Paradise Lost* of the generic imitation of wisdom song is the lyrical reinforcement it provides for themes represented in narrative and the foregrounding it gives for forthcoming narration. During the political debate between Abdiel and Lucifer, Abdiel reasonably recalls God's design in exalting the Son to create not a static meritocracy in Heaven with fixed status for all members under unvarying law, but an evolving organic unity. He derives the plan from his general experience of God and God's proclamation of the Son, "bent rather to exalt / Our happie state under one Head" (5.829–30). Milton does not endorse Abdiel's political ideology of divine monarchy as a model for the human state. The wisdom in Abdiel's words lies in his recognition that, in the political sphere as in the religious, progressive enlightenment is possible. God makes new and contingent decrees "for the very purpose of allowing free causes to put into effect that freedom

[31] But see Robert West, "Abdiel," in *A Milton Encyclopedia* 1:11–12.

which he himself gave them."[32] The social perfection of heaven lies in the continual growth in community, against which Satan rebels to seek self-aggrandizement. To him new law must necessarily be the mark of absolutism; to Abdiel new law if just is reform, the sign of progressive revelation and of augmented freedom. Lucifer proposes not to inquire further but to use force, "our own right hand . . . by proof to try / Who is our equal" (5.864–66).

Throughout the exchange, Lucifer rejects every value of Abdiel's praised by the Father in the wisdom song that ends the first half of their exchange and foregrounds the second. He speaks and reacts irrationally, justifying rebellion neither from personal experience nor necessary logic. He overvalues numbers, rejoicing when "none seconded" Abdiel's words. He chooses force. Then Abdiel leaves:

> From amidst them forth he passd,
> Long way through hostile scorn, which he susteind
> Superior, nor of violence fear'd aught;
> And with retorted scorn his back he turn'd
> On those proud Towrs to swift destruction doom'd.
> (5.903–7)

He departs in the spirit of wisdom Psalm 1.1, "Blessed *is* the man that . . . sitteth [not] in the seat of the scornful," he turns his back on the "seat / High on a Hill, far blazing" (5.756–57) of the scornful, warning Satan with one last cautionary proverb, based on Psalm 2.9–10, "That Golden Scepter which thou didst reject / Is now an Iron Rod to bruise and breake / Thy disobedience" (5.886–88).[33] When they meet again on the battlefield, he produces several more—"Most reason is that Reason overcome," and "few somtimes may know, when thousands err"—before chancing his own right arm. God's testimony of wisdom, greeting him briefly, celebrates the contrary values just established in narrative; it foregrounds the duel to come between Abdiel and Lucifer in the thick of battle, where when "Warr wearied hath perform'd what Warr can do," God himself calls off the all too equal struggle (6.695).

The major value of wisdom psalm in this extended episode is as lyrical highlighting and foregrounding, but it also contributes to multivocality. Milton paid no attention to the many actual speakers of

[32] *YP* 6:160.

[33] "Thou shalt break them with a rod of iron; thou shalt dash them in pieces like a potter's vessel. Be wise now therefore, O ye kings: be instructed, ye judges of the earth" (vv. 9–10).

psalms,[34] but imitated praise, prophecy, or wisdom as angel, bard, witness, or any other speaker in such a way as to produce an overlaid richness of many voices. Abdiel's exchange with Lucifer exhibits a particularly rich interweaving: the bard (instructed by the Heavenly Muse) tells what Raphael (charged by God to instruct man) told Adam that Abdiel (described as unswervingly truthful) said to Lucifer (whose words are called "bold discourse without control") and what testimony he received from God (a voice from a cloud) in return. That multivocality allows Milton to present Raphael's words to Adam as instruction,[35] to create in Abdiel wisdom's *martus*, and, perhaps for the length of God's lyrical witness, to console himself for the pain of the rejection in the Restoration of his own vision of community.

Lament and the Psalm Mixed with Thanksgiving

The rehearsal of "all our woe" in *Paradise Lost* is punctuated by lyrical lament in imitation of psalms, lament ever more pervasive when the epic changes its notes to tragic. Adam grieves, Satan godlessly pities Satan, Eve sorrows to leave her garden, Adam and Eve together make an act of contrition, the poet mourns the decay of nature, and the Father and Son regret man's fall. Nor is it possible to read the Book of Psalms without an overwhelming sense of the sheer volume of lamentation in it.[36] No group of psalms more surely stands forth as a formal kind, long considered a distinctive genre and identified with the penitential psalms. In *Paradise Lost,* Adam is the great and preeminent sorrower. Penitential psalms and private laments govern his personal despair; communal national lament at distresses befalling the entire community governs his "historical" grief during Michael's vision of times to come. These two forms of lament are each presented in three episodes: Adam's abashed discovery of his nakedness (9.1067–98), his nightlong anguish (10.720–844), and his sorrowful acceptance of ex-

[34] He said nothing even of those named in psalm headings, where to David seventy-three are attributed, to Asaph twelve, to "the sons of Korah" eleven, to Heman "the Ezrahite" and Ethan "the Ezrahite" two, to Solomon two, and to Moses one—wisdom songs being among those attributed to Asaph, the sons of Korah, Heman, Ethan, and Solomon, conveying some sense of professional Levitical calling. See Mowinckel, *The Psalms in Israel's Worship*, 2:95; von Rad, *Wisdom in Israel*, 15–23; and Michael D. Goulder, *The Psalms of the Sons of Korah*, 16–22.

[35] For all Raphael's so-called Platonic epistemology, he often himself sounds like a wisdom teacher, and nowhere more so than in choosing the image of the growing tree from Psalm 1 to represent to Adam the ontology of enlightenment.

[36] See C. Westermann, "Struktur und Geschichte der Klage im Alten Testament," 44ff.; see Weiser, *The Psalms*, 66.

pulsion (11.296–333) draw on private lament; his reaction to sickness and death (11.500–514, 547–52), to violence and manslaughter (11.675–82), and to the Flood (11.765–86) draw on communal lament. These are followed by a muted coda of thanksgiving intermingled with serious grief (12.553–73): that modulation is the normal conclusion in the full psalm of lament. All but this coda are introduced or concluded with the words *lament* or *plaint* or a variation of them; many lament psalms are similarly identified.[37]

Adam's first lament is dominated by the guilty impulse to hide; his self-revulsion directs him to a "glade / Obscur'd," where he prays to be covered by boughs of pines and cedars. Ashamed, he confesses he cannot lift up his head, so stained and soiled, so dishonored, so reproached by his body does he feel. All these, with a similar integration of sexual and moral guilt, are the repeated substance of lament in the psalms.[38]

The structure of biblical laments, whether private or communal, builds upon repetition and fluctuation. The sufferer or spokesman confesses despair and then feels enough trust in God to entreat him; the trust drains away and he reverts to anguished confession, only to discover in himself a renewal of entreaty. When that likewise falters, the alternation threatens to become interminable, an endless oscillation between confession and supplication. This crescendo and decrescendo of accusation and petition often secures its difficult closure by modulating at a moment of relief into thanksgiving. The motives organized in this structure differ between individual and public lament, although both circulate around the questions "why?" and "how long?" and both

[37] 9.1063–64, "in face / Confounded"; 10.719, "with sad complaint"; 10.845, "lamented loud"; 11.499, "his plaint renew'd"; 11.675, "Lamenting turnd full sad"; 11.754 "How didst thou grieve then"; 11.762, "utterdst thus thy plaint"; 11.874, "Farr less I now lament for one whole World." In the Book of Psalms, *michtam* or atonement is the superscription of Psalms 16 and 50–60, *shiggaion* or howl of Psalm 7. Neither the Columbia edition nor Sims finds psalm echoes in 9.1067–98, 10.719–844, 11.296–333, 11.500–514 and 547–52, or 11.674–80. Elledge, ed., *Paradise Lost*, 249 notes 27.9 for 11.296–333; the Columbia edition notes 25.10 for 11.762–85; Columbia, Sims, and Elledge all note 145.9 for the coda thanksgiving at 12.552–73. Fowler, *The Poems of Milton*, 963–64 calls 10.720–844 "the first of all complaints" and hears Psalm 69.15, "Let not the waterflood overflow me," in its speech prefix. Lewalski, *Paradise Lost and the Rhetoric of Literary Forms*, 249 notes for the same lament Psalm 77.3, 5, 7–8; on Eve's prayer to Adam for forgiveness, ibid., 250–51, she cites Psalms 38, 51, and 102.

[38] For example, 7.5, "lay mine honour in the dust"; 17.8, "hide me"; 22.6, "I *am* a worm, and no man; a reproach of men"; 31.10, "my strength faileth because of mine iniquity"; 38.4, 7, "mine iniquities are gone over my head. . . . my loins are filled with a loathsome *disease*"; 51.5, "Behold, I was shapen in iniquity"; 55.5, 7, "horror hath overwhelmed me. . . . Lo, *then* would I wander far off, *and* remain in the wilderness"; and 143.9, "I flee unto thee to hide me."

involve the sufferer, his enemies and God. The seven penitential psalms share many common characteristics of personal lament and are prominent in Adam's laments, though not until his final lament does he achieve their ideal contrition.

The penitential psalms—6, 32, 38, 51, 102, 130, and 143—lyrically confess a suffering that has not moved too far from self-pity toward remorse and contrition to apply to Adam. Psalm 6 alternates grief and prayer in impressive simplicity through five repetitions of the cry "O Lord," but confesses little. In Psalm 32, Augustine's favorite psalm and one Luther called Pauline,[39] the poet recollects his sinfulness and penitence, and God's forgiveness. He meditates upon the memory and discovers in it what pious men should learn from trying to conceal their sins—the pain of repression, the relief of confession, the depth of contrition, the joy of deliverance—and then cautions against hardness of heart. Psalm 38 begins with one cry "O Lord" and ends with five; its structure is typically systolic. Its occasion is a morbid illness, caused and punished by sin; its severest pain is a sense of guilt, but the poet's sufferings include persecution by malicious enemies to which he must submit in silence. Psalm 51, the most inward of the group, gives relatively slight attention to physical or material suffering but explores a mood of compulsive self-excoriation. No lament more intensely holds itself to probing and expressing the very heart of loss in the form of repeated alternations of painful confession and serious prayer. Although the Roman Catholic and Anglican Churches included it among the penitential psalms, Psalm 102 is a mixed-mode prophetic psalm, and its structure does not lend itself to Adam's mood of moral desolation as he tries to exonerate himself in accusing God but succeeds in accusing himself and exonerating God. More briefly than any of the others, Psalm 130 forges the link between the anguish of guilt and the relief of forgiveness. The very depth out of which the psalmist has cried becomes his basis of assurance. He fears his God and knows himself absolutely unworthy; his distress comes from the contrast between his sinfulness and God's purity; his sense of grace has the same source. The psalmist of Psalm 130 does not explore his own sufferings; his mood is far from Adam's. Finally, Psalm 143 displays the moods of lament in a twice-repeated sequence: after complaint at his affliction, the psalmist beseeches God to save his life, teach and guide him, and protect him from his enemies.

Adam's "sad complaint" (10.719) "lamented loud / Through the still Night," (10.845–46) begins and ends describing a turbulent alienation. He begins "in a troubl'd Sea of passion tost" (10.718); he ends "Out-

[39] Weiser, *The Psalms*, 281.

stretcht . . . on the cold ground" (10.851) in "black Air . . . with damps and dreadful gloom, / Which to his evil Conscience represented / All things with double terror" (10.847–50). His lament is a protracted confessional determination of his sole responsibility for his sins, "the sourse and spring / Of all corruption" (10.832–33). Since he feels as yet no corresponding contrition, his analysis draws him down into a bottomless despair he describes in horror as an endless falling into an "Abyss of fears . . . from deep to deeper plung'd" (10.842–44). From those depths, as in Psalm 130, he cries for death to end him with "one thrice acceptable stroke" (10.855), but no answer comes and, as in Psalm 38, his lament drains into silence. Though feeling none of God's mercy, Adam acknowledges God's justice and his expressivity results from that candor. He would like to accuse God with the "why" questions of lament, but he is too honest and must resort instead to "how long" questions. Especially when he tries to face his shame that all creation to come will reproach his "propagated curse" (10.729), he cannot accuse his God with "why," for he accepted the conditions of his creation and failed to keep his part of the bargain. But even "how long" is difficult, since the question involves the meaning of death. At the thought of death Adam introduces a veiled adversarial "why," accusing God of either pitilessness in not ending his sufferings by death or incompetence to control death. The veiled accusation is a frequent lament strategy. When accusation is disallowed because God seems both too threatening and too good to provoke it, or because the official reading of man's disobedience is that it justifies God's ways, then laments find oblique means to frame protest.[40] Negative formulations of misassigned anger, for example, as in Psalm 6.1, "O Lord, rebuke me not in thine anger, neither chasten me in thy hot displeasure," transferring to God the speaker's feelings, imply arbitrariness and harshness. In like manner Adam asking his God "how long" implies an accusatorial "why":

> Will he, draw out,
> For angers sake, finite to infinite
> In punisht man, to satisfie his rigour
> Satisfi'd never.
> (10.801–4)

Adam's repetitive and fluctuating lament is structured by the seven exclamations spaced throughout it, taking the form of oxymorons or expressive of antithesis. The first, opening the lament, is "O miserable

[40] The fullest treatment of accusation in personal lament is in C. Westermann, *Praise and Lament in the Psalms*, 183–88.

of happie"; the second, nine lines later, is "O voice once heard / Delightfully . . . Now death to heare"; the third, twelve lines later, "O fleeting joyes . . . with lasting woes"; the fourth, thirty lines later, "O welcom hour . . . delay[ed]"; the fifth, sixteen lines later, "O thought / Horrid, if true"; the sixth, thirty lines later, "O were I able / To waste . . . how would ye bless"; the seventh closes the lament twenty lines later with "O Conscience," implying oxymoron by suspending the conscience between a "sea of passion" in the opening of the lament and the "abyss of fears" at the end. Each of the outcries of "O" represents the crest of a wave, the ebb of which should ideally be a prayer to a trusted God but in Adam's lament is a question—first, "is this the end"; second, "what can I encrease . . . but curses"; third, "Did I request thee . . . To mould me Man"; fourth, "why delayes / His hand"; fifth, "Can he make deathless Death"; and sixth and last, "why should all mankind / For one mans fault thus guiltless be condemn'd, / If guiltless?" Were Adam as trusting and contrite as the penitential psalmists, he could convert those questions into the prayers already latent in them—end my pain, remove the curse, fix a limit to the woe, give me rest, turn wrath away, let me find a refuge. Those are, of course, the supplications of all lament, communal or personal, that follow each swelling of exclamation and question.[41]

Oxymoron, the figure compressing tension into paradox or contradiction, expresses Adam's strained struggle between the poles of self-pity and begrudging justice. No element in his psychology is absent from lament psalms, short of true contrition, which his reluctant acceptance of God's merciless justice is calculated just to miss; and no element in lament psalm is not used in Adam's lament, save the venge-

[41] Some have found Adam's lament Jobean in feeling, and so it is. No formal distinction need be made between Job's laments and the laments of Psalms, any more than a formal distinction need be made between wisdom psalms and the wisdom utterances of Elihu or even of the friends in Job. The use the writer of Job makes of psalm genres in shaping parts of an extended dialogue is similar to Milton's use in shaping parts of a long narrative.

To instance a few typical supplications: Psalm 3, "arise," "save me"; 7, "deliver me," "judge me," "establish the just"; 17, "hide me under the shadow of thy wings"; "deliver my soul"; 22, "be not thou far"; 25, "Remember not . . . my transgressions," "forgive"; 26, "redeem me, and be merciful"; 27, "have mercy," "answer me"; 31, "let me never be ashamed"; 38, "Make haste to help me." Similarly in communal lament: 44, "Awake," "arise, cast *us* not off for ever"; 60, "Give us help from trouble"; 74, "Remember thy congregation," "Lift up thy feet unto the perpetual desolations."

To instance a few typical questions: Psalm 22, "why hast thou forsaken me?"; 42, "why go I mourning . . . ?"; 44, "why sleepest thou, O Lord?"; 77, "Hath God forgotten to be gracious? hath he in anger shut up his tender mercies?"; 88, "shall the dead arise *and* praise thee?"; 89, "shall he deliver his soul from the hand of the grave?"

ful petition in some and protestation of innocence in others.[42] The scene has been called the loneliest in English poetry. Every explanation Adam gives to himself, every question he puts, divides him further from his God and alienates him further from his life. But if the scene is lonely beyond endurance, it is a scene psalmists visited again and again.

By Adam's last personal lament, the contrition so marked in penitential psalms has flowered into obedience in him, prompted by Eve's very personal lament and contrite attempt to move his forgiveness and repair the ruin her sin brought on. The mourning in his last lament is joined by a didacticism also often attached to lament in psalms. At Michael's announcement of the expulsion from Eden, Adam laments anew, incorporating in his new contrition two further themes from psalms—grief at exile and nostalgia for a local and familiar place of worship. Psalm 27.13 suggests Adam's reaction to the news that he must leave Eden: "*I had fainted*, unless I had believed to see the goodness of the Lord in the land of the living"; Psalm 27.8, his pain at losing the sight of God's face in Eden: "*When thou saidst*, Seek ye my face; my heart said unto thee, Thy face, Lord, will I seek." With difficulty he stifles his desire to build altars there (11.323–27). The regret and contrition intermingled in his forgoing local shrines come from lament psalms, perhaps from Psalm 51.16–17:

> For thou desirest not sacrifice; else would I give *it*: thou delightest not in burnt offering.
> The sacrifices of God *are* a broken spirit: a broken and a contrite heart, O God, thou wilt not despise.

When Adam next mourns, he laments publicly the chain of pre-expulsion laments in Book XI that culminate in the brief thanksgiving of Book XII. All widen from personal to communal lament, as the suffering individual becomes the nation of Adam's future children. Milton represents Adam's response to death, to violence, and to the Flood. The first of these laments is divided into two parts, separated by the vision of the Lazar house (11.461–65, 500–514). Adam responds with a pitying outcry to the physical deformities and pains occasioned by intemperance. His outcry generalizes and abstracts from personal lament in a time of sickness, as for example in Psalm 38.3–7;[43] his con-

[42] For the vengeful prayer, see Psalm 58.6, "Break their teeth, O God, in their mouth"; or 79.6, "Pour out thy wrath upon the heathen that have not known thee"; for the protestation of innocence, see 17.3–5; 26.4, 6–8; 35.7; and 59.10.

[43] *There is* no soundness in my flesh because of thine anger; neither *is there any* rest in

trasting the beauty and health of creation when God first made it with its defilement by sickness is a regular feature in the general strategy of communal lament to contrast all God's earlier saving deeds in the history of the nation with current hard times.

Under Michael's instruction, Adam in the second part of the lament over sickness and death (10.547–52) takes refuge in a stoical resignation the angel considers just as overstated as his first revulsion. But whether overemotional or not, both the revulsion and the asceticism have precedents not only in Psalms and Lamentations but also in the Book of Job. "David for piety renowned" and "patient Job" draw identical lessons from sickness and death, and when Milton proves his mortalism in *Christian Doctrine* by citing scriptural texts, he notably turns back and forth from one to the other.[44]

At Adam's second lament—for the violence and inhumanity shown Enoch and staining human history—Michael teaches him to distinguish between the false heroism of might and the true heroism of patient witness and martyrdom. Communal lament regularly contrasts the military with the pious hero, as for example Psalm 44.22 and 6, where the people of Israel are called "sheep for the slaughter," and their spokesman promises "I will not trust in my bow, neither shall my sword save me." The contrast regularly involves a distinction between the purer past and the degeneracy of the rebellious and despoiling present, as in Psalm 74.5–6.[45] Milton's primary source for the action and moral theme of the episode is the story of Enoch, drawn out of Genesis and interpreted in Hebrews and Jude, to say nothing of the apocryphal Book of Enoch, but the passionate dismay of lament colors it.

The psychological climax in Milton's exploration of human depravity through Adam's exemplary grief comes when almost all his sons are extinguished in the Flood, and he despairs. Shown the rainbow sign of covenant, he wrenches his soul from lament to thanksgiving, and no further vision wrings from him a pure lament. He responds to the rest judgmentally, "O execrable Son" (12.64), gratefully, "O sent

---

my bones because of my sin.

For mine iniquities are gone over mine head: as an heavy burden they are too heavy for me.

My wounds stink *and* are corrupt because of my foolishness.

I am troubled; I am bowed down greatly; I go mourning all the day long.

For my loins are filled with a loathsome *disease*: and *there is* no soundness in my flesh.

[44] See, for example, *YP* 6:388, 389, 401, 404–5.

[45] *A man* was famous according as he had lifted up axes upon the thick trees.

But now they break down the carved work thereof at once with axes and hammers.

from Heav'n, / Enlightner" (12.270–71), or replete with wonder, "O goodness infinite, goodness immense!" (12.469).

The double mood of the last book of *Paradise Lost*, grief for sin and loss intermingled with assurance and trust, takes the shape of a mixed mood lament tending toward wisdom song and concluding in thanksgiving. At the end of the search for knowledge, Adam sings a new psalm, his last words in the poem:

> How soon hath thy prediction, Seer blest,
> Measur'd this transient World, the Race of time,
> Till time stand fixt: beyond is all abyss,
> Eternitie, whose end no eye can reach.
> Greatly instructed I shall hence depart,
> Greatly in peace of thought, and have my fill
> Of knowledge, what this Vessel can containe;
> Beyond which was my folly to aspire.
> Henceforth I learne, that to obey is best,
> And love with feare the onely God, to walk
> As in his presence, ever to observe
> His providence, and on him sole depend,
> Mercifull over all his works, with good
> Still overcoming evil, and by small
> Accomplishing great things, by things deemd weak
> Subverting worldly strong, and worldly wise
> By simply meek; that suffering for Truths sake
> Is fortitude to highest victorie,
> And to the faithful Death the Gate of Life;
> Taught this by his example whom I now
> Acknowledge my Redeemer ever blest.
> (12.553–73)

Where lament ends with man's submission to God in assurance that existence is meaningful in communion with him, lament of course moves into thanksgiving. Many psalms actively combine the two modes; Milton has particularly noticed Psalms 22, 31, and 86 in phrasing Adam's obedient praise.[46] Where it resolves into a lesson taught or

[46] Milton put the following passages into Adam's combination of lament and thanksgiving: Psalm 22.24, 26: "For he hath not despised nor abhorred the affliction of the afflicted; neither hath he hid his face from him; but when he cried unto him, he heard. . . . The meek shall eat and be satisfied: they shall praise the Lord that seek him: your heart shall live for ever." 31.8, 19: "And hast not shut me up into the hand of the enemy: thou hast set my feet in a large room. . . . *Oh* how great *is* thy goodness, which thou hast laid up for them that fear thee; *which* thou hast wrought for them that trust in thee before the sons of men!" 86:11, 15: "Teach me thy way, O Lord; I will walk in thy

learnt, lament shades into wisdom song. Of psalms that combine those modes, Milton has noticed 25, adding to it from such composite hymns of trust or wisdom as 107 and 145.[47] Adam's thanksgiving is in effect a Christian profession of faith. The mixed-mode songs to which Milton turned in shaping it were quoted in the New Testament as fulfilled in the Messiah and proper to specifically Christian worship. Adam interprets psalms not yet written in his day as prophetic of a faith not yet founded by a covenant not yet made; as he is the most passionate sorrower in the epic, he is the first Christian worshiper.

If Adam is the most intense exponent of lament in the poem—Eve's contrition only excepted—he is not its highest authority. The ultimate extension of the mode of lament in *Paradise Lost* is its attribution to the Father and Son. The lament of an individual or a community is not only a form of lyrical expressivity but a plea intended to modify behavior, a prayer. The prayer seeks an encounter with God in which he is to show mercy; he is repeatedly asked to do so—to awake, rise up, come down, be near, and help. When the Father laments human disobedience, he inspires the Son's prayer for grace to man; similarly, when man laments in contrition, he inspires the Son's intercession with the Father, the Father answering the Son's intercession for contrite fallen man with mercy. In the intercessory model, the sinless Son can know penitence only on behalf of others, the omniscient Father know regret without remorse. In the intercessory model is the justification for regarding lament or remorse as a mode of worship. When the Son presents the penitence of Adam and Eve to God as the firstfruits of his grace, he acts as God's priest and man's vicar. The intercession produces the Father's proclamation of foreordained mercy. Although the pair must be expelled from the garden and adjudged to death, he explains the mercy in that judgment:

> Death becomes
> His final remedie, and after Life

---

truth: unite my heart to fear thy name. . . . But thou, O Lord, *art* a God full of compassion, and gracious, longsuffering, and plenteous in mercy and truth."

[47] Milton has used 25.12: "What man *is* he that feareth the Lord? him shall he teach in the way *that* he shall choose." To it he has added 107.21, 30, 42–43: "Oh that *men* would praise the Lord *for* his goodness, and *for* his wonderful works to the children of men! . . . Then are they glad because they be quiet; so he bringeth them unto their desired haven. . . . The righteous shall see *it*, and rejoice: . . . Whoso *is* wise, and will observe these *things*, even they shall understand the lovingkindness of the Lord." 145.3, 9, 15: "Great *is* the Lord, and greatly to be praised; and his greatness *is* unsearchable. . . . The Lord *is* good to all: and his tender mercies *are* over all his works. . . . The eyes of all wait upon thee; and thou givest them their meat in due season."

> Tri'd in sharp tribulation, and refin'd
> By Faith and faithful works, to second Life,
> Wak't in the renovation of the just,
> Resignes him up with Heav'n and Earth renewd.
> (11.61–66)

Like his hymns, Milton's laments in *Paradise Lost* stretch across the architecture of the poem, responding to the major incidents of the narrative, giving them multivocal emotional color and affectively integrating them along an arch of natural development, from personal to communal, from anguish through contrition to wisdom and thanksgiving. The wisdom song finds a place in this design, but a smaller role than that it will be given in *Paradise Regained*. What takes the place of the dominance of wisdom song is the poet's adaptation of prophetic psalm to the function of proem in which poesis and worship, inspiration and obedience, are intertwined. This poet finds it possible to join with the angels in praise, to join with the fallen in lament, and to see in the intercessory pattern of lament a way of offering his own song to God in praise of God but to the account of mankind, in a pattern that prompted William Haller to remark that Milton's great argument was written "to justify the ways of man to God."

I need only add that, perhaps for the reason of his conversion of poetry to worship, Milton wrote no imprecatory psalms into *Paradise Lost*. He preferred the denunciation of silence to imitations of the blessing and cursing psalm, however enthusiastic about imprecation he had felt in *Christian Doctrine*, when he noted, "We are even commanded to curse, in public prayer, the enemies of God and the church, fellow-Christians who have proved false, and anyone who commits major sins against God or even against ourselves."[48] As Raphael will not praise ungodly deeds, so Milton will not curse them:

> Nameless in dark oblivion let them dwell.
> For strength from Truth divided and from Just,
> Illaudable, naught merits but dispraise
> And ignominie, yet to glorie aspires
> Vain glorious, and through infamie seeks fame:
> Therfore Eternal silence be thir doome.
> (6.380–85)

[48] *YP* 6:675.

FOUR

"Light . . . from the Fountain of light"

Psalm Themes

THE EPIC POET builds a world into his poem and makes it palpable through passages of varying emotional timbre, now pastoral, now contemplative, now devotional, now celebratory, now tragic. But he builds that world as understandable in terms of the best information or knowledge available to him. Epic places human beings within a cosmos; Milton writes for an audience interested in that cosmos not simply as a storehouse for metaphor but as a structure under investigation by the liveliest minds of his age. He designs his diffuse epic to engage the interest of the seventeenth-century reader in geography, medicine, astronomy, physics, physiology, and psychology quite as much as in theology and philosophy. Epic encyclopedism is the result of the poet's attempt to recreate the present state of his known world not just as backdrop but as a positive value and interest in itself. Milton knew no source of truth better nor regarded any more certain than the Bible. The encyclopedism of his diffuse epic includes the scriptural: ideas, that is, appear in *Paradise Lost* evidenced and argued through Scripture; Milton the epic poet is confident both of his encyclopedic knowledge of Scripture and his own power to interpret the text.

Milton's encyclopedic knowledge of psalm themes and ideas is put to two kinds of use in *Paradise Lost.* One use produces the encyclopedism of copia, the kind of encyclopedism that inspires epic catalogues, for example. When Milton revised *Paradise Lost* from a ten- to a twelve-book poem, he added to the survey of fatal illnesses shown Adam in the Lazar house three new lines of largely psychogenic diseases:

> Daemoniac Phrenzie, moaping Melancholie
> And Moon-struck madness, pining Atrophie,
> Marasmus, and wide-wasting Pestilence.
> (11.485–87)

Milton set enough store by his epic catalogue that, given an opportunity by a resetting of the poem, he increased its copiousness. Literary models for the epic catalogue and encyclopedic sources for the various details in Milton's have been adduced to explain the entire catalogue of diseases.[1] No explanation is required for the epic poet's interest in a density of reference and richness of knowledge; to the modern reader he is defined by his desire to know everything, and in the modern era identifiable by some difficulty bringing his cantos to an end. To find psalm echoes, references, ideas, and themes in the greatest possible density in Milton's encyclopedic epic is no surprise; copia displays his scriptural encyclopedism.

The second use of encyclopedic knowledge, the comprehensive representation of causality or process, is also present in the catalogue of diseases. That processive encyclopedism takes as its goal not simply to show a richness of lore, its universality and comprehensiveness, but to show knowledge in the making, to treat ideas in historical sequences, to view knowledge as learning, to ask who holds what ideas when, and how and why he changes them to what other ideas. Displaying the Lazar house, for example, Michael warns Adam to expect

> Diseases dire, of which a monstrous crew
> Before thee shall appear; that thou mayst know
> What miserie th'inabstinence of *Eve*
> Shall bring on men.
> (11.474–77)

The ensuing encyclopedia of pathology reduces Adam to lament that human beings must undergo so painful a destruction of the being they did not ask for. Michael repeats that illness results from intemperance, "a brutish vice, / Inductive mainly to the sin of *Eve*" (11.518–19). Adam thinks he has taken the point, and when the next vision comes, he parrots, "still I see the tenor of Mans woe / Holds on the same, from Woman to begin" (11.632–33). He has, of course, got hold of the wrong proposition, as Michael informs him curtly: "From Mans effeminate slackness it begins." Temperance, not dominance, is the lesson to be learned, and the scene prefigures in dynamics the later discovery that "a paradise within" hinges not only on the knowledge of obedience but on the addition of deeds answerable to that understanding (12.581–85). Michael's attention to detail reflects both encyclopedic copiousness and encyclopedic progression, an interest in multiplying usable truths and representing the spectrum of those who discover them. Thus Milton presents death not only in encyclopedic

[1] See Svendsen, *Milton and Science*, 202–3, 229–30.

copiousness but also according to an encyclopedic pattern of the progressive human understanding of it based on the Book of Psalms.

Milton's own knowledge of Scripture was encyclopedic in the first sense, full, copious, and precise. It was encyclopedic with reference to a Hebrew Bible, the Geneva Bible, the Junius-Tremellius Bible, the 1612 edition of the King James Version, and the *Biblia Sacra Polyglotta* of Brian Walton.[2] That writing *Christian Doctrine* was a precondition for the writing of *Paradise Lost* is apparent in the density of references in the poem to the biblical texts adduced in the tractate in proof of ideas also present in the epic. Milton's way of collocating psalms into clusters by subject matter is encyclopedic; the transfer of the cluster to the epic is likewise comprehensive.

In *Christian Doctrine* Milton proves the proposition that God is "supremely kind" by referring, in order of appearance, to Psalms 86, 103, 5, 25, 103, 103, and 119. Whenever then in *Paradise Lost* he characterizes God as "supremely kind," he echoes the psalms from that cluster. When in Book III, for example, God assures the Son and spirit elect that "Man . . . shall find grace," Milton describes the scene:

> Thus while God spake, ambrosial fragrance fill'd
> All Heav'n, and in the blessed Spirits elect
> Sense of new joy ineffable diffus'd:
> Beyond compare the Son of God was seen
> Most glorious, in him all his Father shon
> Substantially express'd, and in his face
> Divine compassion visibly appeerd,
> Love without end, and without measure Grace.
> (3.135–42)

Editors have found in the passage an echo of Psalm 86.15, "But thou, O Lord, *art* a God full of compassion, and gracious, longsuffering, and plenteous in mercy and truth." But all the psalms the tractate adduces are present.[3] From Psalm 5.12 comes the response of joy among believers that God "wilt bless the righteous"; from Psalm 25.6 the end-

[2] See Shawcross, "Bibles," and Sims, "Bible, Milton and the," *A Milton Encyclopedia* 1:142–63.

[3] *Christian Doctrine* proves God's mercy by citation: "Secondly, also under the concept of WILL, God is SUPREMELY KIND. . . . Psal. lxxxvi.15 [*But thou, O Lord, art a God full of compassion, and gracious, longsuffering, and plenteous in mercy and truth*] and ciii.8 [*The Lord is merciful and gracious, slow to anger, and plenteous in mercy*] and v.4: *evil will not dwell with you*, and xxv.6: *kindnesses from the beginning of the world*, ciii.11: *his kindness prevails towards those that are afraid of him*, and ciii.17: *Jehovah's kindness is from age to age*, and cxix.68: *he is good and does good*" (*YP* 6:150–51). The whole association comes into play whenever God's compassion figures in the poem.

lessness of the "tender mercies and . . . loving kindnesses; for they *have been* ever of old"; from Psalm 119.68 the distinction between the Father's being good and doing good in the substantial expression of his compassion in the Son. Furthermore, every time God's supreme kindness is referred to, Milton's encyclopedic knowledge of the whole group is brought to bear illustrating it, as at the conclusion of the dialogue in Heaven, when the angels praise the "Father of Mercie and Grace," and the Son for ending "the strife / Of Mercy and Justice in [his] face discern'd" (3.401, 406–7).

But if any one psalm in the cluster has special weight in Milton's epic treatment of God's goodness, it is Psalm 103, the Psalm he three times cited in proving that quality in *Christian Doctrine*. Psalm 103 is full of interest to poet as well as to theologian. A *Te Deum*, where the call to praise God that opens and closes the hymn's particularly full development is couched in the form of a man's dialogue with his own soul, it combines poetical inwardness with intellectual comprehensiveness. Milton cited it to prove God's benevolence because of its encyclopedic examination of just that attribute. In the first five verses, the psalmist asks his soul to thank God for being concerned about the individual and specifies five acts of loving-kindness: God forgives man's sins, heals his diseases, rescues him from death, crowns his life with blessings to the end, and fulfills him. The comprehensive account of personal blessings is then balanced in the next four verses by an examination of God's goodness to the nation Israel in the past: the Lord made himself known to Moses, he was gracious to Israel, he chastised his people but restored them and pardoned their sins, he punished them less than they deserved. The next seven verses contrast God's justice, love, and eternity with man's transience. The last two call for all creation, especially the psalmist's soul, to thank and praise such a god. This copious psalm can be revisited whatever the occasion of God's supreme kindness in *Paradise Lost*.

God's benevolence is also understood in a process of enlightenment; the understanding can be narrated with an organic or progressive encyclopedism. A concept held by some, rejected by some, in time attained by some, has temporal and psychological aspects as well as propositional clarity. Milton is interested by those aspects too, and encyclopedically represents the creatures who can see the truth of God's supreme kindness, their failure or success to realize that truth, and the circumstances that can change their views. Immediately after the Son's full acknowledgment of God's supreme kindness, for example, Milton shows Satan standing on the top of Mount Niphates, bitterly conceding how all that goodness sours in him. Satan chooses to read God's love as a manifestation of a tyrannic desire for self-glorification and chooses also so to argue it before his human victims, as he has already argued it before his angelic peers.

The interest of the Psalter to a mind like Milton's when at work on the ideas and themes of *Paradise Lost*, then, is double. It is an interest in the Book of Psalms as the repository of revealed truths and as the register of the process of their acknowledgment. To illustrate the encyclopedism of psalm themes in *Paradise Lost*, we need only examine two of the ideas Milton considered that he held with special independence, his mortalism and his materialism—the ideas of death and of matter in relation to his reading of psalms. This use of *Christian Doctrine* as providing a skeleton to the constitutive ideas of the poem together with their scriptural sources is capable of extension to a variety of topics. Though the tractate cannot show what the poem "really means," it does show how the poet read Scripture where scriptural themes enter the poem.

Death as Adam's Punishment and Remedy

Milton discusses death in *Christian Doctrine* as part of God's judgment of Adam and the punishment of sin. In chapters 12, "Of the Punishment of Sin," 13, "Of the Death which is Called the Death of the Body," and 33, "Of Complete Glorification, also of Christ's Second Coming, the Resurrection of the Dead, and the Conflagration of this World," he brings together proof texts from the psalms and elsewhere to explain it. Death is a lamentable affair; when Adam laments it, he laments like a psalmist. But death is also a concept verified scripturally and understood existentially. As Milton describes it and has Michael explain it to Adam in *Paradise Lost*, its nature and meaning are thematically represented with encyclopedic copiousness; as Adam and Eve come to think about it, its moral significance is understood in encyclopedic progression. In *Christian Doctrine*, Milton brings together in support of an idea of death that he believes heterodox and a matter of opinion, not faith, Psalms 2, 6, 16, 17, 19, 22, 31, 39, 49, 78, 88, 89, 94, 102, 104, 115, 146, and 148. He makes in *Paradise Lost* out of that cluster of psalms an extended drama of the unfolding of the meaning of death, beginning with oriental and medieval mythology and allegory and concluding with a demythologized rationality that the great metaphysical poets of death in his own century would have thought thoroughly unimpressive.

Milton opens *Paradise Lost* giving death sovereignty over all human history and closes it limiting death's reign of terror to the kingdom of man's mind. At first its fearfulness extends everywhere in time, from "Mans First Disobedience" "till one greater Man / Restore us." But soon we learn with Lucifer that even fallen angels cannot die, and may infer that both time and death belong only to mankind. Moreover dread of death, the impetus in the creation of ornate mythologies, is shown controllable by mind or music:

> Anon [the universal Host of fallen Angels] move
> In perfect *Phalanx* to the *Dorian* mood
> Of Flutes and soft Recorders; such as rais'd
> To highth of noblest temper *Hero's old*
> Arming to Battel, and in stead of rage
> Deliberate valour breath'd, firm and unmov'd
> With dread of death to flight or foul retreat,
> Nor wanting power to mitigate and swage
> With solemn touches, troubl'd thoughts, and chase
> Anguish and doubt and fear and sorrow and pain
> *From mortal or immortal minds.*
> (1.549–59; my emphasis)

To "jocond Music," angels reduce themselves to "less then smallest Dwarfs" and enter Pandemonium, immortal not only in fact but in feeling (1.779). Milton thus synecdochally represents in Book I the treatment of death that he will develop in the remainder of the poem, intellectualizing and demystifying it.

Throughout the epic Milton will show that death consumes the entire human being, body and mind and soul; that death as the punishment of sin is transferred from mankind to his whole world of nature but that the subjective realization of death is limited to human beings in their rationality; and that in fact to understand death deprives it of power, on the purely physical level reducing it to a sleep, on the intellectual level proving it an instrumental good and an eventual nullity. That is to say, death is depicted in *Paradise Lost* encyclopedically as both a physical and mental event; it is understood progressively or historically first as an allegorical concept and then as a literal concept. Death presents to men an intellectual test; when it is properly understood the patience of heroic martyrdom becomes possible. The synonymity of human and mortal is explored across the poem until a reasonable human understanding arises of the unnatural naturalness of death.

Only human beings die. The decease of other created beings occurs encyclopedically in *Paradise Lost*, but that cessation is never generalized by the use of the word *death*. Milton's encyclopedism directs that in

Book X, for example, every order of creation from high to low prove mortal—from the "blasted Starrs" that "lookt wan" and the "Planets, Planet-strook" that "real Eclips / Then sufferd" on down (10.412–14). Created life is variously destroyed, while Milton dramatizes the alternative courses that God's messenger angels may take to adjust the cosmology of creation so as to produce the inimical climate of man's doom—trees are blasted, boughs and vines are lopped, beasts devour each other—but they do not usually "die." On the few occasions when animals or plants "die," face "death," or are shown "dead," Milton gives his readers a picture of natural mortality in the course of being understood by a rational thinker on the scene as the unnatural result of sin. Thus Pharao's "Cattel must of Rot and Murren die" (12.179) to compel a tyrant to know the truth of God. Offering a moral history of the word, its significance as the punishment for Adam's sin, Milton restricts his use of it scrupulously. When, for example, he resumes the allegory of Sin and Death in Book X, Sin within the Gates of Hell feels "new strength within [her] rise" and Death scents "carnage, prey innumerable" (10.243, 268). Together they build a bridge across chaos to the world, exult with Satan when they meet him on his way to Pandemonium, and enter their empire. Milton represents their entrance with a brief definition of death as an ethical phenomenon, distinct from the natural composting of imperishably recycled matter:

> they both betook them several wayes,
> Both to destroy, or unimmortal make
> All kinds.
> (10.610–12)

From the narrator's rational point of view the act of rendering unimmortal can be described as death only if it results from moral judgment. If animals "die," apart from the presence of rational interpreters, their "death" too has a suggestion of moral judgment or punishment; they "die" for turning on each other and their murderous impulse is allegorically represented by a random personification, so the poet amends his allegorical genealogy of death, giving Death for the first and last time in the poem a female sibling, Discord:[4]

> Discord first
> Daughter of Sin, among th'irrational,
> Death introduc'd through fierce antipathie:

[4] See MacCaffrey, Paradise Lost *as "Myth,"* 199. Also, an earlier version of some of the material in this chapter may be found in my own "Psalms and the Representation of Death in *Paradise Regained*," 133–44.

> Beast now with Beast gan war, and Fowle with Fowle,
> And Fish with Fish; to graze the Herb all leaving,
> Devourd each other.
> (10.707–12)

With encyclopedic thoroughness, the drama of the unfolding of the meaning of death presented synecdochally in Book I is played across *Paradise Lost.* In Book II, the universe of Hell is drawn as a locale of spiritual nullity in which Death lives as an allegorical personification. In Book III, the Father and Son meditate the justice of death as a punishment for sin and the mercy of it as a release from punishment. In Book IV, Adam and Eve, who have never seen it, speculate about its meaning as they vow the obedience that would prevent it. In Books VII and VIII, Raphael assures them that without such obedience, death is certain, by his repetitions augmenting their fear and anxiety. In Book IX, Satan lies about death, and Adam and Eve consider experimenting with it. In Book X, allegorical Death steps in brief triumph onto Earth, Adam with experience reconsiders its meaning, Eve proposes sterility or suicide to cheat it, and God denounces ultimate death on Death, his instrument but not his creation. In Book XI, the Son pronounces the judgment of death on the human pair, and in that book and the last of the poem, Michael displays it, expounds its ethical role, and writes its final history.

Milton unfolds his drama of death in a sequence of scenes, showing how death came into the world, what is to be thought of it, what in the end it will amount to. The sequence has both spatial and temporal ramifications. Seen at first allegorically and concretely in the depths of Hell, then predicted judicially and doctrinally in Heaven as conquered by the Son's heroic self-sacrifice, death next enters the garden to be experienced psychologically and physically, then prophetically attacks the future history of the world, and finally is literally understood to be of small moment and religiously understood as a beginning not an end of life. The lesson of death is a lesson of patience and temperance, contained within the large paideutic journey of Adam and Eve, developed like other lessons in the poem, in a pattern of increasing illumination and reasonableness.

Already in *Christian Doctrine* Milton proved a concept of death containing, if not evolution, at least degrees. In the tractate the degrees are known synchronically; they become in the epic a narrative of understanding. He writes of the entry of death into the world and of its stages[5] that the first stage is experienced with the feeling of "guilti-

[5] *YP* 6:393, 394, 399, 414; the psalm verses are cited on *YP* 6:396.

ness," "a sort of partial death or prelude to death in us"; the second produces a darkening of right reason and enfeebling of the will, which does not obliterate all awareness of God, but creates a defectiveness in mankind. Two psalm verses prove that "traces of the divine image still remain . . . not wholly extinguished by this spiritual death": Psalm 19.1, "The heavens declare the glory of God," shows the persistent hearing of the declaration even after the Fall; Psalm 78.8, "a generation *that* set not their heart aright," shows how weak the traces of divine similitude have become. In *Paradise Lost*, Milton represents Adam's dawning sense of the protraction of death, feared as an endless dying:

> But say
> That Death be not one stroak, as I suppos'd,
> Bereaving sense, but endless miserie
> From this day onward, which I feel begun
> Both in me, and without me, and so last
> To perpetuitie; Ay me, that fear
> Comes thundring back with dreadful revolution
> On my defensless head; both Death and I
> Am found Eternal, and incorporate both.
> (10.808–16)

He is soon to understand death as neither that eternal protraction of misery nor the sudden blow with which, when he remembered his creation, God seemed to threaten him (8.329–33).

When Milton takes up the third degree of death, the death of the body, he characterizes it as the death of the whole person—body, soul, and spirit, the crucial proposition in his unorthodox mortalism. He shows that David believed that the whole of man dies and cites Psalms 6, 88, 115, 39, and 146 to prove that all men disappear into silence and the void.[6] Adam has been afraid to die and then more afraid that all of him cannot die. He must learn David's certainty of mortality, a certainty exclusive to human beings. (Belial's dread of death [2.146–54] revisits Shakespeare, not the Psalter.) Since Milton's mortalism is contentious, he contends for it in *Christian Doctrine*. He confutes possible objections that some part of the whole man might be exempt from death by adducing psalms to show the death of the soul, even of the

[6] *YP* 6:401–2. "Psal. vi.5: *there is no remembrance of you in death, who shall praise you in the tomb*, and similarly lxxxviii.11–13, cxv.17: *the dead do not praise Jehovah*, and xxxix.14: *before I go away and am no more*, and cxlvi.2: *I will praise my God while I still exist*. Clearly if he had believed that his soul would survive and would be received into heaven without delay he would not have used this kind of argument, because he would know that he would soon take his flight to a place where he could praise God unceasingly."

soul of the Messiah, and then to show the death of the spirit. The cluster of psalms is extended thus to include Psalms 146.4, 22.21, 78.50, 89.49, 94.17, 16.10, 49.9, 13, 15–16, 104.29–30, and 31.6.

The fourth degree of death is eternal death, the punishment of the damned. In explaining it, Milton assembles citations to Psalms 17.14–15, 49.15–16, 2.8–9, 148.6, and 102.27 to prove that the resurrection of the dead was believed even in the period of the law and to describe the death of the world in a final conflagration. Knowing his views on Christ's Second Coming, the resurrection of the dead, and the conflagration of the world to be less contentious than his mortalism, Milton treats them more briefly. About apocalypse he is terse, or as terse as is consonant with encyclopedic completeness: having set forth "as much as it is useful for us to know about the end of the world and the conflagration," he draws a veil over what "does not really concern us."[7]

In the tractate, Milton's logic of death is argued from Scripture, and psalms prominently buttress each stage. Once his pool of references has been established, he uses the same psalm material in his epic discovery and history of death.[8] The Book of Psalms records how human beings feel about death with encyclopedic copiousness; with the possible exception of Job, no other book of the Bible gives so rich an account of the progressive comprehension of mortality.

Hell's universe of death (2.619–28) draws its remoteness from the land of the living; its dust, aridity, and darkness, its pestilence and unnatural corruption, its joylessness and silence from the psalm proof texts 6.5, 16.10; 22.1, 88.10, 104.29; 49.9, 78.50; 88.10; and lastly 94.17 and 146.4. The personification of death as an allegorical figure, hungry and with a rapacious hand (2.787–809), appears in Psalms 49.14 and 89.48. Christ's faithful offer to die for mankind, his certainty that he will not be left in the grave, and God's promise of resurrection (3.210–338) editors have glossed from Psalms 16.10 and 88.13 from within the psalms gathered together in the treatment of death in *Christian Doctrine*, and 40.6 and 68.18 from outside that cluster; one might add from the cluster 31.4, 49.15, and 94.17. The confirmation that death, unknown in Eden, is promised from the moment of the Fall

[7] See Patrides, "Renaissance and Modern Thought on the Last Things," 169–85, and " 'Something like Prophetick Strain,' " in *The Apocalypse in English Renaissance Thought and Literature*, 207–37. See *YP* 6:627–28.

[8] No psalm echoes have been seen in the key death scenes: 2.619–28, 787–809; 4.425–32; 7.544–47; 9.685–702, 782–84, 953–54, 1000–1004; 10.230–323, 585–640, 706–14, 771–820, 850–59; 11.36–44, 61–66, 462–554; 12.392–435; but Psalms 16.10–11, 40.6–8, 68.18, 88.13 have been seen in the Son's offer to die for man (3.210–338). Sims, *The Bible in Milton's Epics*, 262.

(4.425–32 and 7.544–47) comes from Psalms 39.13 and 104.30. The entrance of death into the human world, wounding nature, and his readiness to eat his way through creation (10.230–323 and 585–640) has the authority of Psalms 49 and 89. Adam's death-wishful meditation (10.720–863) touches on themes from 6.5, 18.5, 88.10, and 89.48; Eve's contrite but sinful proposal of sexual abstinence and suicide to thwart death is Milton's nonbiblical invention, but her anxieties about annihilation derive from 115.17 and 146.4. Adam's responsive contrition (10.1048–53) recalls the protevangelium but also the hope of awakening from death in 16.10, 49.9, and 78.50. And finally, Christ's confirmation of his promise to destroy death (11.36–44), the Father's accord with it (11.61–66), and Michael's narration of the Crucifixion, with his conversion of sleeplike death into the gate of life (12.392–435), recall those hopeful psalms, together with 17.14–15.

Copious psalm reference as the sign of encyclopedic biblical knowledge was considered by Milton valuable in itself, and was so regarded by his earliest readers who made the identification of such biblicism an object of critical interest. For the modern reader, perhaps, a stronger interest lies in progressive encyclopedism, where psalm texts play a role in the drama of *paideia*. That progression exhibits two distinctive views of death, one of which is allegorical, the other natural. First the allegorical is presented in detail in the poem; then it is replaced by the literal, which, like the "single sense" of Scripture, is "a combination of the historical and the typological" (*YP* 6:581). The evolution of a believer's concept of death is present in the epic because Milton thought that he found it in his authorizing texts, the psalms themselves.

Only two psalms in Milton's cluster personify death and so authorize the allegory of Sin and Death in *Paradise Lost*. The psalmists most frequently resort to metaphors of place—death seen as pit or dusty spot or silence region or dim abode to which a man goes and does not return—in explaining death; death as the terminus of a final journey is found in Psalms 6, 16, 22, 88, 115, and 146. A few psalmists represent death as a change in consciousness—as the way time ends in Psalm 39, as a sort of sleep in Psalm 17. More show it as the result of divine or human violence, what God does through his instruments of fire, sword, plague, rod and the like to those who displease him (Psalms 2, 78, 94), or what man does, God not preventing it (Psalm 31). Only Psalms 49 and 89 personify death.

The reluctance to personify recalls how Judaism suppressed the death stories of earlier Semitic religions, such as the Canaanite mythic struggle between Baal and Mot, or Death, Baal's defeat, his resurrection and ultimate victory over Mot. That myth is unthinkable in the

Jewish faith, where the "living God" is not the God once dead but now alive again but the God who cannot die. As Habakkuk puts it, "*Art* thou not from everlasting, O Lord my God, mine Holy One?" (1.12). Hence personification of death is exceedingly rare. Psalm 68 personifies at a remove, referring to a battle with death and a victory over him under the alias "captivity," in the verse "thou hast led captivity captive."[9] And if Psalms 49 and 89 residually authorize the allegory of Sin and Death, they also prefigure its effacement.

Milton's allegory, of course, blends classical and biblical materials. Classical sources allow him first to represent in Satan's encounter with Sin and Death the epic hero's encounter with the guardians of the underworld and to make that heroic encounter both antiheroic or evil and unheroic or bathetic. The scene is rich in irony. Satan's grandeur flares out as he approaches Hell's gate but is undermined when he learns from Sin how she and her son Death came to be assigned its guardianship. She has to inform him, for he has somehow forgotten, that he conceived and bore a daughter, Sin, in circumstances parallel to the ancient myth of Athene springing fully formed from the head of Zeus. Since that myth itself was regularly interpreted by theologians as an analogue of the Father's generation of the Son, Milton's reduplication of it in Hell treats the triad of Satan, Sin, and Death as an infernal parody of the Trinity. Satan also learns from Sin how she seduced him; bore their son, Death, who raped her; and conceived from his assault a pack of dogs who continually rekennel in her womb to eat her bowels, set on by the son whose birth deformed her. All of this lurid story Satan hears as news, having forgotten his "love," and rejects and detests her and their offspring at sight. Nonetheless, he at once grasps the possibilities of turning Death against mankind, the "race of upstart Creatures" (2.834). Satan's revulsion, concealment of it, and prudent rewooing of Sin to unlock Hell's gate has attracted much interpretation, a good deal indicating the richness and variety of Milton's classical and literary sources and the variations he plays upon them.[10]

To that mythological material, rich in potential parody and irony, Milton adds biblical material, susceptible of moralization and dramatic variation but hostile to allegory, which seems to encode polytheism and idolatry. The makers of the Psalter reject personifications that

[9] Jacob wrestles with an angel, who at the conclusion of their fight says to him, "Thy name shall be called no more Jacob, but Israel" (Gen. 32.28). That angel's identity is so carefully veiled that it is equally possible to identify him as God (Jacob's new name, Israel, means "he [who] has striven with God"), or Death, or perhaps even Time.

[10] See Kerrigan, *The Sacred Complex*, 122–23; Lieb, *Poetics of the Holy*, 9–11; Quilligan, *Milton's Spenser*, 84–91.

point to older idolatries and offer a pious account of death. To personify death summons again the dying vegetation god, slain in a mortal combat with Death himself. When Jeremiah, for example, denounces death to Jerusalem for reverting to the Canaanite worship of Baal, he appropriately does so by personifying death, since Mot or Death is Baal's natural enemy. "Because they have . . . walked after the imagination of their own heart, and after Baalim, which their fathers taught them" (9:13–14), they will be destroyed by the death Baal-worshipers imagine. The Lord instructs "the mourning women" how to lament the death that punishes their idolatry in one of the rare Old Testament personifications, death's avatar the reaper who cuts down the children of the vegetation God (Jer. 9.21):

> For death is come up into our windows, *and* is entered into our palaces, to cut off the children from without, *and* the young men from the streets.

The triumph of the Yahwist conception of an eternal God forbids the worshiper to represent uncritically the division of the universe between God and Death, with whom he must at first unsuccessfully struggle, although he may in the end enjoy an annual or even a final resurrection. References to the dying god abound in Scripture, but they manifestly denounce the notion.

To personify Death as God's enemy in the Old Testament period is to repeat the idolatry of earlier Semitic faiths. But not to envisage Death as God's enemy creates a problem in the New Testament period. Unless Death came into the world hostile to God, human beings may consider that God made him. Hence some teachers in the New Testament devised obliquely allegorical parables to take Death off God's hands, and of them Milton draws particularly on James. James 1.13–15 reads as follows:

> Let no man say when he is tempted, I am tempted of God: for God cannot be tempted with evil, neither tempteth he any man: But every man is tempted, when he is drawn away of his own lust, and enticed. Then when lust hath conceived, it bringeth forth sin: and sin, when it is finished, bringeth forth death.

God did not make death; the lust of human beings made it, in an immoral act of mental evil. James offers Milton the outline of an allegory of sin; the allegory exonerates God from afflicting his creation with death by implicating his creatures, but while it gives Milton an allegorical scenario, it does not fill in the content of its relationships.

The allegorical scene at Hell gate presents not only the original of the force that "unimmortalizes" Creation but also the dynamic that deforms an archetypal family. The relationship of the triad is not only a parody of the Trinity, as both Satan and Sin luxuriatingly indicate in appropriating the language of theology to describe their own transactions—"Thy self in me thy perfect image viewing" (2.764), to "Reign / At thy right hand voluptuous" (2.868–69)—it conspicuously perverts what will be involved in the loving relationship of Adam and Eve.[11] The attachments are all merely appetitive, the appetites are fulfilled unpleasurably, the sexuality is contaminated with other motives. Satan fathers Sin when he rebels as a son of God against his own Father. His fatherhood lacks tenderness, and his daughter Sin lacks a mother, so much exclusive maleness telling for sterility, not potency. He fathers Death through an incestuous seduction, but his sexual feelings move through indifference to induced lust to oblivious repression to nausea and, later, to voyeuristic envy. His partner loathes and fears their son who has raped her in hatred, who would cannibalize her if he dared, and who intends parricide. Her children-grandchildren are vicious animals eating her entrails. No detail could be further from the "wedded Love" of Adam and Eve in which "Relations dear, and all the Charities / Of Father, Son, and Brother first were known" (4.756–57). The denunciation of "Death," as it evokes that family, on the human pair originating all society, prophesies the poisoning of the well of human feeling.

Milton concludes the allegorical presentation of Sin and Death in Book X with a scene given from two perspectives. The first perspective is that of the tragic narrator as witness, who assigns to Sin and Death in dialogue, at first together and then with Satan, the development of the action, but makes his own reactions clear. They plan the building of the bridge from Hell to Earth as a heroic work, "a Monument / Of merit high to all th'infernal Host" (10.258–59), as well as useful in "Easing thir passage hence, for intercourse, / Or transmigration" (10.260–61). A great architectural achievement is a traditional ingredient of epic, but the narrator economically indicates that their achievement is far less heroic than the fabrication of the universe: they by "wondrous Art / Pontifical" (10.312–13) make a "new wondrous Pontifice" (10.348). The tautology and the anticlerical pun fix their skill well below that by which chaos was divinely ordered, not simply overbuilt. Standing at Hell's foot of the bridge, Sin and Death receive

[11] See Broadbent, *Paradise Lost: Books I and II*, 44–46; Kerrigan, *The Sacred Complex*, 102–25; DiSalvo, "Blake Encountering Milton," 143–84; and Quilligan, *Milton's Spenser*, 84–91.

Satan on his way back to Pandemonium; he dispatches them to exercise dominion over the earth, and he himself returns to triumph before "great consulting Peers," "What remains, ye Gods, / But up and enter now into full bliss" (10.502–3). The first allegorical episode is completed when Sin and Death arrive meantime on earth and commence to destroy its creatures. And then the second witness, God himself, takes over the exposition of the last scene in the allegory of death.

Between the representation of Sin and Death in Book II and in Book X, Milton silently drops the hellhounds, the offspring of Death's rape of his mother Sin. They entered the allegory, editors tell us, by way of Ovid and Spenser, their classical antecedents the girdle of barking dogs Circe made of Scylla's legs and fastened around her naked belly, their model the misshapen spawn of Spenser's Errour who crept into her mouth when frightened. Like them, Milton's dogs kennel within their mother; unlike them, his violate her womb. Spenser's monstrous creatures destroy themselves in suicidal matricide, but Milton's hellhounds simply do not accompany their parents to Earth; they were not real enough to Milton to make the trip in their allegorical form. Nonetheless, when God takes up the exposition, they are present in metaphor if not in fact, present because Milton replaces his fiction of death from within the psalm cluster proving his mortalism.

God witnesses the end of the allegory of Sin and Death. He calls Sin and Death by the name earlier given to their progeny, as he explains to the angels the destruction they wreak on Eden:

> See with what heat these *Dogs of Hell* advance
> To waste and havoc yonder World, which I
> So fair and good created, and had still
> Kept in that State, had not the folly of Man
> Let in these wastful Furies.
> (10.616–20; my emphasis)

He acknowledges his permission—"I suffer them to enter and possess / A place so heav'nly" and he outlines his motives:

> I call'd and drew them thither
> My Hell-hounds, to lick up the draff and filth
> Which mans polluting Sin with taint hath shed
> On what was pure, till cramm'd and gorg'd, nigh burst
> With suckt and glutted offal, at one sling
> Of thy victorious Arm, well-pleasing Son,
> Both *Sin*, and *Death*, and yawning *Grave* at last
> Through *Chaos* hurld, obstruct the mouth of Hell

For ever, and seal up his ravenous Jawes.
Then Heav'n and Earth renewd shall be made pure
To sanctitie that shall receive no staine:
Till then the Curse pronounc't on both precedes.
(10.629–40)

Sin and Death are "real" in God's explanation, but Milton modulates from a simple personification allegory into another governing mythic mode and commences the historicizing and typologizing of death. An authoritative voice announces a different plot. Satan did not generate Sin and Death in despite of God, any more than he was literally "self-made and self-begot," though ethically that is the case. The finalities that the created being imagines are no more finalities than the origins he imagines are origins. Nothing happens anywhere unbeknownst to or unpermitted by God, but his permission is not sanction. By allegorizing the origin of Sin and Death, Milton has removed the onus of actually creating them from God onto his creatures; he has then removed the onus of instrumentally creating them through his consent by redefining their functions in eschatological terms. The horror in the personification of Sin and Death is reduced through the new animal references by which they become only metaphorical "dogs of death." For God's version, replacing personification allegory with historical eschatology, Milton revisits the psalms of death.

The "dogs of death" came from Psalm 22.15–20; Milton's God refers to that Psalm because it typologically figures the Crucifixion to establish a new theory of death. The psalmist complains, "thou hast brought me into the dust of death. For dogs have compassed me," describes his sufferings in a prefiguration of the Crucifixion, and ends, "O my strength, haste thee to help me. Deliver my soul from the sword; my darling from the power of the dog." *Christian Doctrine* gives that psalm the common Reformation gloss: it predicts the humiliation of the Son. The Geneva Bible, for example, explains, "under his owne person [David] setteth forthe the figure of Christ, whome he did forese by the Spirit of prophecie."[12] An alternative to that reading would see in the psalm vestiges of the repressed pagan ritual, commemorating the annual humiliation of the living god who dies but revives to be honored in a religious service offering a votive sacrifice. Milton converts the suppressed pagan reading of Psalm 22 as containing that vestigial rite into the conclusion of the Luciferian epic in *Paradise Lost*.[13]

Milton contrasts Christ's understanding of Psalm 22 with Satan's

[12] *The Geneva Bible: a facsimile of the 1650 edition*, 239.

[13] See Lieb, *The Poetics of the Holy*, 110; Thickstun, *Fictions of the Feminine*, 60–70.

experience when he returns to Hell to glory in his heroic destruction of mankind. Satan praises his own achievement to the fallen angels in affording them human victims so that they now may enjoy Earth as their empire. While he speaks, he is "punisht in the shape he sin'd, / According to his doom" (10.516–17): he and his followers are changed into serpents. They leave Pandemonium as serpents, go out into the fields of Hell, and eat there the bitter fruit of a nearby grove. At that moment, Milton displays the skepticism about the serpent epic within his human epic so as to contrast the Luciferian false heroism with the true heroism of Christianity. He treats the story of Satan as so merely fictional that many versions of its conclusion may be devised. In the end, no one knows what becomes of Lucifer and the defiant angels, after their metamorphosis into their figurative shape. Some romancers tell one kind of story, some tell another. In one pagan version, all those snakes are

> Yearly enjoynd, some say, to undergo
> This annual humbling certain number'd days,
> To dash thir pride, and joy for Man seduc't.
> (10.575–77)

That version is what a carnal or literal reading of Psalm 22 would suppose to be what Death does to every god. But that pagan version is not the only full-blown myth that heathen romancers made up about the Antagonist and his serpent peers:

> some tradition they dispers'd
> Among the Heathen of thir purchase got,
> And Fabl'd how the Serpent, whom they calld
> *Ophion* with *Eurynome*, the wide-
> Encroaching *Eve* perhaps, had first the rule
> Of high *Olympus*, thence by *Saturn* driv'n
> And *Ops*, ere yet *Dictaean Jove* was born.
> (10.578–84)

Whatever tale that human tradition offers to show the triumph of the Antagonist in devising death for man or god, it is both false and not worth Milton's finishing.

Milton demythologizes the allegory of Sin and Death by subjecting Satan's version to God's correction and by declining to give any decisive end to a diabolical yarn. The true meaning of death in a historical narrative of attested validity was begun back in Book III by the offer of the Son to die for man; it is completed by Michael's instruction in how the incarnation and Crucifixion redeem. In the true account,

Psalm 22 read typologically plays a crucial role. Its prayer, "haste thee to help me," joins with the belief of Psalm 16.10, "For thou wilt not leave my soul in hell; neither wilt thou suffer thine Holy One to see corruption," and with faithful answers to the existential questioning of Psalm 88.10–12, "Wilt thou shew wonders to the dead? shall the dead arise *and* praise thee? Selah. Shall thy lovingkindness be declared in the grave? *or* thy faithfulness in destruction? Shall thy wonders be known in the dark? and thy righteousness in the land of forgetfulness?" From the combination of those three psalms Milton establishes the mercifulness as well as the justice of death as man's punishment. That brings to its end the encyclopedic drama as well as the encyclopedic taxonomy of death in *Paradise Lost*.

Matter and Creation

In writing *Christian Doctrine*, Milton put great stock in another unorthodox concept, not a necessary article of faith but a view he thought substantiated by scripture. He argued that God created all things both visible and invisible out of a preexistent material which he produced from himself, some time between his generation of the Son and his creation of heaven and the angels.[14] He thought this matter was initially chaotic and disordered, but that God tamed it into useful good elements. From them he created the invisible realm of heaven and the angels and the visible cosmos and man, making the invisible well before the six days on which he created the visible world. In the tractate, Milton plainly put the principal arguments against his viewpoint by the orthodox teachers of the view that God made creation out of nothing and initiated time by the creation of the visible world. But first he defined creation as "the act by which GOD THE FATHER PRODUCED EVERYTHING THAT EXISTS BY HIS WORD AND SPIRIT, that is, BY HIS WILL, IN ORDER TO SHOW THE GLORY OF HIS POWER AND GOODNESS," and proved that definition by scriptural texts including Psalms 33.6, 9; 148.5; 135.6; and 19.2, 3. He then distinguished creation into "THINGS INVISIBLE" and "THINGS VISIBLE" and proved the materiality and history of both by scriptural texts including Psalms 7.6; 8.6; 16.11; 33.6, 9, and 15; 51.5; 97.7; 103.20; 104.4, 29–30; and 148.5.[15] When Milton wrote *Paradise Lost*, he had to hand, then, a cluster of eleven psalms, read as containing two opposing interpretations of the materiality and history of creation, his own and the more orthodox. Although both readings

[14] See Kelley, "Introduction," *YP* 6:87–90.

[15] *YP* 6:300, 301–5, 311, 311–25.

were developed to honor God as the creator and to shield his omnipotence and benevolence from dishonor, the very theological controversy gave the poet reason to treat the development of insight into creation encyclopedically as a narrative of the achievement of understanding.

The thrust of epic toward encyclopedic copia is the impulse that causes Milton in *Paradise Lost* to discuss or represent creation in ample detail. To the angel Uriel is entrusted the first description of the act of creation, as he points Earth out to Lucifer in disguise (3.708–34), a description of abstract causality becoming the concrete invisible and visible universe. To Raphael the teacher is entrusted the complementary second description, an encyclopedic natural history of creation in the order in which it came into being.

The progressive encyclopedism, however, is as little absent from the treatment of Creation as from the treatment of death. Once more Milton finds his own heterodoxy represented in Scripture and the orthodox view a misreading of Scripture. The opposition becomes the basis of the encyclopedically detailed account of God's creation of the visible and invisible universe. Satan, the skeptical literalist, does not of course espouse the orthodox theory of creation *ex nihilo*; rather, he opposes to Milton's understanding of creation *ex Deo* a false view of spontaneous material creation. As in the narrative of understanding death, psalms are implicated in the history of understanding Creation. The principal scenes in the unfolding of the meaning of Creation are Raphael's comparing the development of man to a tree growing as the symbol of the Great Chain of Being in 5.469–503, Satan's denial of his creation in 5.853–69, his apostrophe to the Tree of Knowledge in 9.679–733, and Adam's recollection of his creation and that of Eve in 8.250–480.

The eleven psalms Milton adduced in *Christian Doctrine* form a clearly bifurcated group. Almost half of them—that is, Psalms 8, 19, 33, 104, and 148—are self-evident glorifications of God as the Creator and would be cited by anyone exploring the subject of Creation. While Milton does not include in that subset such other creation psalms as 89, 94, 139, and 146, his group is nonetheless comprehensive and thorough in the orders of being it cites and in the creation history it works out, a history he finds consonant with that of Genesis and Job.[16] From that subset he develops the encyclopedic account of Creation in Book

[16] "The creation of the world and of its individual parts is narrated in Gen. i. It is described in Job xxvi.7 etc. and xxxviii, and in various passages of the Psalms and Prophets: Psal. xxxiii. 6, 9 and civ and cxlviii.5; Prov. viii.26, etc.; Amos iv.13; II Pet. iii.5." *YP* 6:315–16.

VII. The other half of the psalms in the creation cluster—Psalms 7, 16, 51, 97, 103, and 135—all relate to interpretative disputes concerning when God made the invisible creation and of what he made the visible world. Milton used those psalms in *Christian Doctrine* to analyze two doctrinal issues that in *Paradise Lost* Satan will bring into question. Thus Milton noticed Psalms 7 and 51 in order to argue that in the original creation of man, God made both the body and the soul, and gave to the material soul the properties of the body: its appetites and its "apprehensibility." He went on to argue that each new human soul is naturally generated by parents and neither created daily by the immediate act of God nor provided from a stockpile of previously existent souls. He quoted Psalms 16, 97, and 103 to prove that God, having begotten the Son by decree, thus initiating time as the measure of motion, created the angels and the highest heaven, his throne and the dwelling place where he and the heavenly beings enjoy perpetual bliss, light, and glory. He went on to claim that God created these "things invisible" well before the first day of Creation on which he made all "things visible." He quoted Psalm 135 to prove that God created all things, invisible and visible, freely and of his own will—to prove that is, that the Holy Spirit played no role in Creation and that the Son played only the subordinate role of the Father's agent in creating.

The copia of creation is shown in two scenes. Uriel, looking down upon the whole cosmology of the created world, praises God as Creator of it, in a hymn formed according to the pattern of hymns deduced from the Book of Psalms.[17] Praising God as Creator, Uriel tells Lucifer, "now a stripling Cherube,"

> I saw when at his Word the formless Mass,
> This worlds material mould, came to a heap:
> *Confusion* heard his voice, and wilde uproar
> Stood rul'd, stood vast infinitude confin'd;
> Till at his second bidding darkness fled,
> Light shon, and order from disorder sprung:
> Swift to thir several Quarters hasted then
> The cumbrous Elements, Earth, Flood, Aire,
> Fire,
> And this Ethereal quintessence of Heav'n
> Flew upward, spirited with various forms,
> That rowld orbicular, and turnd to Starrs.
> (3.708–18)

[17] See Chapter 3, pp. 148–56.

By combining a generalized Platonic enthusiasm with his adaptations of Genesis, Job, and Psalms, Uriel almost avoids materialist or historical controversy. Creation was made by stages: first God by "his Word" organized the "formless Mass" of the world; then by "his second bidding" darkness disappeared and light emerged. Uriel treats this scriptural version of the organization of chaos to a Platonic reading from the *Timaeus*: the "formless Mass" of "[t]his worlds material mould" contained the "cumbrous Elements" and an "Ethereal quintessence" or weightless fifth element.[18] When the heavier elements were organized, that aether rose to form an imperishable heaven and its stars, including the sun on which they stand above the atmosphere. At God's "second bidding," darkness withdrew and those orbs gave light. Although Uriel refers to the matter out of which the visible universe is made, he says nothing of its source; although he confirms the prior existence of an angelic order, he says nothing of its making or the earlier history of Creation. Uriel alludes to the five creation psalms—Psalm 33.6, 9, "By the word of the Lord were the heavens made. . . . For he spake, and it was *done*"; Psalm 8.3, "the moon and the stars, which thou hast ordained"; Psalm 19.1, "the firmament sheweth his handiwork"; Psalm 104.5, "*Who* laid the foundations of the earth"; and Psalm 148.5, "for he commanded, and they were created." Milton devised his hymn as an uncontentious preliminary to Raphael's full account of Creation in Book VII.

Raphael's account is fuller, richer in psalm materials, and a good deal bolder. He begins setting the scene for Creation as Christ returns to the Father, victorious from driving the fallen angels down to Hell. The Father greets him with his decision to create the visible world and to make "out of one man a Race / Of men innumerable" (7.155–56). He charges the Son to work according to his plan, and he then retires from the business of Creation, apparently at the same time withdrawing himself from space—"nor vacuous the space. / Though I uncircumscrib'd my self retire" (7.169–70)—so as to leave behind him matter, the stuff out of which Christ will summon up all the orders of the visible universe. While the angels hymn the benevolence of the decision, its "good will / To future men" in ordaining "Good out of evil to create" and "thence diffuse / His good to Worlds and Ages infinite," the Son surveys uncreation, "Outrageous as a Sea, dark, wasteful, wilde," and begins to order it (7.190–91, 212). The Son stills chaos, draws out the golden compasses and circumscribes the visible universe, and thus distinguishes heaven from earth:

[18] See Samuel, *Plato and Milton*, 39.

> Thus God the Heav'n created, thus the Earth,
> Matter unform'd and void: Darkness profound
> Cover'd th'Abyss: but on the watrie calme
> His brooding wings the Spirit of God outspred,
> And vital vertue infus'd, and vital warmth
> Throughout the fluid Mass, but downward purg'd
> The black tartareous cold Infernal dregs
> Adverse to life: then founded, then conglob'd
> Like things to like, the rest to several place
> Disparted, and between spun out the Air,
> And Earth self-ballanc't on her Center hung.
> (7.232–42)

Milton's procedure from this moment on is to pluck from Scripture each brief creating command and expand it into a picture of natural fecundity, while energetically and spontaneously the individual orders of creation come into existence to fulfill their being. But the scene he has just represented both supports and challenges the view of a spontaneously generative, fruitful, life-producing, and boniform material, the existence of which it announces. Matter—to which the Son brings silence and peace—in itself tumults in apparent rebellion, recalling the consistency of the stuff through which Satan "swims or sinks, or wades, or creeps, or flyes," that "dark / Illimitable Ocean without bound," "the wilde expanse," "the shock / Of fighting Elements" (2.950, 891–92, 1014, 1014–15), matter congruent with the stuff of the fiery lake on which Satan regained consciousness, "a fiery Deluge, fed / With ever-burning Sulphur," "o'rewhelm'd / With Floods and Whirlwinds of tempestuous fire," "A Universe of death, which God by curse / Created evil" (1.68–69, 76–77; 2.622–23). It is the task of the overarching encyclopedic narrative of Creation, affording the reader the opportunity to revisit the experiences and conclusions of the fallen as well as the unfallen, to accommodate both views of Creation. The two senses Milton gives us of matter, its danger and its wholesomeness, are both scriptural: one sense is pitted against the other in *Paradise Lost*, until the moral significance of natural matter be established.

Meanwhile the Son creates on behalf of God the Father as though matter were instinct with its own sexual vitality and he has only to lift the baton for the music of each sphere to sound. The first "Day Eev'n and Morn" is the "Birth-day of Heav'n and Earth" and brings light into being. In Uriel's narrative, Milton has already taught that the visible universe is a stage of creation preceded in time by the more spiritous creation of the invisible universe; some apparent problems of chronology—for example, that visible light appears before the sun, stars, and planets are made—are solved by the recollection that a transfusion of invisible light from heaven would have illuminated the scene of this creation. The second day God produces the firmament and divides the waters; the third he gathers together the waters into one place to let the dry land appear and covers the land with verdure.[19] Milton renders the instinctive, independent fecundity of creation through a series of benignly sexual allusions—Earth, for example, is first seen "in the Womb . . . Of Waters, Embryon immature" and next shown softened by the ocean "to conceave, / Satiate with genial moisture" (7.281–82). But he also works with the greatest care to bring together what Genesis, Job, and Psalms have to say about the originary acts of God in Creation. So he continues:

> when God said
> Be gather'd now ye Waters under Heav'n
> Into one place, and let dry Land appeer.
> Immediately the Mountains huge appeer
> Emergent, and thir broad bare backs upheave
> Into the Clouds.
> (7.282–87)

Milton fits together spontaneous generation and creative act, along with the scriptural texts authorizing both: Genesis 1.9, "And God said, Let the waters under the heaven be gathered together unto one place, and let the dry *land* appear"; Psalm 104.6–8, "the waters stood above the mountains. At thy rebuke they fled; at the voice of thy thunder they hasted away. They go up by the mountains; they go down by the valleys unto the place which thou hast founded for them"; and Job 38.8, 11, "Or *who* shut up the sea with doors, when it brake forth, *as if* it had issued out of the womb? . . . And said, Hitherto shalt thou come, but no further: and here shall thy proud waves be stayed?" The pleasure Milton proposes by his encyclopedic elaboration of the hexameron consists in detail after detail of natural vitality, grounded in the repeated and persistent identification of God's omnific Word in every act of creation.

The creation of man in Raphael's narrative opens onto the second kind of encyclopedism, however, in which the questions about Creation—when or of what it was made—give way to the question of Creation—what it means, what it says of the Creator. The God who makes the visible universe and proclaims that it is for man lives in an

[19] See Gallagher, "Creation in Genesis and in *Paradise Lost*," 163–204.

invisible and distant universe, perhaps so unlike that of man and so incommensurate with man's normal scale that he cannot deduce God from it. Perhaps only in the extremest or least human manifestations of nature can God be revealed; perhaps the Book of Nature can convey only the distance between Maker and man, not the sympathy. To place Job and Psalms so scrupulously in relation with Genesis in communicating Creation is to pose the possibility of its nonmeaning quite as plainly as its meaningfulness.

The education of Adam into the meaning of material creation begins with a brief philosophical lesson by Raphael. He opens his course by suspending scriptural history altogether and by working out instead an analogy between vegetative growth and order in nature. To inculcate the proposition that God made the universe out of himself as its boniform matter and arranged it in a hierarchical chain of spiritual being, Raphael sets forth the great chain of being with abstract synchronic clarity (5.469–79). He then translates that synchronic representation of Creation into a simple image of the history of natural evolution. First he reverses the order of creation from high to low that the great chain of being gave Adam into a picture of growth from low to high, from root to flower to fruit. Then he tracks the alimentary path of fruit from animal to intellectual beings, and draws an analogy between nutrition and human fulfillment (5.496–503). Neither the language nor the imagery of psalms is employed in this lesson on the relationship of body and mind, men and angels, the Creator and his Creation. Not even Raphael's concrete image of the fruitful tree is quite psalmic, although a fruitful tree is familiar in psalms.[20] When Raphael describes a growing tree—

So from the root
Springs lighter the green stalk, from thence the leaves
More aerie, last the bright consummate floure
Spirits odorous breathes: flours and thir fruit.
(5.479–82)

—the tree is the Pauline tree of which Christ is the "first fruits," by way of the analogy between the burial of seed planting and the resurrection of new growth where the body "sown a natural body" is raised "a spiritual body."[21] Behind Paul's spiritual tree are those trees in the

[20] See pp. 98–103, above.

[21] I Cor. 15.35–44: "But some *man* will say, How are the dead raised up? and with what body do they come? *Thou* fool, that which thou sowest is not quickened, except it die: And that which thou sowest, thou sowest not that body that shall be, but bare grain, it may chance of wheat, or of some other *grain*: But God giveth it a body as it hath

Creation (Psalm 104.12, 16–17), where God makes in Nature habitations for each order of creature, habitations each at once accepts as its own:

> By them shall the fowls of the heaven have their habitation, *which* sing among the branches . . .
>
> The trees of the Lord are full *of sap*; the cedars of Lebanon, which he hath planted;
>
> Where the birds make their nests: *as for* the stork, the fir trees *are* her house.

But by not evoking the language and imagery of the creation psalms, Raphael effaces the unacceptable suggestion in several creation psalms that in creation God first had to fight for control with the dragons Leviathan and Rahab who raged forth from the ocean of chaos,[22] or the slightly less unacceptable suggestion in Psalm 104.6–9 that God created by confining and limiting the ocean chaos in which the dragons dwell.

> the waters stood above the mountains.
>
> At thy rebuke they fled; at the voice of thy thunder they hasted away.
>
> They go up by the mountains; they go down by the valleys unto the place which thou hast founded for them.
>
> Thou hast set a bound that they may not pass over; that they turn not again to cover the earth.

---

pleased him, and to every seed his own body. All flesh *is* not the same flesh; but *there is* one *kind of* flesh of men, another flesh of beasts, another of fishes, *and* another of birds. *There are* also celestial bodies, and bodies terrestrial: but the glory of the celestial *is* one, and the *glory* of the terrestrial *is* another. *There is* one glory of the sun, and another glory of the moon, and another glory of the stars: for *one* star differeth from *another* star in glory.

"So also *is* the resurrection of the dead. It is sown in corruption; it is raised in incorruption: It is sown in dishonour; it is raised in glory: it is sown in weakness; it is raised in power: It is sown a natural body; it is raised a spiritual body."

The very differences between Paul here and Milton—that Milton insists on the similarity of all flesh and Paul its dissimilarity, that Milton insists on the goodness of the body and Paul on its corruption, that Milton insists on the connection between body and spirit and between Creator and creation and Paul on the disjunction—makes the submerged reference stronger, not weaker.

[22] See Psalm 74.13–14: "Thou didst divide the sea by thy strength: thou brakest the heads of the dragons in the waters. Thou brakest the heads of leviathan in pieces, *and* gavest him *to be* meat to the people inhabiting the wilderness."

See also Psalm 89.9–10: "Thou rulest the raging of the sea: when the waves thereof arise, thou stillest them. Thou hast broken Rahab in pieces, as one that is slain; thou hast scattered thine enemies with thy strong arm."

When, in the next lesson, Raphael describes human creation to Adam, he frames a special scene: he reports that in the midst of the sixth day God the Father interrupted the Son and reminded him, refixing the conditions of the new Creation, to make mankind in divine similitude, with rule over the visible creation; that the Son took dust of the ground and shaped it and breathed life into its nostrils; and that he made a consort for man, creating a male and the consort female for the sexual procreation of the race. Raphael then concludes his report: God put mankind in the delectable garden, but promised death should he eat the fruit of the Tree of Knowledge of Good and Evil planted there. In his account of man's creation, Raphael emphasizes God's will and deliberation over the spontaneity in which matter became the other living orders; made from dry dust and a little breath, the human being has his existence wholly by God's will. And the delegation of dominion to Adam and Eve goes hand in hand with the threat of punishment for dereliction of duty.

After two such lessons about his own creation, a subject on which he might seem to be himself an authority, Adam might justly sigh. But in exchange for having heard "what was don / Ere my remembrance," Adam offers to rehearse "My Storie" (8.203–4, 205), and begins it with a reservation about "remembrance": "For Man to tell how human Life began / Is hard; for who himself beginning knew?" (8.250–51). But when Eve described her knowledge of her own beginning to Adam, a description so absorbing to Adam that he now imitates it to detain the angel in delightful conversation, she had no such trouble recalling that beginning simply as an awakening ("when from sleep / I first awak't"), nor was she ignorant of it as a creation ("much wondring where / And what I was, whence thither brought") (4.449–52). She knows she was brought to the garden; she wonders where and who she is, however, and not who made her. Elaborating, Adam tells the angel that he too came to self-awareness as though awakening and adds as though just born: "In Balmie Sweat, . . . [and] reaking moisture" (8.255–56). He too knows at once that he was created, but he wonders how to find and worship his "great Maker," "In goodness and in power praeeminent." What he then describes to Raphael in interesting detail is his memory of Eve's creation, not his own.

The expert in retrospective oblivion is Satan, who uses it flatly to deny Creation, first to Abdiel (5.856–63) and then to Eve, elaborating the idea of spontaneous creation into an attack on God as impostor (9.718–23). Between these public disclaimers, alone on Mt. Niphates Satan concedes that God is the maker of all things, visible and invisible. He denies Creation by God in discourse with others, but alone he does not deny it. In solitude Satan has the shrewdest of insights into Creation—the understanding that Creation is epiphany, that God is God because he made the world to reveal himself, to make manifest "I am." In the formulation of both Satan's denials of Creation and his confession of it, Milton makes use both of the second subset in the creation cluster of psalms and of the creation psalms he excluded from that cluster. Satan denies what Milton proved from three of them—Psalms 16, 97, and 103: that God initiated time by begetting the Son by decree and that he then created the angels and the highest heaven in which they dwell, deserving eternal gratitude for eternal grace. Satan represents himself as God's implacable eternal enemy, who seeks at the very least joint empire with him. For this Milton works with the two creation psalms not used in the cluster in *Christian Doctrine*, Psalms 74 and 89. He identifies Satan with "the Dragon, put to second rout" (4.3) that "[brings] within him Hell . . . nor from Hell / One step no more then from himself can fly" (4.20–22). Satan's confession and renewed rebellion claim equal rule with God:

> Evil be thou my Good; by thee at least
> Divided Empire with Heav'ns King I hold
> By thee, and more then half perhaps will reigne;
> As Man ere long, and this new World shall know.
> (4.110–13)

Satan incorporates, here as in his deadly self-justifications to his angelic peers, the polytheistic myth of God's struggle with the preexistent dragon of the deep for control of the cosmos, found in Psalms 74 and 89. Satan too emerges from the ocean of chaos, figured as the hell without and within, to attack God and man.

The creation of Eve as Adam remembers it not only faithfully splices together both of the two accounts Genesis gives of the making of mankind, by doing so it also contradicts Raphael's account. Raphael showed Adam how God simultaneously made man both male and female as reflections of his image, gave them together rule over the whole earth, brought them both into Eden, gave them together all its fruits save the interdicted Tree of Knowledge, and then saw that all he had made was "entirely good." Adam remembers it differently. He remembers that after God and he conferred, responding to the ceremony of the naming of animals and their paying him fealty, and after his experience of his own solitude, God transformed by a special shaping one of his ribs into the secondary creation of the helpmeet for him, "so lovly faire, / That what seemd fair in all the World, seemd now /

Mean, or in her summd up" (8.470–72).[23] The words of gratitude Milton gave Adam are themselves a creation psalm:

> thou hast fulfill'd
> Thy words, Creator bounteous and benigne,
> Giver of all things faire, but fairest this
> Of all thy gifts, nor enviest. I now see
> Bone of my Bone, Flesh of my Flesh, my Self
> Before me; Woman is her Name, of Man
> Extracted; for this cause he shall forgoe
> Father and Mother, and to his Wife adhere;
> And they shall be one Flesh, one Heart, one Soule.
> (8.491–99)

The scene is pivotal in the human understanding of Creation. The material goodness of Creation out of stuff from God himself and the benevolence of the evolution planned by God have been shown by Raphael; Adam's delighted acquiescence in his humanity has been shown in his own account. The destructive Fall will be shown to be their own initiative. What remains for Adam and Eve to understand relates the two topics of death and Creation I have chosen to read in the light of thematic psalm clustering in *Christian Doctrine.*

From the second group of creation psalms there remain two, Psalms 7 and 51, that Milton cited to prove the natural generation of human beings, both body and soul, and hence the natural origin of original sin. They are implicated when Milton expands a final rational understanding of how Creation develops beyond the hand of God. Irene Samuel has observed that "the direction of [Milton's scriptural] nonconformities was never toward greater mystery, greater miracle, but rather always toward greater rationality, greater availability as a guide in living."[24] Adam, struggling to understand both Creation and death after the Fall, concedes as rational a natural inheritance in all future generations of human beings of the acquired trait of sinfulness:

> All that I eat or drink, or shall beget,
> Is propagated curse. O voice once heard
> Delightfully, *Encrease and multiply,*
> Now death to heare! for what can I encrease
> Or multiplie, but curses on my head?

[23] See Quilligan, *Milton's Spenser,* 71–77, 226–29; McColley, *Milton's Eve,* 180–205; and Gallagher, "Creation in Genesis and in *Paradise Lost,*" 183–94.

[24] Samuel, "The Regaining of Paradise," 116.

. . . .

. . . Ah, why should all mankind
For one mans fault thus guiltless be condemn'd,
If guiltless? But from mee what can proceed,
But all corrupt, both Mind and Will deprav'd,
Not to do onely, but to will the same
With me?
(10.728–32, 822–27)

On the purely natural level, Adam's experience of sin would surely teach him to do good: do good, for the consequences of evil are sure and visited most painfully on those he longs to have escape them. On that same level, God is seen to have made a thoroughly rational universe in which cause must lead to effect; as himself a God of reason, his laws of nature are reasonable too. Adam anticipates the psalmist in Psalms 7.3 and 51.5—"if there be iniquity in my hands" and "Behold, I was shapen in iniquity, and in sin did my mother conceive me"; he anticipates too their reactions to doing evil—7.9, "Oh let the wickedness of the wicked come to an end," and 51.10, "Create in me a clean heart, O God; and renew a right spirit within me."

The encyclopedic summoning up of psalmic proof texts in *Christian Doctrine*, then, prepares for Milton's characteristically epic encyclopedism of psalm themes in *Paradise Lost*, an encyclopedism both of epic copia and of epic progression. The two themes, death and the nature of man, creation and the nature of God, could be matched by many other significantly psalmic themes to be found in *Paradise Lost*—work or repentance and the nature of man, for example; covenant and the nature of God; or theodicy and the war in heaven.[25] It would be possible, too, to identify in *Christian Doctrine* clusters of proof texts taken from the other major scriptural groupings that Milton conventionally identified as law, prophets, and history, and to trace the central themes in them as they are worked out in the diffuse epic. But since death and creation were of special interest to Milton, were handled independently by him, and in the end were interlinked, they make a

[25] When Milton treats work in the tractate, he clusters Psalms 15, 18, 19, 25, 26, 40, 62, 81, 106, and 110. When he treats penitence, he clusters Psalms 3, 17, 32, 34, 38, 51, 71, 90, 94, 125, 130. The war in heaven draws on theodicy psalms linked by Milton: Psalms 4, 18, 29, 58, 72, 82, 101. The roll call of fallen angels draws on the psalms treating the renunciation of false gods linked by Milton: 16, 25, 31, 32, 40, 73, 92, 97, 115, and 132. Milton's covenant theory clusters Psalms 5, 19, 26, 29, 30, 33, 54, 72, 73, 90, 103, 104, 105, 147, 148: those are the psalms from which he discusses human history and God as judge of the universe.

natural choice for concentration where space is limited. In both cases, the poet's powerful imagination is put to the service of his equally powerful ethical lucidity. But the journey to that rational subordination of the visionary and the arrival at it are both compelling to one who would understand how Milton read scriptural poetry.

CONCLUSION

In the margins of his own Bible, Milton singled out fifteen psalms in some way: he underlined part of Psalm 2; initialed with "KJ" parts of Psalms 56, 66, and 89; ticked 50, 55, 105, 141, 142, and 146; bracketed 98:12–13; otherwise marked 51, 55, and 96; and smudged 1, 42, and 78 with wear.[1] In *Christian Doctrine* he most frequently cited proof texts from Psalms 2, 18, 19, 33, 37, 51, 78, 94, 102, 103, 104, 119, and 147.[2] He translated or paraphrased Psalms 1 through 8, 80 through 88, 114, and 136. Finally, throughout the English poems, he chose his words in such a way as to recall some psalms in the standard translations of his age more often than others; James Sims, cataloguing verbal echoes identified by a range of commentators and augmented by his own observations, has found most frequently referred to in *Paradise Lost* and *Paradise Regained* Psalms 2, 8, 18, 24, 45, 78, 89, 104, and 139.[3] To isolate psalms that are singled out by at least two of these factors—marginalia, citation, translation, and verbal echoes—produces a small group of Psalms of particular interest to Milton: Psalms 2, 8, 18, 19, 51, 78, 89, and 104. By way of conclusion, I shall review briefly the thematic, generic and figural use Milton made of these eight Psalms and so summarize the value of the Book of Psalms to Milton's two epics.

Before doing so, three observations might be made—observations themselves thematic, generic, and stylistic—on the nature of the group as a whole. First, in terms of theme or content, Milton's preferences compose a Christian selection, each member of which has been given its most common interpretation within the New Testament. All these psalms without exception are themselves quoted in a wide range of New Testament books: in the gospels of Matthew, Luke, and John; in Acts and Revelation; in the letters to Romans, Corinthians, Ephesians, and Hebrews. Although it is sometimes alleged of seventeenth-century English Puritans in general or of the Independents who gave them political voice in particular that they take their theology overmuch

[1] *CE* 18:560–61.

[2] He cited those psalms on at least eight occasions in the tractate. He cited Psalm 119, the wisdom song collecting moral adages, rather more frequently, but his numerous citations occur especially often in Book II of *Christian Doctrine*, the book of moral praxis.

[3] These psalms are found to be echoed on at least five occasions; Psalms 2 and 104, on more than a dozen occasions each.

from Paul, Milton did not privilege in marginal reference, citation in the tractate, translation or verbal echo in the long poems, psalms especially cited by Paul or taken by commentators to be Pauline.[4] Although Psalms 51 and 94 among the Pauline Psalms (Psalms 51, 62, 69, 94, 110, and 116) do appear in Milton's group, they are balanced by Psalms 2 and 89 from those quoted in Luke, Acts, and Hebrews more than once (Psalms 2, 69, 89, 98, 105, 107, 110, and 132).[5] Only Psalms 69 and 110 are common to both the Pauline and Lukean groups; neither is especially important to Milton. If Psalm 51, the great *mea culpa* of the Psalter, is in its fixity on sin so Pauline in emphasis as to suggest such a privileging by Milton, it is balanced by Psalm 89 where not the confession of sin but the expression of suffering drives the lament forward.[6]

Second, in terms of genre, the group is mainly divided between the hymn and lament, with hymn predominating in the group, although not numerically dominant in the Psalter. The group also contains mixed-mode psalms—Psalm 18, a royal thanksgiving modeled on a song of victory that incorporates a theophany; Psalm 78, a wisdom psalm in combination with a historical hymn; and Psalm 89, a royal lament that opens with a recital of past favors, describes present misfortunes, incorporates a visionary theophany, and closes with an appeal to God to remember his people that incorporates a messianic prophecy. The hymns—8, 19, 78, and 104—consist of two creation hymns (8 and 104), one hymn praising God both as creator and lawgiver (19, its themes revealing a psalmist who also uses wisdom song devices) and one historical hymn (78, with a wisdom introduction, proverbial and riddling elements, and an eschatological conclusion). The laments—2, 51, and 89—represent one national or com-

[4] In seven of his fourteen epistles, Paul cited 24 of the 150 psalms (Psalms 4, 5, 7, 10, 14, 18, 19, 24, 32, 36, 44, 51, 62, 68, 69, 94, 106, 110, 112, 116, 117, 119, 140, and 143). The psalms he cited on more than one occasion are 62, 69, 94, 110, and 116; but one might note that Psalm 51, like Psalm 130, which he did not at all quote, is traditionally identified with Paul.

[5] Luke quoted Psalm 2.1–2 at Acts 4.25–26 and 2.7 at Acts 13.33; he quoted Psalm 98.1–2 in Mary's Magnificat at Luke 1.46, 51 and Psalm 18.2 in the Benedictus at Luke 1.69; he echoed 19.8 in Simeon's Nunc dimittis at Luke 2.32; he quoted Psalm 89.3–4 at Acts 2.30, 89.10 at Luke 1.51 in Mary's Magnificat and 89.20 at Acts 13.22; he echoed Psalm 104.2 in Simeon's Nunc dimittis at Luke 2.32 and 103.17 in the Magnificat at Luke 1.50–51. The writer of Hebrews quotes Psalm 2.7 at 1.5; 8.4–6 at 2.6–7; 45 at 1.8–9; and 104.4 at 1.7.

[6] Westermann, *Praise and Lament in the Psalms*, 206–13, gives as the central Pauline contribution based on Psalms the idea of the conviction of sin; he suggests that lament becomes Christianized when the confession of sin is substituted for the theme of suffering.

munal lament (Psalm 2), one individual lament (the great penitential prayer of Psalm 51), and one royal lament. The group broadly represents the generic variety of the Psalter but is independent in its emphasis upon praise, and singular in its interest in generically mixed and complex psalms.

Finally, in terms of the poetical medium, the group invites consideration in terms of thought-rhyme and parallelism through metaphor and rhetorical schemes; naturally all its members share those traits. Some of the Psalms are very ancient (2), but others date from the time of the Davidic kings (18, while Psalm 89 is probably archaized rather than ancient); some are intricate in chiastic arrangements (19), but others move forward episodically by tableaux (78); some are built of a variety of yoked metaphors (8), but others consistently explore only one analogy (e.g., the weeping of man's prayer as an analogue for God's washing of the penitent and watering of faith or renewal of night spirit in 51). All, however, draw on alliteration and assonance to accompany figure and parallelism. While several are Psalms of a high style or heroic scope (18, 78, and 104, for example), others (2, 8, and 19, for example) are remarkable for plainstyle brevity and restraint. In that balance are models for devices Milton used in both brief and diffuse epic. Through the individual members of the group, I summarize Milton's thematic use of psalm materials in the interests of scriptural encyclopedism, illustrate his generic imitations to produce the phenomena of multivocality and dramatic foregrounding, and represent his adaptations of parallelism to both grand and plain style.

Psalm 2

Psalm 2 is thematically crucial to *Paradise Regained*, where the meaning of 2.7, "I will declare the decree: the Lord hath said unto me, Thou *art* my Son; this day have I begotten thee," is tested, and Jesus is shown to merit that proclamation by "firm obedience fully tri'd / Through all temptation" (1.4–5). Satan seizes on the possibility of kingly inheritance in the phrase and construes "begetting" as an institutional transfer of power; Milton shows, however, that to be entitled the Son of God is to be meritorious and to be begotten is to have had that merit acknowledged by the title. The interpretation of sonship dramatized in the debate between Satan and Jesus is drawn from Hebrews, where the psalm is given its Christian reading. Milton's thematic use of Psalm 2 in *Paradise Regained* constitutes a further interpretation, endorsing that of Hebrews but restraining Hebrews to bring it into conformity with his own subordinationism and anticlericism. Jesus, as Satan acknowledges, is "Proof against all temptation . . . firm / To the utmost of meer man both wise and good" (4.533–35); he thereby becomes, as Hebrews explains, "an high priest . . . touched with the feeling of our infirmities . . . in all points tempted like as *we are, yet* without sin" (Heb. 4.15), or, in Milton's version:

> True Image of the Father whether thron'd
> In the bosom of bliss, and light of light
> Conceiving, or remote from Heaven, enshrin'd
> In fleshly Tabernacle, and human form,
> Wandring the Wilderness, whatever place,
> Habit, or state, or motion, still expressing
> The Son of God.
> (4.596–602)

Milton's thematic analysis of psalms enables the kind of ongoing reinterpretation that supports his doctrine of progressive revelation. Psalms thematically clustered in the tractate are contextualized there among supporting passages taken from both the Old and New Testaments, arranged in the order of the canon. The result is a short historical course of biblical reading; on the basis of the tractate's preliminary contextual sorting Milton reinterprets each psalm when he uses it within epic.

Psalm 2 thus becomes one of a class of psalms that Jesus read to deduce his sonship in *Paradise Regained.* It is a prophetic psalm, containing the words of God spoken to his people. Regarded thematically, the oracle in Psalm 2 declares God's sovereignty and power over man and creation, his righteousness and hatred of evil, and his contempt for the earthly power of rebellious nations. That oracle strikingly resembles the messages of the prophets. Regarded generically, the prophetic psalm calls on hymn for topoi through which to praise God, on lament to detail a dark historical moment, on petition to ask for God's help, and finally on thanksgiving or benediction to respond to the help given; it organizes those borrowed features into an independent genre. Milton is just as interested in the psalm as a pattern for the individual's response to vocation as in its treatment of sonship, especially the poet's response to vocation. Milton's exordia in *Paradise Lost,* despite their variety, exhibit a consistent shape, recognizably similar to the structure of motifs in prophetic psalms and filled with some of their invariant motifs. Among other prophetic psalms, Psalm 2 plays its part in *Paradise Lost* in shaping the proems. Just as striking, however, is its confirmation of the poet's complex need to enter his poem in its full flight with the warning voice that opens Book IV. The rich overlay of speakers in the epic, or its multivocality, is particularly enabled by Milton's generic reading of Psalm 2. Its multivocal usefulness in *Paradise Lost* extends even to the formulation of a pithy warning by Abdiel, the angel who is the poet's recognizable avatar: "That Golden Scepter which thou didst reject / Is now an Iron Rod to bruise and breake / Thy disobedience" (5.886–88). Editors have found verbal echoes of Psalm 2.4, "He that sitteth in the heavens shall laugh," in *Paradise Lost* and *Paradise Regained*, when Milton depicts the Father's derision, implying that the poetical medium Milton imitates is the style or idiom of the King James Version. To be sure, Milton often does work with such echoes, but the "artful terms inscrib'd" (*PR* 4.335) in psalms, those poetical traits of parallelism in rhetorical placement or thought-rhyme, and in sound and figure, are of more moment in Milton's echoes of psalmody than the reproduction of catchphrases.

Psalm 8

Psalm 8, a creation hymn like Psalm 104 and half of Psalm 19, but far briefer and less adorned, is thematically woven into Jesus' interpretation of the Father's glory in Creation in *Paradise Regained* and is related to his composure even in the wilderness. His quietness, as wild creatures grow calm in his presence by the dominion God gives the upright man over the animal kingdom, instances thematic use of a psalm to foreground narrative. Psalm 8 also has a generic relevance for *Paradise Lost*, where its topoi and structure influence the hymnody of man and angels. With respect to the poetic medium, Milton's own translation of Psalm 8 suggests that what Milton thought most beautiful in his original was the binary structuring in parallelistic figures of its materials: the opposition of the pastoral goodness of the obedient life to the desert exile of rebellion. Milton enhanced his translation of the central hendiadys *oves/boves* by chains of alliteration and assonance, purifying the merismatic phrase of suggestion of rhyme. He seems to have evinced little pleasure in echoes of others' translations by everywhere replacing the King James Version "sheep and oxen" with the more inclusive and equally Anglo-Saxon "herds and flocks." The sounds and figures that Milton thought most artful and beautiful in Hebrew poetry—represented in devices that review human experience in terms of similarities and dissimilarities, and arrange and judge it in aural mimeses of the acts of its collection and distribution—may be imitated in plain style or grand. Milton's handling of Psalm 8 especially well illustrates plain style parallelism; his handling of Psalms 80 through 88 illustrates parallelisms of the grand style.

Psalms 18 and 78

Psalm 18 represents a theophany of considerable richness, spatial sweep, and detail; God appears to the psalmist in a time of great public peril, saves him, enlightens him, and helps him to a military victory. He in turn both expresses a pious gratitude in genuine thanksgiving and exults in a victory song. Psalm 78 recalls the glorious deeds of God throughout the history of the nation and richly details his just and moral government of the human world down a sweep of time as grandly comprehensive as the sweep of space in Psalm 18. A recollection of these two together must suggest that Milton's imitation of psalms in the epics works simultaneously with theme, genre, and medium. The thematic encyclopedism of *Paradise Lost* comprehends the cosmic scope of the two psalms. It echoes their representations of God as filling all space in epiphany and all time in his governance of history, including apocalypse.

Generic reinforcement of a number of lyric kinds also comes from the very complexity of these two psalms. The different generic traits of the parts of each are subsumed under its constitutive genre, just as the lyrical genres of psalms are folded into the heroic narrative of brief and diffuse epic by Milton. Thus Psalm 18 opens as thanksgiving, then laments past distress at the nearness of death, prophesies by its theophany, teaches wisdom in its analysis of God's fidelity to covenant, and finally vows praise in a renewed thanksgiving. Thus Psalm 78 opens as a wisdom song, then turns to praise and offers a synopsis of sacred history detailing covenant, stubborn and persistent rebellion, deliverance from Egypt, the conquest of Canaan, Israel's infidelity, and finally the election of Zion and David, these instances of God as the Lord of history being subsumed under the initial praise, which is not repeated. These generic combinations of lyrical genres within one lyrical form resembling the high style ode represent for Milton the affective power gained by combining lyrical kinds within the heroic genre.

While they unroll through space and time, the two psalms are composed with iteratively parallelistic figures; these are also variously adaptable to the Miltonic medium—in the first, for example, likening God to rock and tower, his coming to earthquake and storm, or linking his filling clean hands with good things and preserving life like a candle's flame against the darkness; in the second, by the steady pressure of parallel chains of historical events, each rendered in the highly visible emblematic form—the dividing of the sea, the cleaving of the rocks for water, the raining of manna, the plagues sent the Egyptians.

Psalm 51

Decorum Milton thought the grand rule in the creation of any masterpiece. A brief recollection of Milton's severely restricted adaptation of Psalm 51 in *Paradise Regained* and *Paradise Lost* may suggest how decorum governs his own psalm transumptions. Psalm 51 is a confession of sin, inapplicable to the obedient Son in *Paradise Regained* and premature for Adam when he only intellectually exonerates God from injustice by finding no reasonable grounds for accusing him. The very sterility of Adam's merely rational acceptance of the justice of God's punishing his fall is measurable by how far it misses the contrition of the psalm. Hence when Eve expresses her own deep sorrow for causing Adam's fall, her richer sincerity too is measurable in terms of her incorporation of the psalm. Thus Adam's words

> Him after all Disputes
> Forc't I absolve: all my evasions vain,
> And reasonings, though through Mazes, lead me still
> But to my own conviction: first and last
> On mee, mee onely, as the sourse and spring
> Of all corruption, all the blame lights due
> (10.828–33)

sound the psalm's "Against thee, thee only, have I sinned, and done *this* evil in thy sight." Yet his instant thought is of the insupportable weight of his responsibility, even divided with "that bad Woman." Eve's response, however, likewise echoes the confession of Psalm 51:

> both have sin'd, but thou
> Against God onely, I against God and thee,
> And to the place of judgement will return,
> There with my cries importune Heaven, that all
> The sentence from thy head remov'd may light
> On me, sole cause to thee of all this woe,
> Mee mee onely just object of his ire.
> (10.930–36)

Eve's lament is more perfect and more like Psalm 51 (and like Psalms 38 and 102 as well), as Barbara Lewalski has argued,[7] because in contrition she decides to pray that God will hold her responsible for the fall and will lift the blame from Adam. But although Eve's contrition is a good deal more profound in the combination of thought and feeling than Adam's initial aridity, her petition for change is not yet as

[7] Lewalski, Paradise Lost *and the Rhetoric of Literary Forms*, 250–53.

morally rich as that of the psalm's petition, "Purge me with hyssop, and I shall be clean: wash me, and I shall be whiter than snow." Milton's description of the prayer of Adam and Eve in unison at the place of judgment, however, might be used as a summary of Psalm 51.

The stages of the psalm's affective appropriateness to the characters of Adam and Eve, then, govern the increasing fullness with which Milton echoes Psalm 51. Such development or expansion in allusion is enabled by the principle of character decorum. Perhaps inevitably in a work designed to show how one poet reads and adapts a special kind of literary text, psalms may in this book seem somehow to fulfill their destiny when they become visible here or there in Milton's text. The implication of the principle of decorum as it shades Milton's use of Psalm 51, however, may restore a proper proportion. The lexical echo of Psalm 51 to characterize human penitence in *Paradise Lost* is heard ironically; memory of the psalm takes shape outside the poem to supply a context for the less adequate words of Milton's characters. The psalm outside the poem is the sad measure of the value of what is said inside the poem.

Psalms 19, 89, and 104

Finally, some psalms (such as Psalm 2) are made by Milton to enrich each epic and in each to serve purposes connected with genre, theme and prosody. But a brief recollection of the last three psalms, Psalms 19, 89, and 104, may instance the special relevance of some psalms to one use. Douglas Bush once observed that "we cannot feel quite certain what elements in [Psalms 1–8] especially appealed to Milton."[8] Milton's citations of Psalms in *Christian Doctrine*, however, allow us to know what he thought a good number of the verses of many of those psalms meant. Furthermore Milton's generic imitations of psalm kinds allow us to discern the acts of worship he thought psalm kinds could be used for; his poetic echoes enable us to deduce what he thought beautiful in them. Perhaps one can come even closer than that to what Bush thought irrecoverable for the 1653 Psalms and piece out from one practice what special sense Milton had of an individual psalm.

Psalm 19 is a hymn that extols God's revelation of himself both in creation and in his law. It fuses two parts, differing in content and style; the fusion is quite as clear as the difference, however. It says that we read God in Nature—"The heavens declare the glory of God; and the firmament sheweth his handiwork," and we find his perfection in his

[8] *Variorum*, 2:1000.

revealed word, "The law of the Lord *is* perfect, converting the soul: the testimony of the Lord *is* sure, making wise the simple" (vv. 1,7). It then unites these propositions in the human being's consequent self-dedication to God. The wisdom theme, deduction, and prayer are the sources of Milton's interest in the psalm. In the tractate, his citations almost syllogistically alternate among the first theme of God in creation, the second theme of God in the law, and the concluding prayer of self-dedication.[9] In the lexical echoes that Sims has noted, the psalm appears in *Paradise Lost* in relation to the first theme; it appears in *Paradise Regained* in the special relevance of the prayer: "Keep back thy servant also from presumptuous *sins*; let them not have dominion over me: then shall I be upright, and I shall be innocent from the great transgression" (v. 13) to Jesus' obedient witness. By inference from this evidence, Milton valued this psalm for the intellectual strength of its moral didacticism.

Psalm 89 is a royal lament centrally contrasting God's promises to David in the past with the present reality of his reproaches. It finds its place as particularly in *Paradise Lost* as Psalm 19 does in *Paradise Regained*. Psalm 89 interrelates God's epiphany and covenant and man's sufferings; it influences both the poet's own sense of illuminated and inspired strength growing out of loss and weakness, and Adam's discovery under Michael's tutelage of that pattern as the meaning of history. Of great importance to Milton's self-representations in proems is the psalm's acknowledgment that "[God spake] in vision to [his] holy one" (v. 19) and that the covenant of promise did not overrule but made instrumental human weakness and suffering. Like Psalm 19, it responds to Milton's taste for poetry that can teach.

Psalm 104, like 18 and 78, is grand style psalmody on the high theme of Creation. Its characteristic quality, however, is its conversion of especially rich figuration from the delighted contemplation of creatures to joyous praise of their maker. Milton found in it a model for the structure of hymn and a source of hymnal topoi, and he shaped his own account of creation in part on its model. But the heart of his interest in Psalm 104 emerges in his transumption of its strong self-dedication to praising God. The grandeur of creation leads at the end of Psalm 104 (vv. 33–35) to a reflexive vow of praise:

> I will sing unto the Lord as long as I live: I will sing praise to my God while I have my being.
> My meditation of him shall be sweet: I will be glad in the Lord.
> . . . Bless thou the Lord, O my soul. Praise ye the Lord.

[9] *YP* 6:130, 305, 396; 151, 328, 579, 585; 493, 655.

Dedicated worship is Milton's theme whether he sings "the happy Garden," the "paradise within" or "the fairer Paradise," both when the obedience of the Son and the responsive vocation of the poet is at issue, and so it is that Psalm 104 feeds both *Paradise Lost* and *Paradise Regained*.

The existence of the three modes of Milton's readings—thematic, generic, stylistic—does not imply, of course, an invariable schedule of decisions by Milton made in a predictable order and producing a pattern of rigid intentionality. Milton shapes a narrative episode by a reading of psalm themes. He foregrounds the episode by the choice of one of the lyrical genres of the Psalter according to the decorum of voices speaking; and he enhances the affect of that episode by distinguishing the many voices and tones of voice possible to the multiplicity of psalm genres or mixed-mode psalms. He fills the genre under imitation with the individual devices and figures common to all psalms so that delight inheres in ordering pithy and comprehensive suggestiveness, not in the recognition of a word or phrase from this or that psalm translation. Thematic incorporation, generic imitation, and parallelistic echoing are all substantive parts of Milton's biblicism. Neither one nor the other of them appears to enjoy any kind of originary priority over the others. An iron intentionalism to imitate genre does not govern the incorporation of theme; imitating the stylistic effects of parallelism does not demand the encapsulations of genre. Rather, the density of all these modes of biblical poesis reflects a will to charge his own poetry with devotion; the reward of fidelity to his vocation he anticipated would be poetry that had its source in common with the poetry of Psalms:

> what the Spirit within
> Shall on the heart engrave.
> (*PL* 12.523–24)

WORKS CONSULTED

Adams, Robert Martin. *Ikon: John Milton and the Modern Critics*. Ithaca: Cornell University Press, 1955.

Aers, David, ed. *Paradise Lost: Book VII*. Vol. 6 of *The Cambridge Milton for Schools and Colleges*, edited by John B. Broadbent, 6:9–33. Cambridge: Cambridge University Press, 1974.

Allen, Don Cameron. *The Harmonious Vision: Studies in Milton's Poetry*. Baltimore: The Johns Hopkins University Press, 1954.

Alter, Robert. *The Art of Biblical Poetry*. New York: Basic Books, 1985.

Anderson, A. A. *The New Century Bible Commentary: The Book of Psalms*. 2 vols. London: Marshall, 1972.

Anderson, Wayne. "Is *Paradise Regained* Really Cold?" *Christianity and Literature* 32 (1983): 15–23.

Arthos, John. *Milton and the Italian Cities*. London: Bowes, 1968.

Baroway, Israel. "The Hebrew Hexameter: A Study in Renaissance Sources and Interpretation." *ELH* 2 (1935): 66–91.

Baxter, Richard. *A breviate of the life of Margaret, the daughter of Francis Charlton, of Apply in Shropshire, esq; and wife of Richard Baxter*. . . . London, 1681.

Beardslee, William A. *Literary Criticism of the New Testament*. Philadelphia: Fortress, 1969.

Berlin, Adele. *The Dynamics of Biblical Parallelism*. Bloomington: Indiana University Press, 1985.

Boddy, Margaret. "Milton's Translation of Psalms 80–88." *Modern Philology* 64 (1966): 1–9.

Boswell, Jackson C. "Library, Milton's." In *A Milton Encyclopedia*, edited by William B. Hunter et al., 5:23–25. Lewisburg, Pa.: Bucknell University Press, 1978–1983.

Broadbent, John B. *Some Graver Subject: An Essay on Paradise Lost*. London: Chatto, 1960.

———. *Paradise Lost: Books I and II*. Vol. 3 of *The Cambridge Milton for Schools and Colleges*, edited by John B. Broadbent. Cambridge: Cambridge University Press, 1972.

Budick, Sanford. *The Dividing Muse: Images of Sacred Disjunction in Milton's Poetry*. New Haven: Yale University Press, 1985.

———. "Milton and the Scene of Interpretation: From Typology toward Midrash." In *Midrash and Literature*, edited by Geoffrey H. Hartman and Sanford Budick, pp. 195–212. New Haven: Yale University Press, 1986.

Bunyan, John. *Grace Abounding to the Chief of Sinners and The Pilgrim's Progress from this World to that which is to come*. Edited by Roger Sharrock. London: Oxford University Press, 1966.

Carey, John, and Alastair Fowler, eds. *The Poems of John Milton*. London: Longmans, 1968.

Chambers, A. B. "The Double Time Scheme in *Paradise Regained*." *Milton Studies* 7 (1975): 189–205.

Clark, Donald Lemen. *John Milton at Saint Paul's School: A Study of Ancient Rhetoric in English Renaissance Education*. New York: Columbia University Press, 1948.

Colie, Rosalie. "Time and Eternity: Paradox and Structure in *Paradise Lost*." *Journal of the Warburg and Courtauld Institutes* 23 (1960): 127–38.

Collette, Carolyn P. "Milton's Psalm Translations: Petition and Praise." *English Literary Renaissance* 2 (1972): 243–59.

Conklin, George Newton. *Biblical Criticism and Heresy in Milton*. New York: Columbia University Press, 1949.

Crashaw, Richard. *The Complete Poetry of Richard Crashaw*. Edited by George Walton Williams. New York: Norton, 1970.

Cullen, Patrick. *Infernal Triad: The Flesh, the World, and the Devil in Spenser and Milton*. Princeton: Princeton University Press, 1974.

Curran, Stuart. "*Paradise Regained*: Implications of Epic." *Milton Studies* 17 (1983): 209–24.

Dahood, Mitchell. *The Anchor Bible: Psalms I: 1–50*. Vol. 16 of *The Anchor Bible*. New York: Doubleday, 1965.

———. *The Anchor Bible: Psalms II: 51–100*. Vol. 17 of *The Anchor Bible*. New York: Doubleday-Anchor, 1968.

———. *The Anchor Bible: Psalms III: 101–150*. Vol. 17a of *The Anchor Bible*. New York: Doubleday, 1970.

Darbishire, Helen, ed. *The Early Lives of Milton*. London: Constable, 1932.

Diekhoff, John S. *Milton on Himself: Milton's Utterances upon Himself and His Works*. New York: Oxford University Press, 1939.

DiSalvo, Jackie. "Blake Encountering Milton: Politics and the Family in *Paradise Lost* and *The Four Zoas*." In *Milton and the Line of Vision*, edited by Joseph Anthony Wittreich, Jr., pp. 143–84. Madison: University of Wisconsin Press, 1975.

Drijvers, Pius. *The Psalms, Their Structure and Meaning*. New York: Herder, 1965.

"Ecclesiasticus, or the Wisdom of Jesus the Son of Sirach" (Revised Standard Version).

Elledge, Scott, ed. *Paradise Lost*, by John Milton. New York: Norton, 1975.

Elliott, Emory. "Milton's Biblical Style in *Paradise Regained*." *Milton Studies* 6 (1974): 227–41.

Empson, William. *Milton's God*. London: Chatto & Windus, 1961.

———. *Some Versions of Pastoral*. (Published in U.S. as *English Pastoral Poetry*. New York: Norton, 1938.) London: Chatto & Windus, 1950.

Evans, J. M. Paradise Lost *and the Genesis Tradition*. Oxford: Clarendon Press, 1968.

Ferry, Anne Davidson. *Milton's Epic Voice: The Narrator in* Paradise Lost. Cambridge: Harvard University Press, 1963.

Fisher, Alan. "Why Is *Paradise Regained* So Cold?" *Milton Studies* 14 (1980): 195–217.

Fixler, Michael. *Milton and the Kingdoms of God*. London: Faber & Faber, 1964.

Foerster, Donald M. *The Fortunes of Epic Poetry: A Study in English and American Criticism*. Washington: Catholic University Press, 1962.

Fowler, Alastair. "*Paradise Regained*: Some Problems of Style." In *Medieval and Pseudo-Medieval Literature*, edited by Piero Boitani and Anna Torli, pp. 181–89. Cambridge: Brewer, 1984.

Freer, Coburn. *Music for a King: George Herbert's Style and the Metrical Psalms*. Baltimore: The Johns Hopkins University Press, 1972.

Frye, Northrop. *The Great Code: The Bible and Literature*. New York: Harcourt Brace Jovanovich, 1982.

Frye, Roland Mushat. *Milton's Imagery and the Visual Arts: Iconographic Tradition in the Epic Poems*. Princeton: Princeton University Press, 1978.

Gallagher, Philip J. "Creation in Genesis and in *Paradise Lost*." *Milton Studies* 20 (1984): 163–204.

The Geneva Bible: a facsimile of the 1650 edition. Introd. by Lloyd E. Berry. Madison: University of Wisconsin Press, 1969.

Goulder, Michael D. *The Psalms of the Sons of Korah*. (*Journal for the Study of the Old Testament (JSOT): Supplement Series* 20 [1982].) Sheffield: JSOT Press, 1982.

Grant, Patrick. "Time and Temptation in *Paradise Regained*: Belief and the Single Image." In his *Images and Ideas in Literature of the English Renaissance*, pp. 129–53. Amherst: University of Massachusetts Press, 1979.

Greenwood, David. "Rhetorical Criticism and *Formgeschichte*: Some Methodological Considerations." *Journal of Biblical Literature* 89 (1970): 418–26.

Grose, Christopher. *Milton's Epic Process:* Paradise Lost *and Its Miltonic Background*. New Haven: Yale University Press, 1973.

Guibbory, Achsah. *The Map of Time: Seventeenth-Century English Literature and Ideas of Pattern in History*. Urbana: University of Illinois Press, 1986.

Hartman, Geoffrey H., and Sanford Budick, eds. *Midrash and Literature*. New Haven: Yale University Press, 1986.

Herbert, George. *The Works of George Herbert*. Edited by F. E. Hutchinson. Oxford: Clarendon Press, 1941; corr. reprint, 1945.

Hill, Christopher. *Milton and the English Revolution*. London: Faber & Faber, 1977.

The Holy Bible (Authorized [King James] Version).

Hunt, Clay. Lycidas *and the Italian Critics*. New Haven: Yale University Press, 1979.

Hunter, William B. "Milton Translates the Psalms." *Philological Quarterly* 40 (1961): 485–94.

———, ed. *A Milton Encyclopedia*. 9 vols. Lewisburg, Pa.: Bucknell University Press, 1978–83.

Kelley, Maurice. "Introduction." *Christian Doctrine.* By John Milton. Vol. 6 of *Complete Prose Works of John Milton*, edited by Don M. Wolfe. 8 vols. New Haven: Yale University Press, 1953–82. 6:3–116.

Kermode, Frank. *The Genesis of Secrecy: On the Interpretation of Narrative.* Cambridge: Harvard University Press, 1979.

———. "On Being an Enemy of Humanity." *Raritan* 2, no. 2 (1982): 87–102.

———. "*Samson Agonistes* and Hebrew Prosody." *Durham University Journal*, n.s. 14 (1953): 59–63.

Kerrigan, William. *The Prophetic Milton.* Charlottesville: University Press of Virginia, 1974.

———. "The Riddle of *Paradise Regained.*" In *Poetic Prophecy in Western Literature*, edited by Jan Wojcik and Raymond-Jean Frontain, pp. 64–80. Rutherford, N.J.: Fairleigh Dickinson University Press, 1984.

———. *The Sacred Complex: On the Psychogenesis of Paradise Lost.* Cambridge: Harvard University Press, 1983.

Knott, John R., Jr. *The Sword of the Spirit: Puritan Responses to the Bible.* Chicago: University of Chicago Press, 1980.

Kugel, James L. *The Idea of Biblical Poetry: Parallelism and Its History.* New Haven: Yale University Press, 1981.

Lanham, Richard A. *A Handlist of Rhetorical Terms: A Guide for Students of English Literature.* Berkeley: University of California Press, 1968.

Laskowsky, Henry J. "Miltonic Rhetoric and the Principle of Antithesis in Book Three of *Paradise Regained.*" *Thoth* 4 (1963): 24–29.

Lawry, Jon S. *The Shadow of Heaven: Matter and Stance in Milton's Poetry.* Ithaca: Cornell University Press, 1968.

LeComte, Edward. *Milton's Unchanging Mind.* Port Washington, N.Y.: Kennikat Press, 1973.

Lewalski, Barbara Kiefer. *Milton's Brief Epic: The Genre, Meaning, and Art of* Paradise Regained. Providence: Brown University Press, 1966.

———. Paradise Lost *and the Rhetoric of Literary Forms.* Princeton: Princeton University Press, 1985.

———. *Protestant Poetics and the Seventeenth-Century Religious Lyric.* Princeton: Princeton University Press, 1979.

———. "Time and History in *Paradise Regained.*" In *The Prison and the Pinnacle: Papers to Commemorate the Tercentenary of* Paradise Regained *and* Samson Agonistes, *1671–1971*, edited by Balachandra Rajan, pp. 49–81. London: Routledge, 1973.

Lieb, Michael. *Poetics of the Holy: A Reading of* Paradise Lost. Chapel Hill: University of North Carolina Press, 1981.

Low, Anthony. "Milton, *Paradise Regained*, and Georgic." *PMLA* 98 (1983): 152–69.

MacCaffrey, Isabel Gamble. Paradise Lost *as "Myth."* Cambridge: Harvard University Press, 1967.

MacCallum, Hugh. "Milton and the Figurative Interpretation of the Bible." *University of Toronto Quarterly* 31 (1962): 397–415.

MacCallum, Hugh. *Milton and the Sons of God: The Divine Image in Milton's Epic Poetry*. Toronto: University of Toronto Press, 1986.

———. " 'Most Perfect Hero': The Role of the Son in Milton's Theodicy." In Paradise Lost: *A Tercentenary Tribute*, edited by Balachandra Rajan, pp. 79–105. Toronto: University of Toronto Press, 1969.

McColley, Diane. *Milton's Eve*. Urbana: University of Illinois Press, 1983.

MacKellar, Walter, ed. *Paradise Regained*. Vol. 4 of *A Variorum Commentary on the Poems of John Milton*. 4 vols. to date. 1972–75. London: Routledge, 1975.

Martz, Louis L. *Milton: Poet of Exile*. 2d ed. New Haven: Yale University Press, 1986.

———. "*Paradise Regained*: The Meditative Combat." *ELH* 27 (1960): 223–47.

———. *The Paradise Within: Studies in Vaughan, Traherne, and Milton*. New Haven: Yale University Press, 1964.

Milton, John. *Complete Prose Works of John Milton*. Edited by Don M. Wolfe et al. 8 vols. New Haven: Yale University Press, 1953–82.

———. *The Works of John Milton*. Edited by Frank Allen Patterson et al. 18 vols. New York: Columbia University Press, 1931–40.

Miner, Earl. "Milton and the Histories." In *Politics of Discourse: The Literature and History of Seventeenth-Century England*, edited by Kevin Sharpe and Steven N. Zwicker, pp. 181–203. Berkeley: University of California Press, 1987.

———. "The Reign of Narrative in *Paradise Lost*." *Milton Studies* 17 (1983): 3–25.

Mowinckel, Sigmund. *The Psalms in Israel's Worship*. 2 vols. Oxford: Blackwell, 1962.

Nohrnberg, James. "*Paradise Regained* by One Greater Man: Milton's Wisdom Epic as a 'Fable of Identity.' " In *Centre and Labyrinth: Essays in Honour of Northrop Frye*, edited by Eleanor Cook et al., pp. 83–114. Toronto: University of Toronto Press, 1983.

North, Michael. "Language and the Struggle of Identity in *Paradise Regained*." *Renaissance and Reformation*, n.s. 6 (1982): 273–83.

Oesterley, W.O.E. *A Fresh Approach to the Psalms*. New York: Scribner, 1937.

Parker, Patricia A. *Inescapable Romance: Studies in the Poetics of a Mode*. Princeton: Princeton University Press, 1979.

Parker, William Riley. *Milton: A Biography*. 2 vols. Oxford: Clarendon Press, 1968.

———. "Milton and Thomas Young, 1620–1628." *Modern Language Notes* 53 (1938): 399–407.

Patrick, J. Max, and Roger Sundell, eds. *Milton and the Art of Sacred Song*. Madison: University of Wisconsin Press, 1979.

Patrides, C. A. *The Grand Design of God: The Literary Form of the Christian View of History*. London: Routledge, 1972.

———. *The Phoenix and the Ladder: The Rise and Decline of the Christian View of History*. Berkeley: University of California Press, 1964.

———. "Renaissance and Modern Thought on the Last Things: A Study in Changing Conceptions." *Harvard Theological Review* 51 (1958): 169–85.

———. " 'Something like Prophetick strain': Apocalyptic Configurations in Milton." In *The Apocalypse in English Renaissance Thought and Literature: Patterns, Antecedents and Repercussions,* edited by C. A. Patrides and Joseph Anthony Wittreich, Jr., pp. 207–37. Ithaca: Cornell University Press, 1984.

Patrides, C. A., and Joseph Anthony Wittreich, Jr., eds. *The Apocalypse in English Renaissance Thought and Literature: Patterns, Antecedents and Repercussions.* Ithaca: Cornell University Press, 1984.

Patterson, Annabel M. "*Paradise Regained*: A Last Chance at True Romance." *Milton Studies* 17 (1983): 187–208.

Pecheux, Mother Mary Christopher, O.S.U. "Sin in *Paradise Regained*: The Biblical Background." In *Calm of Mind,* edited by Joseph Anthony Wittreich, Jr., pp. 49–65. Cleveland: Press of Case Western Reserve University, 1971.

Phillips, Edward. "The Life of Mr. John Milton." In *The Early Lives of Milton,* edited by Helen Darbishire. London: Constable: 1932.

Preminger, Alex, and Edward L. Greenstein, eds. *The Hebrew Bible in Literary Criticism.* New York: Ungar, 1986.

Quilligan, Maureen. *Milton's Spenser: The Politics of Reading.* Ithaca: Cornell University Press, 1983.

Radzinowicz, Mary Ann, ed. *Paradise Lost Book VIII.* Vol. 6 of *The Cambridge Milton for Schools and Colleges,* edited by John B. Broadbent. Cambridge: Cambridge University Press, 1974.

———. "*Paradise Regained* as Hermeneutic Combat." *University of Hartford Studies in Literature* 15/16 (1983/84): 99–107.

———. "The Politics of *Paradise Lost.*" In *Politics of Discourse: The Literature and History of Seventeenth-Century England,* edited by Kevin Sharpe and Steven N. Zwicker. pp. 204–29. Berkeley: University of California Press, 1987.

———. "Psalms and the Representation of Death in *Paradise Lost.*" *Milton Studies* 23 (1987): 133–44.

———. " 'To make the people fittest to chuse': How Milton Personified His Program for Poetry." *The CEA Critic* 48/49 (1986): 3–23.

———. *Toward* Samson Agonistes: *The Growth of Milton's Mind.* Princeton: Princeton University Press, 1978.

Rajan, Balachandra, ed. *Paradise Lost: A Tercentenary Tribute.* Toronto: University of Toronto Press, 1969.

———, ed. *The Prison and the Pinnacle: Papers to Commemorate the Tercentenary of* Paradise Regained *and* Samson Agonistes. London: Routledge, 1973.

Revard, Stella P. "The Renaissance Michael and the Son of God." In *Milton and the Art of Sacred Song,* edited by J. Max Patrick and Roger H. Sundell, pp. 121–35. Madison: University of Wisconsin Press, 1979.

Revard, Stella P. *The War in Heaven:* Paradise Lost *and the Tradition of Satan's Rebellion.* Ithaca: Cornell University Press, 1980.

———. "The Warring Saints and the Dragon: A Commentary upon *Revelation* 12.7–9 and Milton's War in Heaven." *Philological Quarterly* 53 (1974): 181–83.

Ricoeur, Paul. "The Hermeneutics of Testimony." In *Essays on Biblical Interpretation*, edited by Lewis Mudge, pp. 119–54. Philadelphia: Fortress, 1980.

Sabourin, Leopold, S.J. *The Psalms: Their Origin and Meaning.* New York: Alba, 1974.

Samuel, Irene. *Dante and Milton: The* Commedia *and* Paradise Lost. Ithaca: Cornell University Press, 1966.

———. *Plato and Milton.* Ithaca: Cornell University Press, 1947.

———. "The Regaining of Paradise." In *The Prison and the Pinnacle*, edited by Balachandra Rajan, pp. 111–34. London: Routledge, 1973.

Sanchez, Reuben Marquez, Jr. "Persona and Decorum in Milton's Prose." Ph.D. diss., Cornell University, 1986.

Schaar, Claes. *"The full Voic'd Quire Below": Vertical Context Systems in* Paradise Lost. Lund: Gleerup, 1982.

Schindler, Walter. *Voice and Crisis: Invocation in Milton's Poetry.* Hamden, Conn.: Archon, 1984.

Schneidau, Herbert. *Sacred Discontent: The Bible and Western Tradition.* Baton Rouge: Louisiana State University Press, 1976.

Sharpe, Kevin, and Steven N. Zwicker. *Politics of Discourse: The Literature and History of Seventeenth-Century England.* Berkeley: University of California Press, 1987.

Shawcross, John T. "Bibles." In *A Milton Encyclopedia*, edited by William B. Hunter, 1:163. Lewisburg, Pa.: Bucknell University Press, 1978–83.

———, ed. *Milton: the Critical Heritage.* London: Routledge, 1970.

———, ed. *Milton 1732–1801: The Critical Heritage.* London: Routledge, 1972.

Sidney, Sir Philip. *The Poems of Sir Philip Sidney.* Edited by William A. Ringler, Jr. Oxford: Clarendon Press, 1962.

Sims, James H. "Bible, Milton and the." In *A Milton Encyclopedia* 1:142–63.

———. *The Bible in Milton's Epics.* Gainesville: University of Florida Press, 1962.

Sims, James H., and Leland Ryken, eds. *Milton and Scriptural Tradition: The Bible into Poetry.* Columbia: University of Missouri Press, 1984.

Stapleton, Laurence. "Milton's Conception of Time in *The Christian Doctrine.*" *Harvard Theological Review* 57 (1964): 9–21.

Steadman, John M. *Epic and Tragic Structure in* Paradise Lost. Chicago: University of Chicago Press, 1976.

———. *Milton's Biblical and Classical Imagery.* Pittsburgh: Duquesne University Press, 1984.

———. "Milton's Rhetoric: Satan and the 'Unjust Discourse.' " *Milton Studies* 1 (1969): 67–92.

Stein, Arnold. *Heroic Knowledge: An Interpretation of* Paradise Regained *and* Samson Agonistes. Minneapolis: University of Minnesota Press, 1957.

Sundell, Roger. "The Narrator as Interpreter in *Paradise Regained.*" *Milton Studies* 2 (1970): 83–101.

Svendsen, Kester. *Milton and Science*. Cambridge: Harvard University Press, 1956.

Swaim, Kathleen M. *Before and after the Fall: Contrasting Modes in* Paradise Lost. Amherst: University of Massachusetts Press, 1986.

Tayler, Edward W. *Milton's Poetry: Its Development in Time*. Pittsburgh: Duquesne University Press, 1979.

Teskey, Gordon. "Balanced in Time: *Paradise Regained* and the Centre of the Miltonic Vision." *University of Toronto Quarterly* 50 (1981): 269–83.

Thickstun, Margaret Olofson. *Fictions of the Feminine: Puritan Doctrine and the Representation of Women*. Ithaca: Cornell University Press, 1988.

Treip, Mindele. *Milton's Punctuation and Changing English Usage, 1582–1676*. London: Methuen, 1970.

Verity, A. W., ed. *Paradise Lost*, by John Milton. Cambridge: Cambridge University Press, 1910.

von Rad, Gerhard. *Wisdom in Israel*. Translated by James D. Martin. London: SCM, 1972.

Webber, Joan. *Milton and His Epic Tradition*. Seattle: University of Washington Press, 1979.

Weismiller, Edward R. "Studies of Verse Form in the Minor English Poems." *Variorum* 2.iii: 1007–87.

———. "Versification." *A Milton Encyclopedia* 8:118–35.

Weiser, Artur. *The Psalms: A Commentary*. Philadelphia: Westminster, 1962.

West, Robert H. "Abdiel." *A Milton Encyclopedia* 1:11–12.

Westermann, Claus. *Praise and Lament in the Psalms*. Atlanta: John Knox, 1981.

———. "Struktur und Geschichte der Klage im Alten Testament." *Zeitschrift für die alttestamentliche Wissenschaft* 66 (1954): 44–80.

Whaler, James. *Counterpoint and Symbol: An Inquiry into the Rhythm of Milton's Epic Style*. Anglistica IV. Copenhagen: Rosenkilde and Bagger, 1956.

Wittreich, Joseph Anthony, Jr. *Visionary Poetics: Milton's Tradition and His Legacy*. San Marino: Huntington Library Press, 1979.

———, ed. *Calm of Mind: Tercentenary Essays on* Paradise Regained *and* Samson Agonistes. Cleveland: Press of Case Western Reserve University, 1971.

———, ed. *Milton and the Line of Vision*. Madison: University of Wisconsin Press, 1975.

Woodhouse, A.S.P., and Douglas Bush, eds. *The Minor English Poems*. Vol. 2, parts 1–3 of *A Variorum Commentary on The Poems of John Milton*. 4 vols. to date. 1972–. London: Routledge, 1972.

Zwicky, Laurie. "Kairos in *Paradise Regained*: The Divine Plan." *ELH* 31 (1964): 271–77.

INDEX